Creation
Continues

Creation Continues

Fritz Kunkel

Edited by
Elizabeth Kunkel and
Ruth Spafford Morris

WORD BOOKS, Publisher

Waco, Texas

Introduction

Fritz Kunkel may have been too early for his time. The Ariadne thread which ran through his life and writings was the evolution of consciousness taking place through the interaction of the individual and the living Word of God whom he saw active and revealed in the soul of man. Although he wrote as a scientific psychologist, and from the perspective of an experienced psychotherapist, Dr. Kunkel could not help but extend his influence into the sphere of the religious, for he saw what the Christian writer Tertullian had seen seventeen hundred years earlier, that "the soul is by nature Christian." His Christianity was an "inner Christianity" which gave treasures of meaning to those who were ready for his message, but often fell on stony ground as the message he had to give went counter to the spirit of the times.

Although he himself was a depth psychologist of note, having studied with Alfred Adler and later having integrated the psychology of C. G. Jung into his own outlook, he was also a man of the spirit, who found himself working in the era when most of depth psychology was still dominated by antireligious assumptions and prejudices. Religion, for most depth psychologists, was either an outright symptom of infantilism or neurosis, or, at best, a special field into which the psychotherapist should not venture. But for Dr. Kunkel there was no dividing line between the things of the soul and the things of God, since the unconscious was the inner world of a person where God could be seen most clearly.

At the same time the religious community to which Dr. Kunkel spoke was largely alienated from the spirit of science and the psyche. Christianity, especially, was a matter of institutions, traditions, dogma, and church budgets, and the mystical side of the faith was rejected or ignored. Dr. Kunkel's spiritual perspective was too challenging for the materialistic assumptions of many who called themselves scientists, his scientific attitude was too demanding for those who sought the quiet sanctity of an unreflective faith, and his message of the interaction between the individual and God was too disturbing for those who wanted their God neatly sealed up in the dogma of "Systematic Theology."

Dr. Kunkel was closer in spirit to the early Christian Fathers, those great psychologist-theologians of the first few centuries of the Christian church, who taught that the way to the knowledge of God was through the soul of man. These men, who combined great intellect with great faith, did not hesitate to explore the world of dreams, for they sought to find in the soul of man the imprint of his Creator. Like them, Fritz Kunkel believed that the Word of God is made known in what we now call the unconscious.

But now the spirit of the times is different from what it was even two or three decades ago. There is a disillusionment with a purely materialistic science, and a realization, thanks to atomic physics, that the universe will not yield its secrets to a mechanistic, deterministic philosophy. In matters of religion there are increasing numbers of people who are now searching for their own individual experiences with God. In psychotherapy the narrowly materialistic Freudianism of the "orthodox" era in psychoanalysis is vanishing. Even existentialist psychotherapists acknowledge the necessity for man to find meaning in life, while the psychology of C. G. Jung, which takes into account man's basically religious nature, is gaining ground in many quarters. Many of our young people have shown us their despair with our purely formalized religion, and in their search for an individual spiritual experience in aberrant ways, such as drugs, have drawn our attention to the need in our time for exactly the kind of individual religion which Fritz Kunkel knew and wrote about so well.

My discovery of Fritz Kunkel came in 1953. I was an unhappy seminary student at the time, torn apart by doubts and anxiety. Somehow I had stumbled upon the writings of Fritz Kunkel, and because of them I was led to travel three thousand miles and spend a year away from seminary to study with this Christian depth psychologist. Beyond a doubt this year was the turning point in my adult life, and gave the determining direction to my spiritual and psychological growth. It is not too much to say that the years of my ministry since then have been years in which I consolidated and expanded the base which Fritz Kunkel gave me, culminating in my own book *The Kingdom Within* which owes so much to Dr. Kunkel's *Creation Continues* that I dedicated it to him.

Wherever I go I run across grateful friends of Fritz Kunkel. These will join with me in thanking the publishers for bringing *Creation Continues* into print once more. It could not come at a more fortuitous time. Of all Fritz's books this is the best. It will be welcomed by those searching for a personal religious faith.

It will be welcomed by those despairing of a purely formalized and externalized religion. It will be welcomed by psychologists who seek the religious dimension of the psyche. It will be welcomed by biblical scholars who search for a new biblical hermeneutic.

For *Creation Continues* is, among other things, a daring explanation of the Gospel of St. Matthew. Dr. Kunkel sees the Gospel as a whole. He regards it not as a hodge-podge of isolated recollections of Jesus' life, nor a collection of Jesus' sayings and deeds editorialized by an early Church for short-sighted reasons, but as a whole document, carefully put together with great artistry by the unknown author we call "Matthew." The measure of the Gospel is to be taken by its effect on the reader. Only when we view the Gospel this way can its deepest mystery be revealed, and its carefully woven structure be seen. But this also means that the reader must be revealed to himself. Only if the reader is willing to let Matthew show him himself will he or she be able to see Matthew, and, through Matthew's eyes, see Jesus.

I was happy when I heard *Creation Continues* would be printed once again. I was happy when I was asked to write the introduction. I am happy for you, the new reader of a new decade, that you have ahead of you the experience of reading this book.

San Diego, California   JOHN A. SANFORD
December 1972

───────

JOHN A. SANFORD is Rector of St. Paul's Episcopal Church in San Diego, Calif. He studied with Fritz Kunkel privately in 1953–54, and continued his psychological experience with clinical pastoral education and later with Jungian analysts. In 1962 he attended the C. G. Jung Institute in Zurich for a semester. He is a member of the American Association of Pastoral Counselors and a lecturer on pastoral counseling at Bloy House Theological School in Los Angeles. He is the author of *Dreams: God's Forgotten Language,* and *The Kingdom Within,* a psychological study of the sayings of Jesus.

Editors' Preface

In the revision of this book the editors have attempted to preserve the essential qualities of the original by using Fritz Kunkel's exact words. Where transpositions have been made they are in the interest of lucidity and intensity. A very few small additions have been inserted to round out an expressed idea. The captions inserted by the editors refer to Dr. Kunkel's discussions with the purpose of capturing the essential thought and enabling the reader to refer to it easily. The editors have removed those portions which seemed unnecessary to the flow of Dr. Kunkel's thought.

One purpose was to make room for the Gospel of Matthew, the quotations from which have been placed approximately just before their discussion in the text. Unless otherwise noted, all quotations are from the Revised Standard Version.

Another purpose was to satisfy the many requests of individuals and of religious study groups. These requests arose because the original book fulfilled the need of the human soul in its search for identity, its awakening to higher consciousness, and its struggle for guidance and spiritual leadership as demonstrated by Jesus in his life and message.

Creation Continues is the last book of a series of twenty volumes on psychology by Fritz Kunkel. Throughout his books he has tried to give insight on man's endeavors to relate to himself, to his fellowman and to the universe. He called his psychology, therefore, "We-Psychology," indicating man's longing to know himself, and to relate to men and the spiritual powers beyond himself.

This approach brings the author into close relationship with the thinking of contemporary psychologists such as Assagioli in his psychosynthesis and Maslow in his transpersonal psychology.

Menlo Park, California   ELIZABETH J. KUNKEL
May 1973   RUTH SPAFFORD MORRIS

Note on the Editors

Elizabeth J. Kunkel, herself a licensed professional psychologist, collaborated closely with her husband throughout their marriage. Since his death in 1956 she has pursued and developed the spiritual approach to psychology in her work with individuals and groups. The revision of *Creation Continues* was carried out in response to numerous expressions of interest in the book from the religious community all over the United States.

Ruth Spafford Morris, M.A. Columbia University, has been a student of Fritz Kunkel's psychology for twenty-nine years. Her condensation of Fritz Kunkel's lecture series entitled "Men and Women" was published in the 1964 summer issue of *Inward Light*, a publication of the Friends Conference on Religion and Psychology. She has also edited articles for the magazine *Prevention*.

Preface to the First Edition

The purpose of this book is to investigate, clarify, and increase the influence of Matthew's Gospel on the modern reader. The point of view, therefore, is mainly psychological. Historical considerations have been left out, except for the psychological differences between the original reader (Matthew's contemporary) and the reader of our time. We are not here concerned with the question whether Jesus actually did and said what Matthew recorded. We will try to understand the impact of Jesus' personality on his disciples, through them on Matthew and his students, and through Matthew on ourselves.

This approach enables us to appreciate the artistic values of Matthew's work and to study their effect on modern man, but it prevents theological discussions and philosophical speculations. The essence of Matthew's Gospel is psychological as well as theological. "The coming of the kingdom of heaven" and "the coming of the Son of man" can and should be explored by theologians and psychologists alike. The slightest preparation and the faintest experience of the approach of the kingdom, and even the lack of this experience and the disbelief in its approach have an unmistakable psychological effect on us. This effect is an important object of psychological research, and this research should be a presupposition for the theological discussion of "the kingdom of heaven."

On the other hand, there are many schools of psychology. This book presents only one out of many possible psychological interpretations of the first Gospel. It does not want to convince or convert anybody. On the contrary, by arousing controversies and provoking independent investigations, it will do more for the religious development of the future than by forming a new "school of religious psychology." Christianity should be based on individual experiences, not on "schools of thought." The contribution of this book, therefore, is either the stimulation of individual and genuine religious discoveries—or it is nothing at all.

Los Angeles   FRITZ KUNKEL
September 1946

11

Acknowledgments

I am indebted to all the authors listed in the bibliography at the end of this book, but I want to mention especially three men who have deeply influenced my work. They are C. G. Jung whose exploration of the "Collective Unconscious" has greatly enriched my own psychology; Johannes Wilkens, who made the first attempt at an artistic understanding of Matthew; and H. B. Sharman, whose *Records of the Life of Jesus* helped me to see the dynamic possibilities of the Gospel.

I wish to thank the following for permission to quote from the books mentioned: The Division of Christian Education of the National Council of the Churches of Christ in the U.S.A. for the Revised Standard Version of the Bible, and Harper and Row for *The Moffatt Bible, A New Translation*.

Contents

Part Two
THE CHART OF INITIATION
(The Sermon on the Mount)

Part Three
THE WAY

Part Four
THE CROSSROADS

Part Six
THE NEW CHART

Part Seven
THE NEW GATE

PRELUDE

MATTHEW AND THE EVOLUTION

OF CONSCIOUSNESS

Why Read the New Testament?

Why read the New Testament? Religion has been killed by science. Christianity is a medieval superstition, a mass suggestion, opium for the people. Why bother with it? This is one point of view. But there is another one.

If the psychologist looks at what is printed and listens to what is said about Christianity nowadays, he finds besides cheap literature and shallow talk many valuable discussions and philosophical discoveries of great importance. There are emotional arguments as well as calm meditations and, above all, there are practical expeditions into the realm of the unknown.

Since psychology has learned to experiment with what is called "the unconscious," we are aware of the fact that religion and psychology are concerned with the same thing: the evolution of consciousness. Watching the religious development of our time, nobody can say that this is the agony of a dying faith. It looks more like a new beginning. Christianity, perhaps, is coming of age. It might prove to be the decisive factor in the future of mankind.

If we accept this, at least as a possibility, the most urgent of all our psychological questions should be: What is Christianity? What has it been for nineteen centuries? What will it be tomorrow? Who was Jesus? What was going on in his conscious and his unconscious mind? What did he think about himself? What did he actually teach and do (besides all the legendary things that are ascribed to him)? Is it true that he raised people from the dead?

On what level is Jesus still alive? Was he raised from the dead himself? Is he still alive? And, if so, in what sense, in what kind of reality does he exist?

All these questions can be considered from many different viewpoints, historical, theological, philosophical and psychological. The psychologist must find the starting point for his own answer within himself and within his contemporaries whose experiences he can explore. This psychological starting point is best expressed in a new question: What is this peculiar influence which the New Testament—or Jesus—still exerts in our day? What happens to us when we hear his words? There is no doubt that some people are thoroughly changed by his message.

Can we do what Jesus taught? We have to explore the relationship between the New Testament and ourselves, and we cannot do so without having undergone its influence. It is not enough to read the Bible as an historian reads Julius Caesar, from the outside, with aloof and objective criticism. For the sake of an honest experiment, we have to expose our minds, without restriction, to the impact of the book. We have to do, or try to do, what Jesus taught his disciples. We have to live by his principles; otherwise we cannot decide whether he is dead or alive. "If any man will do his will, he shall know of the doctrine, whether it be of God, or whether I speak of myself" (John 7:17, KJV).

We are forced to search for the real gospel, the message of Jesus behind the four Gospels, and even behind the earliest documents which have been used by the evangelists. And we have to do it practically, by experiment, not only as the hearers, but as the doers of the word. We have to expose ourselves to the full impact of the New Testament, as it is now, regardless of its contradictions and distortions.

Which Gospel will help us? Shall we begin with Mark? His Gospel is supposed to be the oldest and closest to the "historical truth." Like an ancient ballad, it introduces us to a carpenter who is a god. It is true that Mark's Jesus is more "human" in many respects than the Jesus of Luke and Matthew. But the riddles which he presents to the psychologist appear all the more insoluble. Mark's carpenter is at the same time an "avatar," a divine superman. There is no psychological hint to make us understand how this heavenly carpenter felt or how His disciples were changed from fishermen into the pillars of the church. Our psychological curiosity, therefore, makes us turn to the other evangelists.

John's Gospel, this great spiritual symphony, cannot help us at the beginning. It presupposes a reader who has already been initiated into the deeper experiences of the Way, the Truth and the Life. The decisive change of the disciples' inner structure cannot be explored through John.

Luke, the epic narrator, has preserved many revealing remarks which give us priceless information in our quest. But they are scattered like erratic blocks in a beautiful landscape. We can use them as material, but our psychological understanding of Christianity cannot be based on them.

Fortunately, we have in Matthew's Gospel a magnificent record of the inner experience of the early Christians. It is not difficult to find the psychological key and to unlock the door of this treasure house. There is nothing, or almost nothing, esoteric about the first Gospel. Everybody can read Matthew as his first readers did. We simply have to find the standpoint of the man who wrote the book.

Why Matthew?

From Matthew's standpoint, of course, we cannot explore the divine nature of Christ or the human consciousness of Jesus. Matthew took for granted the words and actions of his Master as he found them recorded in the early documents; he was concerned with something different. His own Christian experience and his work with many neophytes made him an expert in religious initiation. He was deeply interested in the reactions of the first disciples. Their fears, doubts and hopes, their amazement, despair and final awakening to courage and creativeness—that was the subject of his lifelong study. It was the same human development that he discovered in his own life history and within the students whom he taught for so many years in the church of Antioch. The form of Matthew's Gospel, the choice and arrangement of the material, the wording, and even the rhythm of its sentences, are conditioned by this main interest of the writer: the inner experience of the initiate.

Outwardly Matthew describes Jesus' way through two or three years of his life. At the same time, however, he teaches step by step the inner experiences of the average disciple (Peter usually serving as an example), and this means he shows us our own way from the first encounter with Jesus up to the final integration of the spirit of Christ. While reading the first Gospel, we should constantly ask ourselves, "What happens to Peter?" rather than "What happens to Jesus?" We should identify ourselves with Peter, and if this is too difficult, with Matthew; and if we cannot do that, at least with Matthew's students for whom the Gospel was written.

Matthew, a literary artist. Matthew was a great writer. But we forget him easily because he subordinated his genius completely to the greater genius whom he served. We know now that he was not one of the twelve disciples and did not write his book before the end of the first century. Most scholars date his Gospel between the years 90 and 95 A.D. We do not know exactly where he lived; but the best guess is that he worked as a leader of the Christian church at Antioch. Our lack of information, however, is strangely compensated by the vivid portrait which comes to life in his book.

Matthew was not a scholar with three or four documents on his desk, comparing them and choosing the best version of the text. He doubtless used reason, but he added to it the creative power of the prophet. He understood his documents because he had experienced the same truth, and he arranged his material, not in order to give an account of Jesus' life or of Christian belief, but in order to create a compass, a tool of guidance for those after him who would have to make the same perilous journey as he had made, through "the valley of the shadow of death."

The remark "For where two or three are gathered in my name, there am I in the midst of them" (18:20), allows the conclusion that Matthew did not think of a great organized Church but rather of small groups within the new Brotherhood. Such groups must have been important to him, and we may assume that it was his experience with them which enabled him to select and change the material of his sources and to alter and polish it until the great work emerged which now bears his name.

Matthew's artistic means are manifold. Sometimes he leads us up many steps to a climax of dizzying height; then there is a gap; the inexpressible takes place in silence, and then the narrative continues on a different level. The stories of Jesus' birth and crucifixion are masterpieces of this kind. The mysterious word "Selah" in the Psalms (e.g., Ps. 3:2, 4, 8) seems to indicate a similar gap. The singer is supposed to pause and meditate. In other cases Matthew uses a method which he probably learned from Jesus himself. A question is answered in a startling way and a picture or symbol is shown which at first sight seems to be meaningless. Later it begins to grow in the reader's imagination like a seed in the field, and finally it answers the reader's question out of his own experience. The writer forces the reader to find the answer within himself.

It is possible to divide the text in many ways, and modern editors have suggested a wide variety of groupings. The best known arrangement is the old division into twenty-eight chapters, which we find in the majority of our Bibles. The person who determined the length of the chapters (as early as the twelfth century) must have had a deep understanding of the inner structure of Matthew's work. In most cases, as we shall see, we can agree with his decision.

Matthew wants to change the reader. Matthew does not want to inform his reader; he wants to change him. Mark and Luke are definitely better sources of information. Matthew uses all his art and experience to force his readers into a process of inner growth, partly against their will and certainly beyond their expectation. He uses symbols which unfold in our imagination, and questions which torture our minds until we dare to answer them on our account. But he possesses even stronger means and handles them in perfect mastery.

He not only arouses compassion and fear, but he also disturbs our peace of mind with well-chosen contradictions (12:46–50 vs. 15:4–6)[1] and magnificently worded paradoxes (5:4; 16:25).[2] As we shall see, Matthew does not hesitate to offend our sense of decency and justice in order to free us from tribal prejudices and conventional patterns (16:23).[3] His confrontations will shock us and, like alarm clocks, wake us up, unless we have already learned to escape into one of three face-saving forms of rationalization.

For instance, we can shun the inner revolution by explaining the depth and beauty of Matthew's work to those who are not aware of it. This is the escape into salesmanship. Or we can investigate the exact historical meaning of Matthew's terms (such as "son of man") as compared with the same terms in Daniel and Enoch. This is escape into historical research. Or we apply Matthew's X-rays to the fate of mankind and the average man instead of to ourselves. This is the escape into philosophy. Matthew, as it were, opens the door for the escapists. He does not initiate anyone who is not ready for his initiation. In Jesus' words he tells the escapists what will happen to them: "And every one who hears these words of mine and does not do them will be like a foolish man who built his house upon the sand" (7:26); but he keeps the door open so that they can come back if they desire: "Come to me, all who labor and are heavy laden, and I will give you rest. Take my yoke upon you, and learn from me; for I am gentle and

---

1. "And stretching out his hand toward his disciples, he said, 'Here are my mother and my brothers! For whoever does the will of my Father in heaven is my brother, sister, and mother'" in contrast to "God commanded, 'Honor your father and your mother,' and, 'He who speaks evil of father or mother let him surely die.' But you say, 'If any one tells his father or his mother, What you would have gained from me is given to God, he need not honor his father.' So, for the sake of your tradition you have made void the word of God" (12:49–50; 15:4–6).

2. "Blessed are those who mourn, for they shall be comforted," and "Whoever wants to save his life will lose it, and whoever loses his life for my sake will find it."

3. "But he turned and said to Peter, 'Get behind me, Satan! . . . you are not on the side of God, but of men.'"

lowly in heart, and you will find rest for your souls" (11:28–29).

This selective power of the first Gospel sifts the readers from the very beginning. If we cannot appreciate the myth of the virgin birth and the three kings, we are not admitted to any kind of deeper understanding. If we reject the central paradox—"For whoever would save his life will lose it, and whoever loses his life for my sake will find it" (16:25)—we are excluded at the very climax of the development. And if we misinterpret the "cruelty" of the king—"For many are called, but few are chosen" (22:2–14)—we had better give up and start all over again.

Matthew does not explain or teach intellectually. He stimulates independent thinking and daring conjectures; but what he wants to convey is practical experience, not theory. In some places, he draws convergent lines but stops before they reach the point of intersection. The reader wants to ask Matthew what his implications are; but actually Matthew asks the reader to draw his own conclusions. The reader, however, cannot yet answer Matthew's question. It may take years until he reaches the level of development on which he understands the final truth. A good example for the dynamic of such a delayed-action bomb can be found in Jesus' two statements: "Love your enemies" (5:44) and "as you did it to one of the least of these my brethren you did it to me" (25:40). The theoretical conclusion is terrifying because we cannot yet live up to it. The practical conclusion is impossible until we reach an unusual degree of maturity.

In each sufferer we are confronted with Christ. If we help him, we help Christ. If we love our enemy we also help Christ. Does this mean: What we do to our enemy we are doing to Christ? Here the lines intersect. Christ approaches us through our enemies as well as through the beggars and the sick. If we find ourselves caught in the high voltage between the two poles of Matthew's dynamo, we have to labor until our own inner structure is changed.

Venture into the unknown. Matthew forces us to set out on our own expeditions into the unknown. If we fail to do so, we are excluded from all further participation in his training. We cannot appreciate Jesus' statement about fasting, praying and giving alms, unless we fast, pray and give alms. Nobody can appreciate a textbook for pilots without ever having flown a plane. And we cannot understand the "night-sea-journey" (8:23–27) if we have not yet done what the Sermon on the Mount tells us to do. Only the practical application of the Sermon will provide the inner experiences which are presupposed in the teaching of the night-sea-journey. To question the "truth" of such a "miracle" without having traveled in the no man's land as the Sermon suggests is just as wise as to criticize the theory of relativity without having practiced higher mathematics. The selective power of Matthew's art prevents the misuse of his treasures. We cannot buy the metaphysical treasure unless we sell our earthly possessions (13:44).

The Dynamic versus the Static Reader

Matthew's readers, therefore, can be grouped into those who expose themselves to the dynamic influence of the book and those who manage to remain static. Either the book changes the reader, transforming him and forcing him into a higher form of evolution, or the reader changes the book, discarding its dynamic qualities and misusing it as material for historical research, philosophical speculation, or emotional excitement.

The difference between static and dynamic reading can be observed even with regard to single words. In static language we are either "just" or "unjust." In dynamic language we are "hungry for righteousness" or "workers of iniquity." The "kingdom of heaven" as a static concept is a certain state of affairs which exists or does not exist in history or beyond space and time. As a dynamic concept, it is a creative process. We can delay or hasten it, but it will influence us and change us for better or worse.

The static reader, if he is naïve, identifies himself with Jesus. The "Imitation of Christ," however, is bound to fail and ends in inner tension and mortification or in self-deception and hypocrisy. If the static reader is less naïve he takes a scientific attitude and considers the Gospel as an object for investigation. He does not identify himself with any character; he only tries to apply theoretical ideas and philosophical principles. He remains outside the precinct of the Gospel.

The dynamic reader is identified with the whole cast of the drama. One day he feels like Peter, trying to walk on the water and failing utterly. The next day he finds himself in the place of Thomas who doubts or even of Judas who betrays. Soon he realizes that while he is consciously Peter, he remains Thomas and Judas unconsciously. The dynamics of the outer drama are transferred to the inner stage of the reader's mind. The pairs of opposites[4] at first exclude each other. Peter and Judas cannot live together.

---

4. *Pair of opposites:* two equal human qualities which complete each other. *Balance of opposites:* no preference for one over the other. Fritz Kunkel, *In Search of Maturity*, p. 45.

Then Jesus says, "love your enemy," and Peter must forgive Judas. The reader must redeem his own inner enemy. The Shadow[5] must be integrated or Christ, the center of the inner drama, will never come to life. Dynamic reading is the mobilization of all the conflicting forces in the reader's soul. Good and evil tendencies, high and low powers, selfish and unselfish goals, must be contrasted and manifested and reconciled. There is no forgiveness, no reconciliation, without our conscious recognition of the negative force that has to be cleansed and accepted.

Matthew's artistic principle can, of course, be recognized by static as well as by dynamic readers. But the latter discover the strangest of all the strange things in this most familiar of our books. If we read one passage many times, and if our reading becomes increasingly dynamic, we observe a kind of spiritual architecture which is based in heaven and reaches down to our earth. What has been a mere word now becomes a bridge between everyday life and eternity.

It is one single thing, being in space and time and beyond space and time, being on earth in history and in heaven in eternity. The dynamic reader, and that means the real Christian, has known this all the time. It is the essential paradox of the Gospel: "Whoever loses his life for my sake will find it" (16:25). Matthew shows us at every intermediate step in every chapter and almost in every verse that the way down is the way up, that facing darkness may mean the discovery of light, and that death can become life.

Jesus' career ascends to its climax (16:16). There the mystery of the "Son of God" is disclosed. And Jesus' transfiguration inaugurates the new life. Then the way leads down to earth again, Jesus is persecuted, arrested and crucified. The anticlimax is the grave, surrounded by some rumors of immortality, like flowers around a tombstone. For the static reader, this is the end of the story.

Those who read dynamically see that the tragedy does not lead down into failure and annihilation. Persecution and crucifixion become translucent. They reveal a deeper, so far unknown, aspect of reality. Every event, every sentence, which at the first reading meant a new danger and a new step down towards crucifixion, now reveals its creative power and its value for the final victory.

---

5. Fritz Kunkel, *In Search of Maturity*, p. 118, note: "Shadow . . . the crystallization-point of all the powers which are repressed onto the unconscious." See also Frances Wickes, *The Inner World of Man*, Ch. VI. A part of oneself containing qualities considered inferior which have been excluded from consciousness but that hold values which, if consciously accepted, would make one's life more enjoyable and creative.

The dynamics of redeeming creation become visible; they begin to work within the reader himself. They blow through him like a strong wind. But he is not permitted to lose his grasp on our bloody earth. Death remains death, and the cross the cross. No idealism or easygoing spiritualism is allowed. The gate is still the tomb. Yet the tombstones become transparent. The light appears in the darkness. The grave opens beyond space and time, and Spirit finds itself in eternity.

Part One

THE GATE

Chapter 1

GENESIS

Jesus—Human or Divine?

> The book of the generation of Jesus Christ, the son of David,
> the son of Abraham. Abraham begat Isaac; and Isaac begat
> Jacob; and Jacob begat Judas and his brethren (1:1–2, KJV).

In the Greek version, the word *Genesis,* which has been var-
iously translated "generation, genealogy, origin," means also
"lineage, descent, nativity, birth," and even "nature, life, existence." Matthew promises to tell us all he knows about the most
fascinating personality in history; and in the very first sentence
he says extraordinary things. This man bears the divine title of
Christ, which means at the least that he is superhuman; but, at
the same time, he is an offspring of Abraham, a Jew, a human
being. The relationship between the human and the divine aspect
of his life will be the most disquieting problem for most of Matthew's readers. First, for their own sake, they will need to know
what the divinity of Christ really means. Second, in order to
understand history, they need to know how people could believe
in the "dual nature" of Jesus, how they could die for this belief.
Matthew's initial words "Book of Genesis" repeat the title of
the first book of the Old Testament. We are to witness a second
Genesis, a re-beginning, a rebirth. With Jesus starts a fresh phase
of creation. At the same time the values of the past are preserved.
Abraham and David carried "the blessing of the Lord," which was
the promise of an all embracing Jewish empire established by a
spiritual hero, the Messiah. Does this promise hold good for
Jesus? Matthew, however, calls him not Messiah, but Christ. The
two words have the same meaning, "the anointed one," but their
historical implications are as different as night and day. Thus,
the New Testament begins with a bewildering enigma, and we
anticipate that the transition from the old to the new, from the
Messiah to the Christ, will not be achieved without crises.

With some foreboding we read the solemn genealogy. Strange

names, unknown personalities, are connected by the ever-repeated statement that a father begat a son. The word "begat" occurs forty-one times, striking upon the ear with the monotonous insistence of a gong in a temple. We realize that the power of procreation was an integral part of the Divine Blessing when it was given to Abraham. But we know in advance that the Blessing which rested on Jesus was of a different kind. It is as if the powers and values of creation were suddenly stopped: they recoil and change their direction. Jesus begat no son. He is a strange son of Abraham.

Through fourteen generations the lineage soars to its climax in David the King. Four times, however, the solemn rhythm of the temple gong is interrupted. In opposition to the ancient custom four women are mentioned—famous women it is true, but each one representing a taint in the ancestry of Christ: Tamar—incest; Rahab—a harlot; Ruth—a foreigner; Bathsheba—adultery and murder. The more the power of the Blessing manifests itself in political success, the more it is endangered by human blindness and deviation. Four times we are reminded of human weakness. Four questionable women: should the fifth one, Mary, the mother of Jesus, be questionable too?

Scandalons

The best word to denote the mixture of sorrow and indignation which the average reader—ancient and modern alike—feels when he thinks of those old stories of incest, adultery and murder, is the Greek word *scandalon*. It is usually translated "offense, hindrance, stumbling-block"; its original meaning is "trap." In the New Testament it always indicates a situation of great dynamic potentiality, a crossroads in history, the possibility of failure and deviation as well as of victory and spiritual growth. Matthew has a deep knowledge of the significance and value of "scandalons." He does not spare his readers. Disquieting as it may be, he trusts that even the scandalous truth will make us free, if we can stand it. Commentators and preachers may try to smooth over the difficulties; Matthew puts his finger straight on the sore spot.

The story of Abraham's family is not pleasant at all. After King David, through fourteen generations, his progeny descend to the misery of the Babylonian exile; and then through fourteen more generations they wait in the darkness for the promised light. The last descendant, Joseph, has nothing left of David's inheritance but his spiritual nobility, the title "son of David"; otherwise he is but a poor carpenter working hard for a living. Then suddenly we hear he is not the father of Jesus at all.

> Jacob begat Joseph the husband of Mary, of whom was born Jesus, who is called Christ (1:16, KJV).

Jesus is neither Joseph's son nor David's nor Abraham's; a new "scandalon"! From the ancient point of view Jesus, not being the bodily offspring of Joseph, could not inherit the Blessing and therefore could not be the potential Messiah. The physical inheritance which we connect with the nobility of the blood is missing. He is not the princely heir of ancient kings. The text shows frankly that the whole birth-roll of forty-two generations is after all meaningless.

> So all the generations from Abraham to David are fourteen generations; and from David until the carrying away into Babylon are fourteen generations; and from the carrying away into Babylon unto Christ are fourteen generations (1:17, KJV).

Matthew, knowing that he has hurt his reader, inserts the calm and comforting statement about the three times fourteen generations. He wishes us to see that God controls the rhythm of history in spite of all the "scandalons" which his creatures produce. Then finally our question is answered: "The origin of Jesus was this . . ." Again the Greek version uses the word "genesis," linking the second half of the chapter with the first. Then follows in seven short verses one of the greatest dramas of mankind.

> Now the birth of Jesus Christ took place in this way. When his mother Mary had been betrothed to Joseph, before they came together she was found to be with child of the Holy Spirit; and her husband Joseph, being a just man and unwilling to put her to shame, resolved to divorce her quietly. But as he considered this, behold, an angel of the Lord appeared to him in a dream, saying, "Joseph, son of David, do not fear to take Mary your wife, for that which is conceived in her is of the Holy Spirit; she will bear a son, and you shall call his name Jesus, for he will save his people from their sins." All this took place to fulfill what the Lord had spoken by the prophet:
> "Behold, a virgin shall conceive and bear a son,
>   and his name shall be called Emmanuel"
> (which means, God with us). When Joseph woke from sleep, he did as the angel of the Lord commanded him; he took his wife, but knew her not until she had borne a son; and he called his name Jesus (1:18–25).

Mary is pregnant, but not from Joseph. He loves her. He feels that higher values than his own masculine pride are involved. He does not wish to disgrace her, but if he leaves her with an illegitimate child, that would disgrace her almost as much as a public trial. Thus he is caught and torn by conflicting impulses. All through human history, innumerable men have found themselves in the same situation, though not many have found Joseph's way out.

Jesus, the Son of David or the Son of God? Here we see Matthew's art. He has forced upon us the unanswerable question whether Jesus be the son of David or the son of God or both or neither one. Now, in his dynamic way, he gives us the answer. He makes us feel that every one of us is in Joseph's situation. We face the same dilemma: Who is Jesus' father? Joseph worried about the origin of his first born son; we worry about the origin of the most important man in history.

We experience the dynamic of the "scandalon." We may explode in impatient fury, calling it moral indignation, or we may refrain from acting until the deeper insight begins to speak to us in the night. The more we listen to the voice of our inner life, the sooner we shall know what God wants us to do. Thus it dawns on Joseph that Mary's motherhood is the will of God. Joseph is confronted with the dark forces of his own nature; hurt pride fights against love, and anger struggles with self-control. Joseph, and that means everybody in such a decisive moment, has to face himself. He has to face destiny. The weird power which has cornered him is greater than he is. He feels its presence in the dark. He stares at this strange power which is his own fate, and he senses it looking at him. It looks and speaks: "Thou son of David . . ." and it arouses the answer in his own inner depth: "Yes, I am the son of David, and of Bathsheba, the offspring of royal adultery and murder." All pride is gone; there is only human misery left, his and Mary's; and the future of the unborn child.

Mary is not a harlot. What happened to her? Joseph will never know the exact truth, nor shall we. The angel in Matthew's text says, ". . . that which is conceived in her is of the Holy Spirit." For a moment it seems clear, but then all our questions recur: What does it mean, "of the Holy Spirit"? We do not know. Like Joseph, we have to act on faith. It is the will of the Eternal that Mary have a child, and if Joseph and Mary accept their destiny the child will be exactly the person who is needed for the eternal goal of creation.

Now Joseph knows his task. He arises from sleep a new man, mature, determined, and faithful; he understands and accepts his role. The vision has taught him that he carries a great respon-

sibility. Creation continues, and Joseph has to make his contribution. The Messiah, perhaps, does not need to be a son of
Abraham? The future, perhaps, is more important than the past.

This is Matthew's first lesson to us modern readers as well as
to his students in Antioch: Understand that you are in Joseph's
position, facing the "scandalon" of the unanswerable question, "Is
Jesus the son of David or the son of God?" Whenever life is creative, it has to break through the walls of our individual pride. Our
scientific, moral, and religious convictions will time and again
prove to be obsolete. They will collapse in a painful crisis and
open the way for a new phase of creation. What hurts us as a
"scandalon" may become the beginning of a new life.

Chapter 2

THE NEW LIGHT

The Gate

> Now when Jesus was born in Bethlehem of Judea in the days of Herod the king, behold, wise men from the East came to Jerusalem, saying, "Where is he who has been born king of the Jews? For we have seen his star in the East, and have come to worship him." When Herod the king heard this, he was troubled, and all Jerusalem with him; and assembling all the chief priests and scribes of the people, he inquired of them where the Christ was to be born. They told him, "In Bethlehem of Judea; for so it is written by the prophet:
>> And you, O Bethlehem, in the land of Judah,
>> are by no means least among the rulers of Judah;
>> for from you shall come a ruler
>> who will govern my people Israel.' "
> Then Herod summoned the wise men secretly and ascertained from them what time the star appeared; and he sent them to Bethlehem, saying, "Go and search diligently for the child, and when you have found him bring me word, that I too may come and worship him" (2:1–8).

Between Chapters 1 and 2 there is a gap, like the silent night between two tumultuous days. In the secrecy of this gap, the great event takes place. Chapter 1 ends with the words, ". . . until she had borne a son." Chapter 2 begins, "Now when Jesus was born . . ." Luke fills the gap. He describes the Christmas night in an unforgettable way, with the manger, the shepherds, and the angels singing (Luke 2:1–14).

Matthew's Christmas message is not formulated in words. Between his Chapters 1 and 2, the reader is supposed to pause and think. Looking back to the wearisome genealogy and to the puzzle of Jesus' "irregular descent," looking forward to the bewildering stories of the three kings and the slaughter of the children in Bethlehem, we might say that Matthew's message is confusion and suffering rather than peace on earth and good will.

The contradiction between Luke's sweet harmonies and Matthew's shrill discords forces us into a new meditation. Did Jesus come to bring peace or the sword or both? Who will ever fathom the mystery of this child, high and low, born in King David's family, but in a manger? Some readers may decide that all this is interesting mythology or beautiful art, but nothing more. "If the most modern religion cannot offer more than the virgin birth and the three wise kings, then we have done with religion forever." They drop the book, and the book drops them. They are not admitted. Other may complain: "It does not make sense. All these angels, dreams and miracles are not authentic, of course, yet there is something fascinating in Matthew's presentation, so let us go on reading." These are admitted partially; with their hearts they enter the precinct of the Gospel, but their intellects are still excluded.

The gap between the two chapters turns out to be a gate. An invisible power seems to stand at the threshold, sifting the readers who believe they are sifting the text. The first interval in Matthew's symphony indicates the entrance of the Christchild into our world and at the same time the admission or rejection of those who are attracted by the child's magnetism.

Luke illustrates the fascinating power which emanated from the Child. He records at length the adoration of the shepherds and of Simeon and Anna (Luke 2:15–18, 25–28). Matthew gives a single instance, but a more effective one: the visit of the Magi. These three astrologers from Persia recognized in the stars the time and place of the Child's birth. Though "heathen," they were keenly aware of the signs of the times, and were therefore admitted to the mystery. But first they had to meet another "King of the Jews," Herod.

Violence Confronting Light Destroys Itself

> When they had heard the king they went their way; and lo, the star which they had seen in the East went before them, till it came to rest over the place where the child was. When they saw the star, they rejoiced exceedingly with great joy; and going into the house they saw the child with Mary his mother, and they fell down and worshiped him. Then, opening their treasures, they offered him gifts, gold and frankincense and myrrh. And being warned in a dream not to return to Herod, they departed to their own country by another way.
>
> Now when they had departed, behold, an angel of the Lord appeared to Joseph in a dream and said, "Rise, take the child and his mother, and flee to Egypt, and remain there till I tell you; for Herod is about to search for the child, to destroy him." And he rose and took the child and his mother by night, and departed to Egypt, and remained there until the death of

Herod. This was to fulfil what the Lord had spoken by the prophet, "Out of Egypt have I called my son."

Then Herod, when he saw that he had been tricked by the wise men, was in a furious rage, and he sent and killed all the male children in Bethlehem and in all that region who were two years old or under, according to the time which he had ascertained from the wise men. Then was fulfilled what was spoken by the prophet Jeremiah:

"A voice was heard in Ramah,
wailing and loud lamentation,
Rachel weeping for her children;
she refused to be consoled,
because they were no more."

But when Herod died, behold, an angel of the Lord appeared in a dream to Joseph in Egypt, saying, "Rise, take the child and his mother, and go to the land of Israel, for those who sought the child's life are dead." And he rose and took the child and his mother, and went to the land of Israel. But when he heard that Archelaus reigned over Judea in place of his father Herod, he was afraid to go there, and being warned in a dream he withdrew to the district of Galilee. And he went and dwelt in a city called Nazareth, that what was spoken by the prophets might be fulfilled, "He shall be called a Nazarene" (2:9–23).

Herod not only represents the irritability and selfishness of all human tyrants; he also illustrates the historical background of Jesus' life; namely the cruelty and pettiness of the Jewish government under Roman supervision. Palestine, at that time, was not the idyllic land that some writers would have us believe it to be. The whole population was torn by political seditions. Riots and bloody retaliations were daily occurrences. During his childhood Jesus probably witnessed a very large number of crucifixions. Herod's slaughter of the children in Bethlehem must be understood as a typical illustration of this reign of terror.

King Herod pretended to share the common hope for "peace on earth" and honesty and decency (and he may even have deceived himself that he truly cherished these values), but as soon as the real representative of the Light appeared, he felt compelled to destroy him. Mass murder is the unavoidable reaction of innumerable Herods, whenever the Light tries to win a foothold in the dark country. It is as if Matthew wants us to learn something about the strategy of the Light in its unending warfare against darkness. The casualties are inexplicably high, it is true; yet, if we were in charge of the armies of Light, could we think of a better policy? Could we spare casualties without depriving the dark powers of their free will? We have to conquer them in full freedom, not by violence. Therefore, they must, first of all, be-

come manifest in their destructiveness. They must appear in all
their deadly negativity before they can be overcome; indeed they
must begin to destroy themselves.

The terrible rage of Herod proves his helplessness. He cannot
destroy the little child who frightens him; and this failure,
though it is paid for with the lives of hundreds of innocent
children, is the inevitable cost of our spiritual growth. The process
has worked all through history, and is still operating in our day,
with all the great and little Herods who surround us, especially
the Herod who resides in our own souls.

The Light cannot be destroyed, but it can be forced to withdraw; it can be shut out. The three wise men, as well as Joseph,
are servants of the Light, and are therefore able to receive and to
understand its commands. Herod is cheated, and the child is
brought to Egypt. Such a temporary withdrawal, as we shall see,
is one of the great moves which can be found wherever the
creative power is in operation. We should hardly appreciate this
principle, however, had not Jesus developed it into a definite and
conscious strategy, and had not Matthew understood and described it in his book.

The Light withdraws. Darkness enjoys its temporary superiority, and lashes out in all its destructiveness and ugliness. Then,
when darkness begins to wane, disintegrating through the exag-
geration of its own horrors, the Light returns, and the course of
history changes.

It has been said that Egypt itself stands for darkness, and that
Jesus, in his childhood, had to pass through a period of "Egyptian
errors." It is more likely, however, that Matthew wished to em-
phasize the parallelism between Jesus' childhood and the history
of the Jewish nation. This outstanding child had to go through
all the important experiences of Jewish history. It is an ancient
expression of the modern idea that every child, during the first
few years of his life, repeats the whole evolution of his race.
For Matthew and his students Egypt probably had the double
aspect which it shows all through Jewish tradition, namely, the
"fleshpots," the carefreeness and irresponsibility of early childhood, and, on the other hand, "slavery," lack of freedom, dependence; thus it symbolizes our bondage to the power of the past.

When Joseph finally received the order to return, he chose his
new home not at Jerusalem, but in an inconspicuous place on
the outskirts of his country. Nazareth, an unknown village, becomes the headquarters for the impending campaign of the Light.
The decisive battle would have to be fought one day in the very

center of the spiritual world (which meant at that time in the temple at Jerusalem), but the preparation of the commander and the training of the army had to be achieved behind the front.

Meditation: The New Light

The first two chapters in Matthew's Gospel are characterized by definitely mythological features. This separates them from the rest of the book, and the experts are inclined to discard them as "unhistorical." Moreover, Matthew, here, is hopelessly at variance with the corresponding chapters in Luke. Even the genealogies do not tally.

Mark and John have no record about Jesus' parents and childhood; and Paul, the earliest and most reliable of all the New Testament writers, does not mention the virgin birth, though his philosophical interest in the preexistence of Christ could have biased him in this direction. He discouraged the discussion of Jesus' genealogy (1 Tim. 1:4; Titus 3:9), but he stressed that Jesus was "made of the seed of David according to the flesh; and declared to be the Son of God with power according to the Spirit of holiness, by the resurrection from the dead" (Rom. 1:3–4).

The situation is bewildering for the historian but it yields important results to the psychologist. Why did Luke and Matthew speak about Jesus' parents at all, and why did they insist—though in different ways—on the virgin birth? The oral tradition of the first century seems to have developed several stories about Jesus' supernatural origin. Was it the emotional enthusiasm which wanted everything in his life to be superhuman and miraculous? It certainly was not the biographical interest which we feel today. However that may be, our question is not only why and how the stories about the virgin birth arose, but why Matthew chose to write his first two chapters as he actually did.

The answer is here the same as it will be time and again in the course of our investigation: Matthew chooses what serves his purpose best; and his purpose is to initiate his students into Christianity. He wants not only to increase their knowledge but to influence them emotionally and to change the very structure of their character. Here we discover the method of Matthew's teachings; and if there were any doubt about its effectiveness, we would only have to look at the Middle Ages and our own childhood. The Madonna has guarded and guided the lives of innumerable people for many centuries. The Christmas tree still warms and lights the memories of our early years.

The Christmas tree links Jesus of Nazareth as the bringer of the new Light with the old sun-gods and heroes who caused the light to come back and the days to grow longer at the end of the year. Prometheus was a bringer of light as well as Jesus, but on a different level; he stole the fire and was punished by Zeus. Jesus brought us the Light at God's command and was punished by man. This new Light, as we shall see, can appear within every man, freeing him from the past, endowing him with new creative power and guiding him toward a higher and more spiritual life. Paul described it by the words: "Christ lives in me" (Gal. 2:20); Meister Eckhardt called it the "birth of the Son in the castle of our soul";[1] the Quakers call it "The Light Within."[2] All of them agree that this light appears "by grace." The human soul, as it were, is its mother; the father is the eternal spirit. It is a virgin birth. At Christmas we celebrate this coming of the light, this virgin birth of Christianity within each one of us.

Matthew's drama in the outer world is good psychology; it gives an exact account of the inner drama which occurs in the human psyche before and while the birth takes place. It depicts the favorable as well as the unfavorable factors surrounding the great event: a propensity to worship and to search for the new light all over the earth—symbolized by the three kings traveling across the outer and inner desert, a mysterious star guiding them; Joseph struggles and conquers his pride; Herod kills much potential life, outside and inside himself, but he misses the point; Mary in amazement and unspeakable joy accepts the new life as if it were the most natural thing in the world. And so it is.

---

1. Meister Eckhardt, *Meister Eckhardt, A Modern Translation*, Sermons 23 and 24.
2. Thomas Kelly, *A Testament of Devotion*.

Chapter 3

BAPTISM

John's Message: Confession, Repentance, Baptism

> In those days came John the Baptist, preaching in the wilderness of Judea, "Repent, for the kingdom of heaven is at hand." For this is he who was spoken of by the prophet Isaiah when he said,
> > "The voice of one crying in the wilderness:
> > Prepare the way of the Lord,
> > make his paths straight."
> Now John wore a garment of camel's hair, and a leather girdle around his waist; and his food was locusts and wild honey. Then went out to him Jerusalem and all Judea and all the region about the Jordan, and they were baptized by him in the river Jordan, confessing their sins.
> But when he saw many of the Pharisees and Sadducees coming for baptism, he said to them, "You brood of vipers! Who warned you to flee from the wrath to come? Bear fruit that befits repentance, and do not presume to say to yourselves, 'We have Abraham as our father'; for I tell you, God is able from these stones to raise up children to Abraham. Even now the ax is laid to the root of the trees; every tree therefore that does not bear good fruit is cut down and thrown into the fire" (3:1–10).

Between Chapters 2 and 3 there is an interval of about thirty years. What did Jesus do, how was he brought up, what did he learn? Matthew omits the many stories which (as we know from the later apocryphal gospels) were told in the Christian communities. He leads us right to the Baptist, preaching in the wilderness.

John's personality and his message fitted exactly the popular expectation of his time. Many Jews were awaiting the Messiah; and, according to their tradition, another prophet, a reincarnation of Elijah, should precede him. The Baptist understood that this was his role. Modern psychologists would say that he incorporated the tribal idea; he carried the collective image[1] of the

---

1. *Collective image:* An inherited unconscious symbol which has appeared in dream and myth throughout countless ages. Frances G. Wickes, *The Inner World of Man*, Ch. VI.

forerunner of the Messiah. He was completely conditioned by it and was unable to outgrow it. Thus he remained in the precinct of the Old Testament. His concept of the kingdom of heaven corresponded to the visions of the apocalyptic prophets. His success, therefore, was enormous; but nothing new happened. Without Jesus' appearance, John's life would have been futile. Not the incorporation of a collective idea, but its development and change against the wish and expectation of the people is what precipitates evolution.

The first three gospels use the Greek imperative *metanoeite* to indicate the Baptist's message. All English translations render it by "repent," and the Latin by *poenitentiam agite* (do penitence). This gives too narrow an impression. It is true the Baptist was a moralist, but he knew that good works alone do not suffice. He wished a real inner change of the human character, including thinking, feeling and volition. "Bear fruit that befits repentance" (3:8).

John had two means of producing this effect: the confession of sins and baptism. Both were needed. The Pharisees and Sadducees who came to his baptism were denied the ceremony presumably because their confessions were not sincere or not complete.

With the plain folk of the countryside, confession is a simple thing. They know what they are and the deeds they have done. With sophisticated city-dwellers, however, it is altogether different. These might have a good conscience, though they are unconsciously deviated. Confession then becomes a long and intricate process of discovering "secret sins," or in modern language, of analyzing unconscious content.

The Baptist appeals to the simple mind but has no access to the leaders of the nation. His message, therefore, turns into the old revolutionary pattern of Amos. He knows his weakness, and relies on the strength of the one who is "mightier than he," whose shoes he is not worthy to bear, and who will baptize with fire.

> "I baptize you with water for repentance, but he who is coming after me is mightier than I, whose sandals I am not worthy to carry; he will baptize you with the Holy Spirit and with fire. His winnowing fork is in his hand, and he will clear his threshing floor and gather his wheat into the granary, but the chaff he will burn with unquenchable fire."
>
> Then Jesus came from Galilee to the Jordan to John, to be baptized by him (3:11–13).

Then follows the great scene which contains the highest example of Matthew's humor. The revivalist proclaims in thun-

derous fury that the Messiah is near. The people listen, aghast and
frightened. He shouts at the top of his voice, ". . . the chaff he
will burn with unquenchable fire!" Then he stops, and in the
silence which ensues the inconspicuous carpenter appears, exactly the opposite of what the Baptist has foretold. Yet everybody
feels: This is He!

It is difficult to imagine a moment more embarrassing for a
great preacher and more amusing for the friends of the carpenter.
Mark's and Luke's records contain the same elements; but Matthew alone achieves the dramatic climax, and he does so by exag-
gerating the Baptist's sermon and lowering the tone of the
following sentence which introduces Jesus upon the scene. The
contrast between verse twelve and verse thirteen in the original
Greek is so striking that most translators have imitated it, even
if they were not aware of the humorous effect.

The Baptist is stunned by Jesus' arrival, and it is a tribute to
both his courage and his humility that he recognizes Jesus as the
potential Messiah, different though he be from traditional expectation. This acknowledgment may be due, however, just as
much to the strength of Jesus' personality as to John's open-
mindedness. Later, as we shall see, the Baptist had serious misgivings, and probably could never forgive Jesus for not living up
to the picture he had painted.

Baptism as Jesus Experienced It

> John would have prevented him, saying, "I need to be bap-
> tized by you, and do you come to me?" But Jesus answered
> him, "Let it be so now; for thus it is fitting for us to fulfill all
> righteousness." Then he consented. And when Jesus was bap-
> tized, he went up immediately from the water, and behold, the
> heavens were opened and he saw the Spirit of God descending
> like a dove, and alighting on him; and lo, a voice from
> heaven, saying, "This is my beloved Son, with whom I am well
> pleased" (3:14–17).

Jesus wanted to be baptized, and this means he wished to
confess his sins. Many commentators try to avoid this difficulty,
since "Jesus Christ knows no sin." They agree that John's
baptism was granted to all who had a good conscience and that
the confession was necessary only in case the initiate's conscience was not yet clear. Matthew was convinced also that Jesus
had no sin on his conscience; yet the argument in his record
about who should baptize whom allows a fuller interpretation.
If we assume that confession and baptism are two inseparable
factors of "metanoia," and Jesus could have baptized John as well

as John baptized Jesus, and if we add that the story of Jesus'
temptation in the desert was known soon afterwards among his
disciples, we are forced to the conclusion that "confessing one's
sins" must have been more than the words now convey. It
must have been what we would call in modern language "discussing one's inner problems." The discussion between Jesus
and the Baptist was certainly not a one-sided "confession" in the
present sense of the word. It seems to have been a giving and
taking, a mutual searching, an exchange of ideas. The Greek
word for "confessing" allows at least such an interpretation, and
perhaps even suggests it.

If we accept this hypothesis, we understand that the encounter
between the Baptist and Jesus was the latter's initiation, regardless of the spiritual inferiority of John. It was Jesus' "metanoia,"
the shake-up of his mind, the turning point of his life.

Jesus' first temptation. The Baptist's offer to change roles
appears as a serious danger; indeed, it was Jesus' first great
temptation. It would have been easy for him to accept the leadership, to become the head of John's movement and to live and die
as a famous miracle-worker and pseudo-Messiah. Here, as in
many other instances, Jesus found his way with clairvoyant
certainty. These stories cannot have been invented by his disciples.
Both the temptations and his resisting them are so extraordinary
and at the same time so subtle that they surpass the limits of
understanding for the average disciple and possibly for Matthew
himself.

Jesus was aware of the dangers which surrounded him, and
therefore he was eager to discuss them with this experienced
father-confessor. The content of this first temptation is closely
connected with the three classic temptations which Matthew
describes in the following chapter. Thus, we may safely infer
that his "confession" was actually a discussion of his chief
problem; and this problem was the possible misuse of his power.

Jesus first decisive step then was that he did not misuse his
power over the Baptist. He understood that he could overcome
this inner danger by going through the age-old process of initiation, regardless of his being more advanced than the initiator.
"Thus it is fitting for us to fulfil all righteousness" (3:15).

Baptism: gateway to a new reality. The majority of interpreters
throughout the centuries have said that the immersion of the
initiate into flowing water symbolized cleansing. They were right,
but they did not know the whole story. Other authors interpret
baptism as a drowning of the old personality, to make room for

the birth of a new. In Saint Paul's language, "old Adam must die." The past form of character is melted and washed away, together with the dust that covers the body, while the submerged individual for a few moments faces death in drowning; but this is not the whole story.

We know from a comparison of the Jewish baptism with similar initiation rites of other ancient cults, that this going down into the water symbolized a regression into the primeval state of existence. The human body, for a moment, ceases to be the carrier of individual consciousness. The participant becomes an unconscious part of the material substance of the universe. He goes back into the womb whence the Creator called him. He becomes matter again, and then emerges, breathing anew, on a higher level, as a conscious spirit; he is actually "reborn."

If the baptized person takes his experience as a symbol in the sense of a visible substitute for something invisible that might or might not happen, nothing will happen indeed. He will consider himself baptized, but his inner structure, his tendencies and limitations will remain as they were, with the addition only of a new self-deception; he will believe erroneously that he has made a step forward. If this experience has real meaning for him in the sense of being a visible part of an actual, though mostly invisible, inner evolution, it must express itself in the discovery of a new aspect of reality. The one who emerges from the water, as someone who has passed through death, is definitely more mature. He knows more, feels more deeply, wills more powerfully, and lives more truly than the one who came to be baptized.

In Jesus' case, both the discourse with the Baptist and the symbol of baptism itself must have been so real and so effectual that the last part of the ritual became an experience of utmost impressiveness, not only to himself but also to those who witnessed it. "The Heavens were opened"; he saw the Spirit descending like a dove. It was an experience of ecstasy. Matthew describes it in the same terms as other mystics: a light, a bright shining figure, a white or fiery something, perhaps a bird, comes down from Heaven. At Pentecost it was "cloven tongues of fire" (Acts 2:3); and when Jesus spoke of initiation to Nicodemus (John 3:5), he described it as a rebirth "of water and of breath." (The exact meaning of the Greek word for "Spirit" is "breath.") He was apparently describing the experience of his own baptism, but he left no doubt that he wished every Christian to undergo the same process.

Matthew does not permit us to identify ourselves with Jesus.

We cannot yet participate in his initiation. We can only look at him in amazement, and see that something unheard of has happened. Soon, however, we shall understand that the same thing might happen to us, and the sooner and the more thoroughly, the more we can follow him. Thus Jesus' experience of initiation becomes for him the gate leading into Messiahship, and for us it becomes the gate leading into discipleship.

What we want to know now, of course, is the real meaning of the expression "Son of God." But Matthew seems to answer: "You will learn it later. It takes a long time and much inner development until you can grasp it. So you had better go on reading."

Chapter 4

TEMPTATIONS

The First Inner Steps: Three Temptations

> Then Jesus was led up by the Spirit into the wilderness to be
> tempted by the devil. And he fasted forty days and forty nights,
> and afterward he was hungry. And the tempter came and said
> to him, "If you are the Son of God, command these stones to
> become loaves of bread." But he answered, "It is written,
> 'Man shall not live by bread alone,
> but by every word that proceeds from the mouth of God.' "
> Then the devil took him to the holy city, and set him on the
> pinnacle of the temple, and said to him, "If you are the Son
> of God, throw yourself down; for it is written,
> 'He will give his angels charge of you,'
> and
> 'On their hands they will bear you up,
> lest you strike your foot against a stone.' "
> Jesus said to him, "Again it is written, 'You shall not tempt
> the Lord your God.' " Again, the devil took him to a very high
> mountain, and showed him all the kingdoms of the world and
> the glory of them; and he said to him, "All these I will give
> you, if you will fall down and worship me." Then Jesus said
> to him, "Begone, Satan! for it is written,
> 'You shall worship the Lord your god
> and him only shall you serve.' "
> Then the devil left him, and behold, angels came and min-
> istered to him" (4:1–11).

At the beginning of Chapter 1 the reader was confronted with
the question: Who is Jesus' father? The question has been
answered: God is the Father. Now, in Chapter 4, the question is
raised: What will the "Son of God" do with his sonship? He found
his Father, and he experienced an overwhelming increase of
creative power. He is the "mightier one" whom the Baptist foretold, the one who will "baptize with the Holy Spirit and fire."
What kind of baptism will this be? He is supposed to bring the
"kingdom of heaven," and we wonder what kind of a kingdom

this is. Will he carry out one of the visionary dreams set forth by the Old Testament prophets?

Decisions of utmost importance had to be made. They were made silently in Jesus' own mind and in communion with his Father. Again we see that we are not admitted to the secrets of Jesus' inner life, but are told exactly as much as will be helpful for our (meaning the disciples') spiritual development. It is likely that Jesus himself decided how much he wanted his followers to know about the great inner struggle which made him in reality what the "voice" had appointed him to be, the "Son of God."

The first verse of Chapter 4 is loaded with theological and psychological problems—loaded indeed, with the fate of mankind. "Then Jesus was led into the desert by the Spirit to be tempted by the devil" (4:1, Moffatt).

Almost all great men, when they are initiated, feel the need of being alone. They give up the traditional form of life; they leave behind the master who initiated them and the crowds who expect a new leader. There, in the desert, Jesus finds himself face to face with the unknown. The future will be different from all expectations. Neither John the Baptist nor any other person, neither books nor rites, can help him. He has outgrown all of them. The past is past. Mark tells us that "he was with the wild beasts" and that "the angels ministered to him" (Mark 1:13). The more we are humanly alone, the more we are haunted by the conflicting powers which sway the lives of individuals and races. The future is fighting to overcome the past. The wilderness outside corresponds to the wilderness within: the battlefield of the soul.

Jesus was keenly aware of the fact that God's creative power forces us, and cannot help but force us, to meet with temptation almost every moment of our lives. There is no step forward which does not present the possibility of error, and the great step forward which Jesus had to take was surrounded by so many dangers and included so many possibilities of mistake and failure that he, more than anyone else, might have experienced the need of his prayer, "Lead us not into temptation." In modern language this prayer says, "Help us to become creative without being misled by our new possibilities."

Two features stand out clearly when we think of Jesus facing his temptations in the desert, and both apply to us as much as they do to him. The first of these is his freedom with regard to God. The Spirit leads him to the place of utmost danger—the place of encounter with the devil—then leaves it to him as to how he will cope with the situation. The Spirit does not hold our hand, showing us every step of the way. We are not allowed to be blind tools of God, as hand and foot are our own tools. We are always left with our own free will, to decide on our own account how to interpret and how to fulfill the will of God.

The second feature is individual independence: Jesus' freedom with regard to men. He turns away from tribal traditions and conventional expectations. The new way cannot be found by large groups. The birth of the future takes place within the mind of the individual. This segregation from the collective support of the tribe is the most difficult part of the forty days in the desert.

Whenever the inner awakening takes place in an individual mind, powerful negative images arise: the power of the past, the fear of the new, and the inertia of matter which resists further creation. If under the guise of loyalty we offer our creative forces to a part, the past part, and not to the whole of creation, we succeed for a short time in serving this limited image rather than the imageless whole, and then fail utterly.

Three great, though one-sided, images of this sort have time and again captured the creative imagination of mankind, and in the desert Jesus withstood them all. They are: (1) The "Great Provider," offering bread and physical welfare for all, and nothing more; (2) the "Great Conqueror" who enslaves nations under the guise of promising glory and security; (3) the "Great Priest," performing miracles and prescribing for the masses just what they should and should not believe.

The lure of these three images is so similar to the will of God that the inner voice which propagates them may easily be confused with the creative command of the Eternal. Their goal, however, is a finite goal, absolutized for a moment, and therefore a goal of a pseudogod, a devil, or more correctly speaking, it is our own fiendish delusion, our inertia, which worships the part instead of the whole, and changes our creative forces into destructive ones.

Temptation of material power: the Great Provider. The first temptation refers to nourishment. The most simple and natural need of mankind may be answered if the "Son of God" concentrates his creative power on this fundamental problem. If bread can be manufactured by some new device, not only Jesus' hunger but the hunger of all the poor people in the world can be satisfied. The "greatest happiness of the greatest number" can be expected.

In modern phraseology it is the temptation of materialism. In Jesus' time, it corresponds to the hedonistic ideals of the Sadducees. Psychologically, it means that if Jesus had yielded, he would have impersonated an inner image which was alive in the Jewish people since the prophecy of Amos: "my people of Israel . . . shall plant vineyards and drink the wine thereof; they shall also make gardens, and eat the fruit of them. And . . . they shall no more be pulled up out of their land which I have given them, saith the Lord thy God" (Amos 9:14–15, KJV).

The great dream of the Golden Age, bread for all, has poisoned the imagination of innumerable reformers; and they have perished in the tempter's net. Jesus saw through the delusion. He knew that bread, the satisfaction of physical needs, would not change the character of man. Old Adam, well fed, remains as egocentric, ambitious and cruel as he ever was; the more bread he has, the more lazy he becomes, and the less inclined to enter the painful struggle toward spiritual evolution, for which we need dissatisfaction. We need the nourishment of mind and spirit as much as the nourishment of the body. The higher evolution of mankind cannot start with the providing of bread and nothing but bread. Only if the hunger of mankind is understood as spiritual, even where it expresses itself as physical hunger, can the food be provided by a new step of creation.

Jesus was not the prophet of materialism. Social justice, and that means bread for all, in his school of thought had to come as a result of the inner development of man, not as its presupposition.

Temptation of political power: the Great Conqueror. Matthew's second temptation corresponds to Luke's third one, the most important temptation for Jesus, as for every other person. Luke's logical pattern puts it as a climax at the end of the temptations. We will follow here Luke's arrangement. The image of the King-Messiah arises. The hope and love of millions of people is invested in this ideal, and from early childhood Jesus' imagination had been fed with its heroic beauty. The son of David, a national hero, had to come.

Jesus must have felt strong enough to mobilize the revolutionary forces of the subdued nations and to conquer "all the kingdoms of the world and the glory of them," yet he refused this way. By this decision Jesus condemned nationalism and imperialism once and for all as a way of further human evolution. Spiritual development cannot be achieved by coercion; it presupposes freedom. And no imperialism is possible without violence and power policy. Jesus' answer, therefore, is—and our answer in a similar situation should be—that the Creator and His creative power represent the highest value; new forms of life will be created.

Thus, the image of the King-Messiah is removed from Jesus' inner life. He will be immune to all attempts of individuals and groups which may offer him political leadership. He will face their disappointment and take the risk that they may feel betrayed and even cooperate with his enemies in bringing about his destruction.

Jesus established the spiritual center of his life, not by means of conquest and war, nor by means of material abundance, but by relying on "the Lord God." What, then, would be the most efficient and infallible way to spiritual victory? This question forms the basis of Jesus'—and our—most dangerous temptation.

Temptation of magic power: the Great Priest. If a person were to leap from the topmost pinnacle of the temple without hurting himself, the result of this event would be unique in history. First, the one who did it would have definite proof that he was a "Son of God," and that he was free to use his power in whatever way he thought fit. Moreover, nobody else could question his power. The supremacy of the spirit over the body would be demonstrated; and not only the Jews, but also the Greeks and the Romans would have to acknowledge his divine authority. How simple it would be then to introduce the kingdom of heaven on earth! If necessary, the performance could be repeated every Sunday, and the spiritual result would of necessity follow.

Here is the weak spot in the devil's argument. The miracle, misused as scientific evidence of divine power, presupposes the guarantee that this miracle will occur as often as we provoke it. God has promised that His angels will protect the "Son of God." If this promise be as rigid a certainty as are all natural or mathematical laws, it can be used like electricity or gunpowder. God is no longer free. To "tempt God" is a terrible thing, because it is the effort to destroy God's freedom, and not only God's but all freedom throughout the universe. If the Messiah forces God to act according to His promise, the essence of his messianic mission, namely, to bring freedom and maturity to men and to turn them from "servants" into "sons" of the Eternal, will be frustrated by the very means which the Messiah applies. The more we need miracles, the more we sink into spiritual slavery. The nearer we come to spiritual maturity, the more we are opposed to miracles, and the less we need them. Whenever Jesus was forced to use his "miraculous" power, he tried to avoid all publicity.

All this, of course, applies to us as well as to Jesus. The ninety-first psalm (v. 6), "He will give his angels charge. . . ," quoted by the tempter, is not addressed to the Messiah alone. The psalmist speaks to all those who experience some direct relationship with God. Moreover, each human being who prays seriously has experiences of this kind. Some miraculous coincidence, some unforeseen help or guidance, some happening against the law of averages, will make him feel that he is protected in a special way, and the infinite power of creation cooperates with him. Then why not rely on this power? Spend your money! The Great Treasurer in Heaven will send you a check in due time. This is tempting God; be aware not to become the wrong kind of Messiah.

The New Goal

Jesus rejected the three ideals of his time, and of ours: the materialism of the Sadducees, the power policy of the Romans, and the spiritual totalitarianism of the Pharisees. It was not for him to follow the beaten track. If creation were to continue, he had to find a new way altogether, and this way had to be based on a new relationship to the Eternal. On the one hand, God was his Father; His will was supreme; the initiative always had to come from Him. On the other hand, there was no guarantee that God would protect him if he misused the divine power. But the Son was not to be a blind fool or an obedient slave. On the contrary, a new degree of freedom and responsibility was indicated by the words "Son of God" in contradistinction to a "servant of God." The new task could not any longer be expressed in the language of the Old Testament. Jesus had to live—to make real the new ineffable truth.

At the end of the forty days in the desert, his mission was clear to Jesus. He turned away from the well-known paths of human life, and set out into the unknown future. By doing so, he entered a new phase of creation.

The First Outer Steps: The Beginning Mission

> Now when he heard that John had been arrested, he withdrew into Galilee; and leaving Nazareth he went and dwelt in Capernaum by the sea, in the territory of Zebulun and Naphtali, that what was spoken by the prophet Isaiah might be fulfilled:

"The land of Zebulun and the land of Naphtali,
toward the sea, across the Jordan,
Galilee of the Gentiles—
the people who sat in darkness
have seen a great light,
and for those who sat in the region and shadow of death
light has dawned."
From that time Jesus began to preach, saying, "Repent for the
kingdom of heaven is at hand."
As he walked by the Sea of Galilee, he saw two brothers,
Simon who is called Peter and Andrew his brother, casting a
net into the sea; for they were fishermen. And he said to them,
"Follow me, and I will make you fishers of men." Immediately
they left their nets and followed him. And going on from there
he saw two other brothers, James the son of Zebedee and John
his brother, in the boat with Zebedee their father, mending their
nets, and he called them. Immediately they left the boat and
their father, and followed him.
And he went about all Galilee, teaching in their synagogues
and preaching the gospel of the kingdom and healing every
disease and every infirmity among the people. So his fame
spread throughout all Syria, and they brought him all the sick,
those afflicted with various diseases and pains, demoniacs, epileptics, and paralytics, and he healed them. And great crowds
followed him from Galilee and the Decapolis and Jerusalem
and Judea and from beyond the Jordan (4:12–25).

As soon as Jesus in his inner development entered the new life,
facing the dangers and accepting the conditions of his "Sonship,"
a corresponding change took place in his outer life. His missionary life began. His predecessor, the Baptist, was arrested by
King Herod, the son of Herod the Great. The present was dark
and the light had to fight its way through the clouds. The Baptist
would be executed in all likelihood, just as all his forerunners
had been, as a rebel against the Herodian dynasty or the Roman
Empire. There was no reason to assume that his successor would
meet with a better fate.

The paradox that light comes out of darkness was well known
to the old prophets. Since the Babylonian exile they had said that
Israel had to undergo utmost darkness in order to see the light of
"the day of the Lord." The average Jew, however, expected the
new light at the very moment that the Messiah would appear.

Jesus' first move is a step of great importance. He goes from
Nazareth to Capernaum; from the little village in the hills to the
busy town by the lake; but he does not yet go to Jerusalem.

Jesus began exactly where the Baptist left off. He took over
the latter's slogan, "Repent, for the kingdom of heaven is at hand."
But the words "kingdom" and "at hand" meant for him something

far more powerful and real than anything imagined by the Baptist. Yet it took much work to bring out that greater meaning. Indeed, it took his death to make his disciples understand that the new life had not only drawn near, but had actually begun.

Soon people were fascinated by the magnetism of the new prophet. Many chose him, but out of those many he chose four, Peter, Andrew, James and John, the leaders of the future army of the Light. They renounced their professions, their families and their traditional ideas, following him with complete trust into the unknown future.

Meditation: The Old and the New

Matthew's dynamic mind saw and wanted to express a deeper truth. In that Jesus' life broke out of the traditional casting-mold, the structure and essence of evolution vaguely foreseen by ancient visionaries now made its appearance in history. The myth became truth: and reality by far outgrew all prophecies.

The splendor of the new historic cycle is so dazzling that we would be frightened by it, unable to grasp the meaning, were it not for some familiar traits which allow us to connect the new with the old. Not so much the outer events in Matthew's narrative but the reader's inner experiences—if he can read dynamically— are utterly bewildering. We are blinded like Luke's shepherds when "the glory of the Lord shone all around them" (Luke 2:9), and we need a comforting voice: Have no fear. All this is not new; for thousands of years the sages have expected such a spiritual revolution. Open your eyes; you can learn to look into the eternal fire.

Part Two

THE CHART OF INITIATION

The Sermon on the Mount

Steps on the Way to the Kingdom of Heaven

The Sermon on the Mount has been labeled in a thousand
different ways: "The proclamation of the kingdom of heaven,"
"An exposition of Christian morality," "The goal of human living,"
"A means of communion with God." Each writer reads it through
his own eyeglasses and praises or condemns it from his point
of view. Seen through the eyeglasses of a religious psychologist, all
those statements are unsatisfactory. To him the Sermon on the
Mount is the chart of initiation as taught by a great adept. This
adept dared to divulge the secrets of the kingdom, knowing that
they would be misunderstood and misused by countless followers
and yet rediscovered time and again when circumstances would
permit.

The practical nature of this Sermon has been rightly stressed
by Gerald Heard: "The Sermon on the Mount tells us what to do,
what will happen to us if we do it and what will happen to us
if we don't. It is the spiritual law of human life rather than a
moral law. It does not condemn us morally if we prefer the 'wide
gate that leadeth to destruction.' It simply states that in this
case we shall be destroyed. The choice of the road is ours, and
the study of the map also."[1]

The Sermon on the Mount is not a good example of oratory.
It is unlikely that Jesus ever loaded one single discourse with so
heavy a weight of truth; yet he may have repeated these terse
statements again and again, as the summaries of longer teaching;
and what we study now may be the epitomes of a hundred lessons.
Luke's parallel passages (especially Luke 6:20–26) are un-
doubtedly better as examples of Jesus' method of teaching. But
Matthew gave us an unsurpassed sequence of instructions for
spiritual expeditions into the unknown. He arranged them in such

---

1. Gerald Heard, *The Creed of Christ*, p. 6.

a way that we can actually use them for our self-education; and if we dare to do so, they lead us into the fathomless depths of religious experience.

The whole Sermon on the Mount can be understood as a treatise on spiritual diet; it teaches us that spiritual evolution means acceptance and assimilation of experiences, joyful and painful alike. The Lord's Prayer (6:9–13) is the center of the whole Sermon. This, of course, will not surprise us; and if we take the center as the essence and the clue of the whole, the Sermon on the Mount evidently is the answer to the question, What shall we do to find the way into the kingdom? Jesus' answer is "Pray." And the center of the Prayer is the demand for daily bread.

The Lord's Prayer is surrounded by the passages on giving alms and fasting (6:1–18). The three sections together form the central instruction of the whole Sermon. The material preceding this central part is clearly divided into two sections. We can distinguish them as the proclamation of the kingdom or "Magna Charta"—the nine Beatitudes (5:3–16)—and the five earthly steps leading into the heavenly kingdom (5:17–48).

Chapter 5

THE MAGNA CHARTA
OF SPIRITUAL EVOLUTION

Introduction

The outer frame (5:1 and 7:28–29) of the Sermon on the Mount indicates that different circles began to form around Jesus from the very beginning, the "multitudes" being the outer circle, and the disciples the inner. Jesus here teaches both groups with the same words, but the disciples are supposed to understand him more thoroughly. Later, in Matthew's chapter on parables (13) the teaching for the outer circle and the special instructions for the inner are separated from each other.

We may read the Sermon first as members of the crowd perfunctorily; later, rereading it, we may find a deeper meaning in every sentence; and finally some of us will realize that we have been admitted to the inner circle. But the growth of our insight does not end by our initiation. The nearer we draw to the personality of Jesus, the more deeply we experience his power and the more firmly we grasp the content of his words. The Sermon on the Mount, by virtue of its own dynamics, is exoteric and esoteric at the same time.

THE KINGDOM OF HEAVEN ON EARTH

So far we have heard only two sentences from the mouth of Jesus: the repetition of the Baptist's slogan, "Repent, for the kingdom of heaven is at hand!" and the injunction, "Follow me and I will make you fishers of men." Evidently he had a far-reaching plan, a spiritual policy which surpassed the vision of his forerunners. What did he mean by the kingdom of heaven? Matthew gives us the answer in a form so condensed and powerful that we need years of experience and meditation to appreciate it.

The first section of the Sermon provides nothing less than the Magna Charta of the kingdom of heaven on earth. It does not refer, however, to the kingdom of heaven as a realm beyond space and time. If we suppose that the promise of "rewards" in the

Beatitudes can be fulfilled only after death, we deprive the Sermon of its actuality and efficacy. If we understand it as a statement about actual events in the spiritual realm here on our earth, taking place within us and within our fellowmen, it will prove not only to be true, but also to be charged with power almost to the extent of being dangerous.

Through nineteen centuries Matthew has forced his readers to form their own ideas about the kingdom of heaven. We see that the kingdom has been a magnet which attracts mankind. It causes evolution and history. We see its influence when we watch the early Christians in their struggle to become "children of God." And if we compare the reports of the New Testament with the experiences of our contemporaries, we see a parallel development. The facts repeat themselves almost exactly, psychologically, as well as sociologically.

Emergence of Individual Consciousness

St. Paul, for instance, relinquished his nationalistic endeavor and sacrificed his reputation as a Pharisee. Jesus said, "Who is my mother, and who are my brothers?" (12:48). He told his disciples: "If anyone comes to me and does not hate his own father and mother and wife and children and brothers and sisters, yes, and even his own life, he cannot be my disciple" (Luke 14:26). In psychological terms this means that the individual emerges from the tribe; his personal consciousness begins to differ from the conventional consciousness of his relatives and friends. Not only do the content of his consciousness and the objects of his interest change; his judgments, his point of view, the dynamic of his personality are also metamorphosed. The change can be compared with puberty. The human character comes of age. As a result of all this he is alone, an outlaw, a dangerous innovator, or a madman, or a criminal. How does he know and how do we know whether he is insane, or a criminal, or a reformer?

Our psychology provides the terms which link our experiences closely with the development of the early Christians. Our time, like the first century, is characterized by the decay of national structure on an international scale. The individual must stick to old conventional values which are obsolete, or he must set out on his own account to find the entrance into the realm of the future. The new outer structure is developing within the character of the average individual. We are witnessing a psychological mutation; the old species, *homo feudalis* (feudalistic man), is changing into the new species, *homo communis* (common man). But every mutation has to be paid for with much loss of life. There will be many criminals and madmen for each single "reformer" who finds the entrance into the kingdom.

The danger in individualism: egocentricity. The new form of consciousness is broadly indicated by the term *individualism*. The transition from feudalistic to individual consciousness reached its climax in the Renaissance and the Reformation. The personal capacities and responsibilities of the individual were developed far beyond the traditional patterns of medieval society. In feudalism the individual exists for the sake of the group. Since the Renaissance, the individual exists for his own sake; if he exploits the group in the service of his private ambition, the result is egocentricity and competition. Then society disintegrates into a battle of everybody against everybody. The madmen and the criminals have their heyday.

Practically, we manage to maintain some decency and lawfulness in our outer appearance but we transfer our egocentricity to the next generation. Every child is imbued with the wrong kind of individualism—selfishness, fear and greed—from the very beginning. The question, therefore, is whether individualism is essentially wrong. Is it always identical with egocentricity? If that is the case, mankind is doomed. The development of individualism cannot be prevented. We cannot go back to the feudalism of tribal life. What is the way out? In religious terms: how can we act unselfishly, get rid of sin? How can we reach forgiveness and enter the kingdom of heaven?

Mature individualism: individuation. One way out is Christianity. There is a form of individualism, of self-reliance and independence, which allows the individual to become responsible for himself and for the group also. Individual freedom and collective responsibility coincide. The psychological process of this development is characterized by the terms *individuation* and *integration*. Its religious goal is stated in St. Paul's description of the mystical body of Christ (1 Cor. 12:12–31).

Our question now is: how can we avoid egocentricity and reach individuation? Or, since we are egocentric already, without exception, how can we get rid of egocentricity and replace it by individuation?

The Kingdom Proclaimed in the Beatitudes

> Seeing the crowds, he went up on the mountain, and when he sat down his disciples came to him. And he opened his mouth and taught them, saying:

"Blessed are the poor in spirit, for theirs is the Kingdom of heaven.

"Blessed are those who mourn, for they shall be comforted.

"Blessed are the meek, for they shall inherit the earth.

"Blessed are those who hunger and thirst for righteousness, for they shall be satisfied.

"Blessed are the merciful, for they shall obtain mercy.

"Blessed are the pure in heart, for they shall see God.

"Blessed are the peacemakers, for they shall be called sons of God.

"Blessed are those who are persecuted for righteousness' sake, for theirs is the kingdom of heaven.

"Blessed are you when men revile you and persecute you and utter all kinds of evil against you falsely on my account. Rejoice and be glad, for your reward is great in heaven, for so men persecuted the prophets who were before you" (5:1–12).

The Beatitudes, the proclamation of the kingdom of heaven, convey an inner experience, a new discovery, which overthrows our natural philosophy of life. A step of development, an achievement of conscious growth, is proclaimed in appalling, though simple terms: nonsensical oratory to those who are not ready for it; clarifying insight and unquestionable truth to those who have passed the test of evolution; help, comfort, and remedy to those who struggle in the midst of the painful transition.

The proclamation of the kingdom is a series of paradoxes, built in pairs around the center,[2] the fourth beatitude, "Blessed are those who hunger and thirst for righteousness, for they shall be satisfied." Hunger for righteousness means in modern language "hunger for spiritual evolution." Even in the Old Testament the righteous one is the mature one who lives up to the will of God. To be discontent with our spiritual situation, to crave for something better with all the violence and recklessness of people who are starving to death, that is the inner situation of those who are blessed.

Nobody has this new blessing as a birthright. We have to deserve it by our own endeavor. We must, therefore, first understand that we do not have it. We are like landless peasants, like settlers without farms, hungry, thirsty, demoralized. Suddenly, the message comes that there is land to be had. Claims can be staked with the government, and everyone who is aware of his poverty joins the surging crowd of pioneers, shouting for land.

Jesus was well aware of this riotous feeling among his disciples. He described it exactly like the setting out of settlers going West. "The law and the prophets were until John; since that time the

2. This is the way we shall consider the Beatitudes. [Ed.]

kingdom of God is preached, and every man presseth into it" (Luke 16:16, KJV).

There is, of course, the danger that good news may be misunderstood and the new property misused. The hardships of the journey are a safeguard, but not a sufficient one. Matthew, therefore, surrounds the fanfare of the spiritual riot by two restrictions: only the meek and the merciful are accepted.

Who inherits the earth? The meek and the merciful. That the meek shall inherit the earth has always been considered as a paradox of almost sarcastic poignancy, and the more so, the more the word "meek" was misunderstood as meaning "soft, weak, and helpless." Moffatt translates it "humble," Goodspeed "humble-minded." Gerald Heard contends it means "tamed," or, more exactly "disciplined" by spiritual practices such as were developed by the Essenes.[3] The Greek word allows of such an interpretation; but it is not likely that Matthew would have used it for readers who hardly knew about esoteric practices. We might come closer to the truth if we transcribe "meek" by "sensitive," "open-minded," or, in more psychological language, "without inhibitions and repressions," and especially "without blind spots, callousness or dullness." We then understand that these people are able to hear the inner voice, to distinguish between the creative voice of eternity and the destructive voice of egocentricity. These people, therefore, will be creative and in the long run successful, in spite of temporary failures.

The fifth beatitude allots the blessing to the merciful. The Greek word for mercy corresponds to the Aramaic *hisda,* which means a mature state of mind characterized by understanding, sympathy and justice.[4] On the other hand, the Greek refers to the alms which we will discuss later. The "merciful," therefore, might be described as a person who is completely individuated, so that he acts out of his own resourcefulness; but, at the same time, he is so open for the calamities of his fellowmen that he feels them as if they were his own. Individuation includes love and empathy. The word "mercy" refers to that aspect of individuation which is usually described as "the heart"—in modern psychology, "integration." The merciful is the mature of heart.

The two beatitudes about the meek and the merciful form a pair of opposites surrounding the central beatitude about the hunger for righteousness. The meek will receive the whole earth, while the merciful will give away all they have. The more we give

3. Gerald Heard, *The Code of Christ,* pp. 63–65. Cf. Ps. 37:11.
4. T. H. Robinson, *The Gospel of Matthew,* p. 30.

away, the more we shall get. If we are sensitive to other people's suffering, we are sensitive also to the guiding intimations from beyond. Sharing our small resources with our fellowmen, we are allowed to share the "mercy," the creative love, of the Eternal. The two opposites are two different aspects of one and the same evolutionary process.

"Those who mourn" and *"the pure in heart."* The next pair of beatitudes again form a unit contradicting and completing each other. If we learn to mourn in the right way, our mourning will turn into the experience of inner growth and the discovery of a new world with new values and new goals. It has been said that this "congratulation for bereavement" is the most paradoxical of all the beatitudes.

To lose a dear friend by death always means the possibility of a new contact with the beyond, and of a new turning away from the past towards the future. Such a spiritual evolution, however, takes place only if we accept simply and honestly, without bitterness and without self-pity, the suffering which is involved, and search with patience and an open mind for its deeper meaning. Then desolation will be replaced by consolation and the suffering will change into a hunger for spiritual growth.

The corresponding beatitude, therefore, concerns the "pure in heart," or we might prefer to call them "pure in mind." To "see God," to understand His dealings with men and His purposes in history, presupposes the same lack of inhibition and absence of blind spots which characterize the meek and the merciful—in other words, a lack of egocentricity. The nonegocentric heart is courageous and honest; it is full of love and creativeness, and that means it is pure.

Purity of heart has a new dynamic quality; it either grows or decreases; and it grows by experience. At least half of our experiences are negative, dealing with "evil," within ourselves or within other people. We shall have to mourn. Our problem therefore is: How can we suffer without decreasing our "purity," without becoming egocentric, negative, bitter? How can we increase our purity in spite of the suffering which is an unavoidable factor in evolution? Answer: By trying to see God, to discern the divine purpose within or behind our difficulties. Let us look at our predicament from the standpoint of the eternal educator. This should enable us to discover deeper reasons for our suffering and to change our point of view. "Seeing God" is more than sensing some contact with eternity. It presupposes a humble acceptance of the evil of life and a forgiveness of those who wrong us. This beatitude describes the wisdom and maturity of those who have become accepted as "children of God."

"The poor in spirit" as *"peacemakers."* The first and the last beatitudes (5:3 and 9) complete the description of the dynamic process which may be called the way to Christianity, in the individual as well as in mankind. The poor in spirit will enter the kingdom of heaven, and the children of God will be the peacemakers on earth. The poor in spirit will find the kingdom, not after death but here and now; otherwise they could not become peacemakers on earth—and to be a peacemaker is a final condition without which the title for the true Christian, namely, to be the Son of God, cannot be attained.

You cannot make a good peace by compromising. You have to "create" it as a new and higher form of human relationship, or else you will become a miserable appeaser. The word "creativity" is missing in Greek, Aramaic and Hebrew, as far as human beings are concerned. All ancient languages are tribal, and therefore dumb with regard to individualism. God alone is the Creator. The fact that man should be created individually can be expressed only by the almost sacrilegeous statement that he shall become a "Son of God," a divine, creative creature.

This new dignity harbors a terrible temptation. Jesus was able to conquer the danger, but how can we be individuated, endowed with creativity, without falling into the temptation of egocentric willfulness? How can we be peacemakers instead of warmongers? Answer: By remaining "poor in spirit."

The Greek means literally "beggars regarding the spirit." Begging for spirit presupposes the knowledge that there is Spirit, and that we do not possess it; and this again is identical with the maturity of heart and mind as described in 5:7 and 8. The medieval praise of utter emptiness and poverty, as derived from this beatitude, was completely mistaken. All the intellectual forces that we can muster, all the energy of volition and all the strength and subtleties of the human heart are required as the tools of the Spirit. We must know that we are poor, but only in Spirit, not in intellect nor in emotions.

We must create peace on earth, or mankind will destroy itself. If we pretend to be Christians, we have to bring about this peace, because nobody else can do it. In spite of all our intelligence and our growing emotional maturity, we are completely unequal to the task. We need a superhuman amount of courage and creativity; we need the divine Spirit. We must try to be accepted as "sons of God," sharing the responsibilities and sorrows of creation, cooperating with the creative power of eternity, or mankind will collapse and we shall have not heaven on earth but hell.

The Central Paradox of the Magna Charta

"Blessed are you when men revile you and persecute you" (5:11). The proclamation of the kingdom of heaven is a paradox. It conveys an inner experience, a new discovery, which over-throws our natural philosophy of life.

At first this paradox is stated with philosophical aloofness: "Blessed are *those* . . ." (5:10). We should consider it as a general law of spiritual development. Then the text turns with sudden violence, like a pointed dagger, against the reader him-self: "Blessed are *you* . . ." There is no escape; we have to answer. Is it a blessing to be reviled and persecuted? Do we feel it? Do we actually rejoice? Do we experience the reward in heaven (5:12)? No, we don't; and that means that we have not yet signed the Magna Charta. The kingdom does not yet exist for us.

The "reward in heaven" must be realized immediately; loss must be felt as gain here and now, not after death. The kingdom must be an experience of growth and evolution before we die; it may continue after death, but it must begin on earth.

Matthew adds "for righteousness' sake" and "for my sake" (KJV). Those who "hunger and thirst for righteousness" are usu-ally at odds with the majority of their contemporaries, and so were the prophets of the Old Testament. There is not a blessing in every persecution; but where spiritual progress arouses the fear and fury of reactionaries and revolutionaries, there the suffering which the opposing forces inflict helps to speed the inner growth of the sufferer.

The text does not say that the people who persecute the fol-lowers of Jesus are bad or selfish or malicious. They are simply "people," neighbors, friends, relatives, everybody. They are like us. We are persecutors as far as we do not participate in the evolu-tion of mankind. We may be outstanding members of progressive or revolutionary organizations. "The world should progress," we may say; "our economic system should change. The millennium of the classless society should come tomorrow." But the expansion of our consciousness is something different.

Conscious growth, the evolution of the human character, is a painful and exclusively personal task. It implies the acceptance and assimilation of our unconscious fears and faults, the removal of our inhibitions and prejudices, the reformation and integra-tion of our passions and compulsions.

Are we on the side of the "prophets" or of those who persecute them? Do we correctly understand the final issue of this ever-lasting persecution? What is this kingdom that has to be paid for with persecution and which changes suffering into joy?

Matthew is not able or is not willing to answer our question. He forces us to venture our own answer, cautiously, tentatively, hypothetically. A variety of possible approaches is indicated, food for unending meditations, all of them related to each other and finally leading to the same situation: our active participation in the evolutionary process, "co-creation."

The Salt and the Light-Bearers

> "You are the salt of the earth; but if salt has lost its taste, how shall its saltness be restored? It is no longer good for anything except to be thrown out and trodden under foot by men.
> "You are the light of the world. A city set on a hill cannot be hid. Nor do men light a lamp and put it under a bushel, but on a stand, and it gives light to all in the house. Let your light so shine before men, that they may see your good works and give glory to your Father who is in heaven" (5:13–16).

The central part of the Magna Charta (5:10–12) describes the dynamics of individuation with regard to the individual. The first part (5:3–9) shows what will happen to us if we set out on the way. This third part (5:13–16) refers to the relationship between the individuated person and his environment. The more he advances on his way, the more he will influence his fellowmen. Finally he will force them through their own crises into their own evolution.

The symbolism of the light. The center of this passage is: "You are the light of the world." No personal pride, no individual superiority is meant—rather a great responsibility and a high mission. The flame is not ours. We remain beggars in spirit, temporarily entrusted with the privilege of being consumed by the heavenly fire. All danger of pride and self-righteousness disappears when we experience that to be creative means to be consumed.

The fact remains, however, that the one who burns cannot conceal his flame. He can extinguish it, for instance by pride, but as long as he is burning, he will set others afire. His influence will spread. People will admire him and hate him, and his creative mission of being a peacemaker will be thwarted time and again by the interference of his nearest friends as well as of his opponents.

The Christian is, and always will be, poor in spirit, mourning and hungry, and at the same time, the salt of the earth and the light of the world. Humbleness and power, poverty and wealth, suffering and success, will coincide in his life. He will be in the kingdom of heaven and in the dust and the dirt of the earth.

The symbolism of the salt. The statement about the light is flanked by the statements about the salt and about the bushel. The salt is one of the profoundest symbols in the New Testament. It is the same as fire but without the destructive violence of the latter. Christianity is not fire as such; it is light, one aspect of fire; and it is salt—another aspect—stimulating, cleaning, smarting if it touches a wound, helpful in protecting against decay, arousing opposition because of its taste; yet without the salt, all food would be tasteless.

Again, it is no merit or reason for pride to be salty. It is an inherent feature of the Christian character, though for centuries the misinterpretation of the words "meekness" and "humility" has almost eclipsed the stimulating power and initiative which the word "salt" implies.

The balance of opposites now becomes more startling. How can we be meek, in the sense of being sensitive, and at the same time salty, in the sense of being provocative; peacemakers, without being conquerors? Nobody can play such a role at will. No actor can learn or teach it. It has to be genuine, growing out of the creative evolution of the new life. There are innumerable people who pretend to be Christians, but very few who are at the same time merciful and salty, and that means creative.

FIVE CHALLENGES TO SPIRITUAL MATURITY

The New Code of Spiritual Laws

> "Think not that I have come to abolish the law and the prophets; I have come not to abolish them but to fulfil them. For truly, I say to you, till heaven and earth pass away, not an iota, not a dot, will pass from the law until all is accomplished. Whoever then relaxes one of the least of these commandments and teaches men so, shall be called least in the kingdom of heaven; but he who does them and teaches them shall be called great in the kingdom of heaven. For I tell you, unless your righteousness exceeds that of the scribes and Pharisees, you will never enter the kingdom of heaven" (5:17–20).

This part of the Sermon on the Mount (5:17–48) is usually understood as the discussion of Jesus' relationship to the Mosaic law. But his words contain more than that. On the one hand, the old tribal code is acknowledged in its value: "not an iota, not a dot will pass from the law until all is accomplished" (5:18). On the other hand it is superceded by a new kind of rule solemnly and boldly introduced by the six-times repeated words, "Truly, I say to you. . . ." It is the beginning of a new code of spiritual law as part of the new spiritual revolution.

The new rules are voluntary. They cannot be enforced. The form, as Jesus explains, is a system of practical experiments leading those who dare to face the tests into a new kind of religious "perfection" (5:48 and 7:24). It is as if the disciples had asked him: How can we achieve meekness and purity in heart and all the other qualities of the Beatitudes? Jesus' answer is: There are five different fields in our soul that we can till. Do so, and the harvest will be yours. These are the five steps that lead into individuation.

1. Cope with Your Resentments

> "You have heard that it was said to the men of old, 'You shall not kill; and whoever kills shall be liable to judgment.' But I say to you that every one who is angry with his brother shall be liable to judgment; whoever insults his brother shall be liable to the council, and whoever says 'You fool!' shall be liable to the hell of fire. So if you are offering your gift at the altar, and there remember that your brother has something against you, leave your gift there before the altar and go, first be reconciled to your brother, and then come and offer your gift. Make friends quickly with your accuser, while you are going with him to court, lest your accuser hand you over to the judge, and the judge to the guard, and you be put in prison; truly, I say to you, you will never get out till you have paid the last penny" (5:21–26).

The tribal law "Thou shalt not kill" was limited to the tribesmen among themselves; outside the tribe it was honorable to kill as many Gentiles as possible. The law forbids crimes only between relatives. Jesus knows that the overt crimes are but the flowers and fruits of hidden roots, and that we cannot truly love our brothers and sisters unless we unearth those forgotten and repressed roots of evil. There are old resentments and grievances; there is fear and competition from early childhood, well covered up under politeness and sentimental consideration.

Such an unconscious hatred poisons the human mind like unknown germs; it might grow like cancer and lead into bitterness, pessimism and despair, indeed into "the fire of Gehenna."[5]

---

5. The word Gehenna, wrongly translated "hell," better "purgatory," originally referred to the valley of Hinnom where the people of Jerusalem burned their garbage. It was an "unclean" place of decay and destruction. Later the

What can we do against this deadly evil if we do not know it? Jesus answers: There are symptoms which can be diagnosed early enough. Undue anger is the first of them. Our brother makes an insignificant mistake and we explode as if he had wounded us to the quick. Then, there is an exaggerated criticism, or a blunder, a slip of the tongue, instantly followed by the assertion that we did not mean it and are sorry. All this shows that the cancer of negativity in us is growing. We must release and change the repressed forces, or they will kill us. All our religious efforts, therefore, are futile until we clean our house.

Even if there were no symptoms of repressed negativity we might discover that the basement of our mind is filled with "dead men's bones" (23:27)—namely when we try "to see God." When we come "to the altar," when we hope, in prayer or meditation, to reach the awareness of the eternal presence, the inner "altar," the inner center of our spiritual life remains inaccessible, and the outer altar remains meaningless, until we discover and remove the cancer of our unconscious negativities.

However, the text says we remember our brother's grievances and accusations against us, not ours against him. We have to make peace with him. If this fails something must be wrong with our own inner attitude. Then the task switches from the outer dealings with our real brother to the inner dealings with our unconscious tendencies. Now we discover the inner figure of our "dark twin-brother," our Shadow, our unlived life.[6]

We have to redeem this inner image, that is, become aware of it at whatever cost in pain—accepting it, forgiving its faults, changing its reactions and assimilating its energy. Only then will fear turn into joy and hatred into love.

All this can be done while we are "on our way with him," namely, with the inner figure of the opponent, the Shadow, which we project[7] so easily on brothers and strangers in the outer world. When all the outer brothers are gone and our inner twin-brother is not yet redeemed, the redemption must be achieved otherwise:

---

common belief was that the unclean souls would be judged and punished in this valley "where their worm dieth not and the fire is not quenched." There is no indication, however, that Jesus thought of an everlasting punishment. The fire in Gehenna was burning unceasingly, but only because there was an unending supply of garbage coming out of the city.

6. *Unlived life:* Buried talents and repressed possibilities, which have turned negative. Cf. Fritz Kunkel, *In Search of Maturity*, p. 159.

7. Projection occurs when an unconscious identity with an outer object (person) becomes disturbing and is automatically perceived as a negative feeling caused by the object (or person). Cf. C. G. Jung, *Psychological Types*, p. 582.

"in prison," in the agony of loneliness and despair, until pain and horror finally clean and redeem our hidden viciousness.

2. *Sex versus Love*

> "You have heard that it was said, 'You shall not commit adultery.' But I say to you that every one who looks at a woman lustfully has already committed adultery with her in his heart. If your right eye causes you to sin, pluck it out and throw it away; it is better that you lose one of your members than that your whole body be thrown into hell. And if your right hand causes you to sin, cut it off and throw it away; it is better that you lose one of your members than that your whole body go into hell.
>
> "It was also said, 'Whoever divorces his wife, let him give her a certificate of divorce.' But I say to you that every one who divorces his wife, except on the ground of unchastity, makes her an adulteress; and whoever marries a divorced woman commits adultery" (5:27–32).

The central purpose of our religious self-education is to grow into individuation without misusing our freedom egocentrically. We cannot achieve this, however, by simple will power. The good intention alone could only make us more self-conscious and more egocentric. Other practical steps are required. We must learn to control our natural impulses, especially our sex drive, lest we misuse them egocentrically.

The exact interpretation of Jesus' statement is of extreme importance because the vulgar misunderstanding may produce, and indeed has produced, infinite misery. Many teachers have taught their students to turn away from sex altogether, and to repress it rather than to develop it. The equation "sex equals sin" has wrecked innumerable lives, destroyed marriages, and caused neuroses throughout the world. The repression of sex is exactly as stupid and dangerous as the egocentric misuse of sexual possibilities.

Our question is—and Jesus' question was also—how can sexuality be lived and employed for the sake of new creation, without selfish use and distortion? Jesus' words refer to man's attitude toward woman; but in our day they have to be applied to woman's attitude toward man also. The following statements refer to both sexes alike.

"To look at a woman lustfully" means to misuse her, in reality or in our imagination, in the service of egocentric satisfaction. If we looked at her with love instead of lust, we would admire her beauty, enjoy the privilege of admiring her, and perhaps tell her that we envy her husband, past, present or future; but we would not offend her femininity. If we loved her, we would strive to help her on her way, while misusing her as a tool for our selfish satisfaction would wreck her life rather than make it richer.

If, on the other hand, we are both lonely and have no other responsibilities, both of us knowing and accepting that we only wish to be happy for one night, then why not? Again, the answer is that we do not know the future, and cannot judge how much harm we do to one another. If we knew what it means for individuated people to become "one flesh" (19:4–6), we would look at each other with joy and wait until love transforms us into mature lovers, able to unearth the creative treasures which are hidden between manhood and womanhood.

The treasures are indeed so great, and somehow our intuition tells us so insistently about their value, that we imagine time and again we have found them; we are fascinated, we idolize our partner, we feel the hurricane of passion, until suddenly the mirage disappears, and we understand that this again was an egocentric self-deception.

The power of waiting. Matthew is wise enough not to give the solution of the whole problem in so early a part of his book. We shall have to wait until we come to Chapter 19. What he gives us here is exactly what we need at the beginning of our way: Jesus' teaching about the great art of waiting. Keep the wild horses in check. Do not starve them to death; do not kill them; but do not let them loose either. Wait! Do not repress your lust; admit it, accept it, and force it to wait until it turns into love.

The simile of the eye plucked out and of the hand cut off seems at first sight to describe complete mortification, and that is what thousands of ascetics have read into the text. As a matter of fact, the sex drive cannot be annihilated. It will remain alive, however deeply we repress it. It will return as a specter, haunt us as nightmares, or explode our virtuous career by the most foolish of all escapades.

If we look at the beautiful woman with love, everything is all right. To wait, then, will be a creative sacrifice. We shall suffer and grow. But if we look at her with lust, we must, according to Jesus, force ourselves to refrain from doing anything impulsive. Such self-restraint will be painful. Sleepless nights, nervousness, sweat and blood will be our lot. If we go through this experiment, regardless of its costs, it will lead us from one amazing discovery to another. If our egocentricity melts away, individuation teaches us real love, and we experience its creative power. This principle is valid within marriage as well, as is shown by the special reference to divorce.

Is divorce the answer? As far as the tribal law is concerned, divorce should be easy; the Mosaic code allowed it without restrictions. But as far as we wish to become individuated—and that means to become lovers—we should refrain from divorce as long as possible. Matthew gives here "fornication" as the only reason. Later (19:8) he mentions egocentricity (the hardness of the heart) in the same connection. Here, however, the question is not what husband and wife should make of one another, but what they should make of themselves. Marital difficulties are a great opportunity for individuation. To run away from each other is often just as egocentric a mistake as to come together too hastily. Again the rule is: Wait! But do not let the time pass without using it for your spiritual growth. You may overcome a large part of your egocentric rigidity by looking at your opponent. The first task was to look "not with lust"; now it is to look not with hatred nor with indifference. If we cannot learn to love, at least we can learn to be fair and kind and unselfish, and that too means evolution.

3. God Is Not Your Weapon

> "Again you have heard that it was said to the men of old, 'You shall not swear falsely, but shall perform to the Lord what you have sworn.' But I say to you, Do not swear at all, either by heaven, for it is the throne of God, or by the earth, for it is his footstool, or by Jerusalem, for it is the city of the great King. And do not swear by your head, for you cannot make one hair white or black. Let what you say be simply 'Yes' or 'No'; anything more than this comes from evil" (5:33-37).

These words deal with an apparently obsolete problem: the oath. Jesus is not speaking here about the oath before the law courts. The Jews forbade the use of the name of their God for solemn promises regarding the future. "You shall not swear by my name falsely, and so profane the name of your God" (Lev. 19:12). This shows a deep religious instinct; but Jesus says: "Do not swear at all."

Orientals liked to forswear themselves: "My daughter shall never marry that man, so help me God!" or "You wish to buy my house? I'll be damned if you ever get it!" But we are not better than they; we only express ourselves more politely. We may say, "If my daughter elopes with that man, I don't know what I shall do." In all these cases we try to settle the future, to eliminate certain possibilities which appear unbearable to us. We build, as it were, dams which supposedly prevent life from flowing in a certain direction. By this (half-conscious) magic we try to browbeat not only people but destiny. We assume a power which belongs only to God.

Jesus wanted the individual to emerge from tribal life. The reborn individual finds himself in possession of creative powers and new possibilities which constitute a temptation of unexpected severity. He is free to create and to destroy. He feels as if he were God. But if he misses the right road, individuation is replaced by egocentricity, and man tries to match himself against God as his equal. The temptation is not new. Adam and Eve succumbed to it. But in tribal life, the lawbreaker is an outcast and will perish. In the new era of creation, the danger of confusing egocentric stubbornness with creative individuation is so great that the whole purpose of evolution may be thwarted by it.

The decisive achievement which Jesus wants his disciples to attain is a new kind of responsibility equal to the new creative power which will be given to them. They are the "salt" and the "light"; but only if they remain "poor in spirit." They may participate in the divine life beyond space and time, but if they issue rigid orders for the future, they are lost souls.

Jesus' prohibition, "Do not swear at all," can be transcribed in psychological terms: "Do not identify yourself with any plan, any work or value which you want to pursue. Be determined, yet remain flexible! Be persevering, but not stubborn! Do not give up because men want you to do so; but resign gladly if you see that creation itself is going the other way."

4. Meet Violence with Nonresistance

> "You have heard that it was said, 'An eye for an eye and a tooth for a tooth.' But I say to you, Do not resist one who is evil. But if any one strikes you on the right cheek, turn to him the other also; and if any one would sue you and take your coat, let him have your cloak as well; and if any one forces you to go one mile, go with him two miles. Give to him who begs from you, and do not refuse him who would borrow from you" (5:38–42).

The Authorized Version says, "That ye resist not evil"; Moffatt and Goodspeed have "not to resist an injury," and Weymouth "not to resist a wicked man." All these translations are correct. Psychologically, the term "evil" should be preferred because then our passage becomes a profound lesson on the dynamics of evil.

Jesus was not thinking of a new civil code without police, where bullies are allowed to exploit their victims. If we do not protect our children against perverts and aggressors, we are cowards and murderers. Innocence must be defended. But Jesus speaks here of something else; he is teaching self-education. How can we exploit evil, injuries, and wicked men for our own spiritual growth? Jesus' answer describes a rich man who does not mind if someone steals his purse. If our dignity is rooted in our creative relationship with God, a slap in the face cannot harm us. Jesus' own attitude when he was struck by the high priest's officer (John 18:22–23) was bold and calm and of an unshakable peacefulness. If we are aware of our power, feeling the contact with our Father in heaven, we are not inclined to resist evil, to fight back; we only want to serve creation.

However, it would be a poor and merely static imperative if Jesus or Matthew were to tell us: "Pretend to be rich, confident, and powerful," while actually we feel poor and insignificant and frightened. Nonresistance must be a dynamic device, a way of inner strength and development, or it remains a foolish ideal. If it is not the result of our spiritual wealth, it should become its cause.

The principle of nonresistance must not lead to the repression of our natural urge for retaliation. The repression of our self-preservation would be as disastrous as the repression of our sexuality. The problem is not how to get rid of our natural instincts but how to discipline them for the sake of inner growth.

The way, as far as we can see, is this: "Evil" comes from outside. The evildoer attacks us. This arouses our "evil" response; fear, hatred, bitterness, revengefulness; therefore we resist, fight back, and the sum total of evil increases. But if we relax, letting the attack sweep through our body and mind, the suffering wakes us up more completely, removes •our blind spots and enables us to see the deeper meaning of our fate.

One who can honestly respond with generosity is freed from evil within. But we should not expect that our calm reaction will change the evil attitude of our opponent into something good. Even Jesus could not achieve this. His creative nonresistance led him to the cross. Why should we be more successful than he? Pain remains pain, the evildoer remains an evildoer, but he cannot inflict "evil" on us. Our response remains positive, and the sum total of evil decreases.

5. *Hate Yields to Love*

> "You have heard that it was said, 'You shall love your neigh-
> bor and hate your enemy.' But I say to you, Love your enemies
> and pray for those who persecute you, so that you may be
> sons of your Father who is in heaven; for he makes his sun
> rise on the evil and on the good, and sends rain on the just
> and on the unjust. For if you love those who love you, what
> reward have you? Do not even the tax collectors do the same?
> And if you salute only your brethren, what more are you doing
> than others? Do not even the Gentiles do the same? You,
> therefore, must be perfect, as your heavenly Father is perfect"
> (5:43–48).

Jesus is concerned with religious self-education and nothing
else. The imperative "Love your enemies" cannot refer to a legal or
administrative attitude under a future government. Justice and
fair treatment should certainly be granted to all, friend and foe
alike. The democratic society should not hate; it should be just;
but above all it must be firm and ready to eliminate "enemies"
who cannot be changed.

To love our enemy is a psychological task, not a political one.
It relates to emotional reactions, and therefore to the structure of
our character. The law of love cannot be enforced. Even to formu-
late it as an imperative is dangerous. "Love!" is as impossible an
exhortation as "Grow!" or "Be mature!" Such imperatives cause
hypocrisy, self-deception and repression. We try to love, conceal
our hatred, force ourselves to express something which we do
not yet feel, act as if we were better than we are, and finally believe, or pretend to believe, that we have become better. In reality,
we are just as wicked as we used to be, only our wickedness has
become more intricate and the outer mask more deceptive.

Conquest of our hostilities. What Jesus meant was different.
He taught us how, in a slow and laborious way of self-education,
our positive and creative powers can be developed, and how our
negative and destructive deviations can be undone. Consider at
which place of the way we are confronted with the "impossible"
possibility that we might love our enemies. This fifth and last of
our tests follows after we have experienced in the fourth test, that
the evildoers cannot inflict "evil" upon us if we do not resist evil.
They can make us suffer, but this does not increase our inner
darkness; all pain becomes growing pain, and we recognize the
power which makes us grow. Moreover, the fifth test forms a pair
of opposites with the first one. There we discovered the shadowy
figure of our "dark inner twin-brother" which we projected occa-

sionally onto our best friends so that they appeared for a moment
as enemies. Our outer enemy, who truly endangers us and whom
we hate fullheartedly, might still be the carrier of such an unconscious projection. How can we discern, then, between the objective danger which the enemy actually represents and our subjective excitement which results from the projection and which
prevents the sober settlement of the issue?

"Pray for those who persecute you" (5:44). These few words
convey all we need, if we have worked our way through the foregoing experiments of Matthew's initiation. Praying, among other
things, means the attempt to look at our situation from above,
from the standpoint of the guiding power of life. Why did this
power allow our enemy to become so powerful? What kind of
power does he possess? What can he do to us? And why should
this be allowed? Could it be for our own benefit? Is it the removal of our blind spots, to make us see more clearly, less emotionally? Perhaps it is our liberation from those unconscious
projections. Could the outer enemy help us to get rid of the last
and deepest inner image of negativity, the figure of the fiend, the
great and dreadful symbol of universal hatred and destruction?

Let us pray for the outer enemy as the text says, looking at him
as much as we can with the eyes of the Creator, with fatherly
love. He might appear very bad, an evildoer; but we would give
him a chance, in sunshine and rain. Maybe we could rescue him
somehow, if one day we were to become peacemakers in the fullest sense of the word.

However, in order to become peacemakers, we must do away
with our fear, hatred, horror, bitterness; indeed, with the whole
store of negative and destructive energies which the enemy con-
jured up from the hidden depths of our mind, and which we
would never have discovered without him. He has shown us what
prevents our becoming "sons of God": the dead men's bones
within our own soul.

The outer enemy forces us to face our inner enemies. Our
inner spirit of darkness and despair is more important and more
powerful than the outer enemy. Now we pray for the inner foe:
God, change him, he is part of me, he is the larger part of my
life. How can I rescue him, redeem him, turning his darkness
into the light of creation?

When we look from above, from the higher third point, at our
enemy and ourselves, we begin to discriminate between the real
person, the adversary in the outer world (who was bad enough)
and the fiendish inner image which we projected on him and

which was worse than he. Now, again, we try to pray, and that means to find the "third point" and to look from above, objectively, at the two fighting forces within us.

Here is point One, our conscious personality, the Ego, incomplete, insecure, frightened; and there is point Two, the inner foe, the symbol of darkness, the fiend, the counter-Ego, frightening and irresistible. How can the two come together? Can thesis and antithesis be combined in a creative synthesis? What does the Creator want us to do? Jesus says: "Love your enemy." Can we love our own hatred and our own anxiety? Can the ego love its own undoing? If we look from above, objectively, we discover that our hatred once was love, in early childhood, and our anxiety then was caused by frustration of our unprotected and unlimited eagerness for life. We discover the virtue behind our vices, and we understand that darkness may be changed into light again, if only we can face it, accept it, sustain its horror, and believe in the light beyond.

Jacob wrestled with the demon until he turned out to be the angel of the Lord. Jesus faced utmost darkness in Gethsemane, and by so doing entered a new phase of creation. What is our task when the unconscious opens its gates and anxiety floods our conscious mind? Let us do what all the pioneers of the inner life have done; in the battle between the opposites let us appeal to the creative center which can reconcile them on a higher level of reality. "Though I walk through the valley of the shadow of death, I will fear no evil; for thou art with me" (Ps. 23:4, KJV). Why should we be less courageous than the psalmist? But we cannot yet pray, nor love our outer enemy.

Matthew understands this and therefore he admits us, in spite of our failures, to the next endeavor, the practice of the eternal Presence. Without this deeper and more central experience we certainly would fail again.

Chapter 6

THE PRACTICE
OF THE PRESENCE OF GOD

Introduction

This part of the Sermon on the Mount (6:1–18) teaches us what we can do to improve our relationship with the Eternal, to clarify our position in the universe, and to cooperate with Creation. The center of this section contains the core of the whole Sermon: the Lord's Prayer. The sections on either side of the Prayer deal with problems which might appear to be out of date: giving alms and fasting. We shall see, however, that they provide the best opportunities for religious expeditions into the unknown. They are the two main training grounds where the higher consciousness can be learned. Therefore we will consider them before studying the Lord's prayer.

THREE SPIRITUAL PRACTICES

1. Giving Alms

> "Beware of practicing your piety before men in order to be seen by them; for then you will have no reward from your Father who is in heaven.
> "Thus, when you give alms, sound no trumpet before you, as the hypocrites do in the synagogues and in the streets, that they may be praised by men. Truly, I say to you, they have their reward. But when you give alms, do not let your left hand know what your right hand is doing, so that your alms may be in secret; and your Father who sees in secret will reward you" (6:1–4).

As long as we are egocentric, we cannot help thinking, "It is our duty to succor the poor. If we do it, we are good; if not, we are bad; so let us do it in order to be good." All morality which preaches to egocentric hearers must result in great deviation; the individual seeks to be moral for the sake of his own Ego. This is what Jesus denounced as hypocrisy (6:2).

Modern psychology adds that the egocentric moralist is not only looking for "glory of man." His Ego pattern may be more subtle nowadays; he may do his good deeds anonymously and then say: "Look, Lord God. Am I not a good Christian? I did that in secrecy. I am not one of the vainglorious ones."

Sharing. Jesus shows the right way with amazing simplicity: "Do not let your left hand know what your right hand is doing" (6:3). The inner attitude which Jesus describes must refer to a new standpoint and a higher plane of consciousness, where giving is a natural, inconspicuous activity of the heart. Sharing then becomes the unavoidable expression of a "spiritual We-experience."[1]

This higher form of consciousness cannot be achieved by thinking and understanding alone. It is not a merely intellectual process; nor can it be reached by praying alone. Though it is given "by grace," it has to be explored by practice and proved by experiment—giving alms and fasting—which are hard work.

It is clear that we should give alms not for the sake of the poor alone. God has other means of providing for them. Jesus' main concern in his statement is the giver himself. He wished his disciples to understand the deeper meaning of the spiritual experiment, the "giving of alms," which may transform an egocentric person into a selfless one.

There are at least two aspects of giving which can be pointed out by means of our present psychology, leaving other and deeper interpretations for later generations to explore. The first aspect is that of sharing. If you are lost in the mountains with, let us say, three companions, and the small piece of bread you have saved in your pocket is all the food for the four of you, then to "give alms" would not mean to give your bread to one of them and to go hungry yourself; but to share it equally with them all. The "reward" would be that your joy over the joy of your comrades and their joy over your joyfulness would cause your bodies to enjoy the quarter portion of bread far more than ever you could have enjoyed the entire piece. Physiologists know that our bodies use the food much more effectively if we eat with joy. Your quarter portion may have given you more strength than the whole piece would have done, if you had eaten it clandestinely with a bad conscience.

This experience of sharing which causes the shared substance to "grow" is the basis of the miracle of the Lord's feeding of the multitude in the desert (14:15–21). Such sharing is the beginning of the spiritual We-experience. It is the first aspect of the

---

1. See Fritz Kunkel, *In Search of Maturity*, pp. 192–96.

evolutionary process which is called in our clumsy translation, "giving alms."

Trusting in the higher guidance of life. The other aspect of giving alms is included in the first one: it is the trust in the higher guidance of life. The widow who gave "all her living" for the temple treasure must have trusted God enough to eliminate all fear of starving upon the following day (Luke 21:1–4). If we share our abundance, the miracle does not work. Only if we give away what we urgently need, do we fulfill the conditions of the experiment. We give away our daily bread, trusting that through some unknown channels we shall get what we need tomorrow.

Here the borderline between the honest risk and the careless gamble is extremely subtle. The only means of finding the right way between many temptations and mistakes is to resort again and again to the Great Prayer. "Give us this day our daily bread," and "deliver us from evil." The nearer we come to the right attitude, the sooner we shall discover our reward. The new kind of consciousness, the unity of our individuated consciousness with the tribal unconscious, is our recompense. It is the growing experience of spiritual brotherhood, and above all the realization of our being guided and supported by the Eternal. Then, finally, the giving of "all that we have," the crucial experiment of faith, might become as natural to us as walking and breathing. We walk and forget that we breathe or breathe and forget that we walk. Thus our right hand might give to men what we need, while our left hand takes from God what we need, in perfect serenity.

2. *Fasting*

> "And when you fast, do not look dismal, like the hypocrites, for they disfigure their faces that their fasting may be seen by men. Truly, I say to you, they have their reward. But when you fast, anoint your head and wash your face, that your fasting may not be seen by men but by your Father who is in secret; and your Father who sees in secret will reward you" (6:16–18).

The passage on fasting is built parallel to the one on giving alms. For Jesus, fasting was not a general religious duty. His answer to the disciples of John (9:14–17) allows no doubt about this. On the other hand, he did not advise against it. He wished his disciples to fast individually, at the right time and in the right way. From his remark that his disciples would fast "when the bridegroom is taken away from them" (9:15), we understand that he considered fasting necessary for those who have to undergo crises and suffering.

Overcoming self-indulgence. The majority of people in distress try to compensate by indulging themselves. Someone who cannot love is prone to eat too much and too heavy food. While going through a serious crisis, we crave talk. We want to be understood, pitied, and comforted. We need advice or we wish at least to pour out our misery to a sympathetic friend. If we understand the deeper meaning of fasting, we would see that by all this eating, reading, and talking, we evade the purpose of our suffering. Caught in the breakdown of our egocentricity, we try to escape into a kind of infantile or tribal retreat, while we are meant, by means of our very pain, to emerge into a new form of independence and self-responsibility.

Self-discipline. Fasting means to refrain not only from eating when we are hungry, but also from smoking if we have developed this habit; from sleeping, if this is our escape; and from gossiping when we should go through utmost loneliness.

If our suffering results in a strange and new inner experience, a great thought, a spiritual discovery or a vision, we shall be tempted to share our new insight with our friends. If we do so, the spiritual process will not continue. Our eagerness to tell them what has happened to us might look like "giving alms" in the sense of sharing. But the more we feel the urge of sharing in such a situation, the more we should fast. Otherwise we create a leakage through which we relieve our inner pressure, and prevent the spiritual explosion and the beginning of the new life. Fasting means facing reality when the crisis comes, staying sober, without escaping into cheap consolations and delusions.

The reward of fasting. By silence and withdrawal we confine our inner forces and cause them to flow, as it were, in the centripetal direction, instead of being disseminated into the outer world. This is one meaning of the forty days in the desert, which we find in the lives of so many saints. It could be the meaning of forty days in a hospital, a prison, or any miserable environment, if only we and our friends and doctors and jailors knew about the method and purpose of fasting and silence and loneliness.

If we fast for a long period, the pent-up power of our deeper unconscious images may cause us all kind of inner and outer disturbances. We may become easily irritated, oversensitive. A small offense may hurt us as if it were a deadly wound, a simple truth may appear like a fatal judgment; and a slight glimpse of love will make us overexuberant like little children. We feel almost as if we had no skin; and if we did not already know what the words "inner evil" and "outer evil" mean, during this period of fasting we should certainly discover it. All evil must become manifest before we can alter it into something positive; and fasting, silence, loneliness, whether voluntary or involuntary, mobilizes all the inner and the outer evils against us. We are thrown back violently upon the central source of spiritual power; and if this power fails us, we are lost. We should not choose this way, therefore, unless we have enough experience in the practice of the presence of God, and this means in secret, individual prayer.

3. Private Prayer—The New Form

> "And when you pray, you must not be like the hypocrites; for they love to stand and pray in the synagogues and at the street corners, that they may be seen by men. Truly, I say to you, they have their reward. But when you pray, go into your room and shut the door and pray to your Father who is in secret; and your Father who sees in secret will reward you.
>
> "And in praying do not heap up empty phrases as the Gentiles do; for they think that they will be heard for their many words. Do not be like them, for your Father knows what you need before you ask him" (6:5–8).

For Jesus and his followers prayer became a new and powerful event which had to be distinguished carefully from the old, pious habits of the Jewish congregation. So far, prayer had chiefly been a tribal ceremony and it was the stronger and the more potent the more the whole tribe was united in worship. The greatest prayer took place when the High Priest entered the holy of holies and the whole congregation knelt about the temple. Jesus' new discovery was that each one can be his own High Priest. The temple now is inside ourselves. Each must enter the holy place and experience what self-responsibility is, for in prayer he stands alone before God.

The word "secret" refers to the seclusion of the individual whose worship should not be watched by his fellowmen. All prayer, meditation, and contemplation, if performed in secrecy, defended against intruders from without but not against the truth which intrudes from within, leads to the inner room into which we have to withdraw. This symbolizes the heart of our heart, the center of our soul, which in our day is at least half, and sometimes completely, surrounded by the repressed and therefore negative forces of the unconscious. Indeed, we cannot enter the inner room—and this means we cannot contact Eternity—if we do not contact and face our own unconscious life.

However, the transition from tribal to individual life is slow. The old tribal and feudal form of worship must be preserved for the majority of the people for a long time. But for the more in-dividuated person, the new form should be taught and practiced. If this is not done, people who outgrow the tribal form of life are forced to behave as though they still felt and thought with the tribe, while actually they feel and think individually. They then cannot help using the tribal form of prayer for egocentric pur-poses, becoming, as Matthew describes it, conscious or uncon-scious hypocrites. The new form of worship would help them to overcome their egocentricity and replace it by individuation. The egocentric prayer always attempts to use God as a means in the service of the Ego.

The way to overcome egocentricity is to pray secretly in our innermost room, and that means, as much as we can, "in the presence of God." We can tell Him only what He knows anyhow, but by reviewing our egocentric needs, fears, desires and ambi-tions "in His presence," we expose our innermost troubles and confess them to God.

THE LORD'S PRAYER

The Climax of the Sermon on the Mount

> "Pray then like this:
>   Our Father who art in heaven,
>   Hallowed be thy name.
>   Thy kingdom come,
>   Thy will be done,
>   On earth as it is in heaven.
>   Give us this day our daily bread;
>   And forgive us our debts,
>   As we also have forgiven our debtors;
>   And lead us not into temptation,
>   But deliver us from evil.
> For if you forgive men their trespasses, your heavenly Father also will forgive you; but if you do not forgive men their tres-passes, neither will your Father forgive your trespasses" (6:9–15).

This prayer is not only the climax but also the summary of the Sermon on the Mount. The experience of fasting and giving alms enter into it as integral parts of the practice of the eternal Pres-ence. The prayer then becomes practical life, not a special activity in addition to other activities, but the basis and the goal, the background, and the motivation of all activities. It becomes the essence of life.

This prayer can and should be understood in innumerable different ways. It satisfies the needs of people in all possible stages of evolution. It helps children and adults, fools and sages, feudalists and individualists alike. But it irks and bores our egocentricity. Its dynamic is so strong that it sometimes changes our point of view before we have finished it, so that we can begin it over again on a higher level. Often it ceases being a prayer and changes into a vow of commitment, and then, changing again, it becomes a commission entrusting us with creative power and unforeseen tasks.

"Give us this day our daily bread" (6:11). The center of the Lord's Prayer is the request for bread.[2] Before Jesus teaches his disciples the great prayer he reminds them of the fact that God knows what they need (6:8), yet he teaches them to ask for bread. He knows that our fear of starvation is so strong that it would interfere with all other religious considerations. At Gethsemane he himself prayed for something that he knew would not be granted. This emotional honesty in our relationship with God is the first lesson we should learn in our study of the art of prayer.

The second lesson begins when we compare the central clause of the Lord's Prayer with the central beatitude. The parallelism of both the Prayer and the Beatitudes proves the oneness of the underlying religious truth. The clauses of the Prayer and the Beatitudes will interpret each other.

The fourth beatitude promises that those who "hunger and thirst for righteousness shall be satisfied" (5:6). Keeping in mind that "righteousness" refers to the development of the new spiritual life, we begin to grasp the dynamic implication of Jesus' thought. The hungry pray for bread. Bread does not only support them; it makes them grow. They might pray for something to keep them as they are. They want to remain static; but the heavenly dietician does not fulfill such a foolish desire. He wishes them to grow and to develop.

There is no doubt that the term "bread" includes physical food and all the material goods we need; but it also covers emotional and mental nourishment, and the spiritual vitamins indeed must not be lacking. We learned this from Jesus' temptation. "Man shall not live by bread alone, but by every word that proceeds from the mouth of God" (4:4; see Deut. 8:3). Moreover, we often need food which we do not relish. When we were children, we asked for chocolate and were forced to eat spinach. Now that we are adults, we may ask for promotion or financial security and we

---

2. We shall consider the Lord's Prayer as we did the Beatitudes, working out in pairs from the center. [Ed.]

may be forced to swallow public disgrace and bankruptcy. The better we understand our deepest longing for spiritual development according to the fourth beatitude, the better we shall see that by praying for daily bread we are praying, without knowing it, for the bitter medicine which we abhor.

Now the adjective "daily" appears in a new light. The supplication means: Give us joy and pain to grow rather than to remain static; but do not give us more than we can endure; especially, do not give us meat for adults while we are still babes needing milk (see 1 Cor. 3:2). Our state of development is well known to the Great Dietician. It is for our own sake that we should pray and meditate about our diet. If we hunger, not after the bread of static self-preservation, but after the bread of dynamic evolution, our prayer itself will become this bread.

People, helpers, friends, and enemies are part of the food (and bitter medicine) that comes to us every day. We are part of the daily bread that is given to others, to make them grow. To be good food, to become better food, glad to be eaten, not pampering the eater by our sweetness, not poisoning him with our vengefulness, not intoxicating him with cheap enthusiasm, but nourishing him even if he blames us for being indigestible, that is our commission.

"Thy kingdom come, Thy will be done, On earth as it is in heaven" (6:10). Our request for bread is granted; new growth, new power is granted to us. What shall we do with it? Which goal shall we serve? The requests on either side of the center petition answer these questions.

The Prayer says "Thy kingdom come." Is this still a petition? If we fullheartedly wish that His kingdom come, we must ourselves do—indeed, we cannot help doing—everything in our power to hasten its coming. Our demand turns out to be our oath of allegiance to God: I shall serve the kingdom of heaven with all my might, conscious and unconscious; otherwise my praying for the coming of the kingdom would be a lie.

However, we do not know what this "kingdom" is. It seems to be the goal of spiritual evolution or even of all creation, but there is no objective information about any details. We are still limited to our subjective theories and hopes. How can we serve such an indistinct goal?

The Prayer goes on: "Thy will be done, On earth as it is in heaven." The orders of the heavenly government are clear enough, but they are issued (and obeyed) "in heaven," beyond space and time. If we could receive and understand them here on our earth, if our receiving sets were not always clogged with earthly fears and desires, we should know what we have to do, now and here, and we should not have to bother about the final purpose of history and the evolution of mankind. "The pure in heart see God."

God, of course, could tell us directly what His will is, in spite of all our egocentric deafness and blindness; that would be easy for Him. But He wants us to find out by ourselves, repairing our receiving-sets, deciphering the code, applying general principles to special situations. This is hard for us; we often go astray; we waste time and energy and do harm to others; but it is an important part of our training for the future life.

Now we begin to see in detail what the term *individuation* means. We have to learn to do our work without the unceasing voice of the tribal instincts or of God's spirit whispering into our ears what we should do every moment. We have to make decisions, taking responsibility of our own; therefore we have to understand more fully the strategy of the kingdom of heaven. How can we learn this?

The answer comes from the corresponding beatitude: "Blessed are the meek, for they shall inherit the earth" (5:5). It is our egocentricity which prevents our deeper understanding of God's strategy as well as the reception of his direct orders. If we were meek, and that means not egocentric, we would efficiently co-operate with creation; we would hasten the coming of the kingdom; and, so says the beatitude unmistakenly, we should inherit the earth: the kingdom of heaven would actually begin on earth. Even if our contribution were only a small drop in the ocean, in the service of this goal it would be important enough.

We do not yet know what the "kingdom" means; and we are not able to know it as long as our egocentricity deafens and blinds us. The impure cannot see God. Our prayer for the coming of the kingdom here turns into the petition for our liberation from egocentricity. In Jesus' master prayer, this is the demand for forgiveness and the promise to forgive our fellowmen.

"*Forgive us our debts*" (6:12). Our demand for the coming of the kingdom includes our commitment to the fullest cooperation. Our demand for forgiveness presupposes that we forgive too; but that is less obvious and therefore expressed in the prayer itself. Matthew repeats this statement twice (6:14 and 15), indicating that it is of utmost importance. We should understand and apply every letter of it.

The words "debt" and "debtors" might surprise us; we would

expect something about sin or guilt. Jesus, however, wants us to
see that great values have been entrusted to us, for special
purposes, like the "talents" lent by the king to his servants
(25:14–30). We are stewards owing capital and interest to the
Creator.

In modern language: We are endowed with consciousness, intellect, feeling, and all the rest, in order to promote the spiritual
evolution of mankind. Earth is a training school for the higher
life. If we lag behind schedule, misusing our loans, we increase
our debts, and we fail in our examination. We may be demoted
and have to pay back. Creation does not like to lose its invest-
ments.

Some of these debts are conscious. We misused our capital;
we refused to learn our lesson, and we know it. But we often
thought we did the right thing and were mistaken, unwittingly
and unwillingly: this constitutes our unconscious debt. The question is not whether we are good or bad; the concept of "unconscious debt" eliminates all moralistic judgments. The question
is whether or not we did our share in God's unceasing creation.
Did we grow? Did we co-create? Did we help the evolution of the
Spirit on earth? That's why we need this prayer.

Yet our spiritual growth is arrested time and again by the
memory or discovery of what people have done to us. Why did
my father not understand me better? Why was that first grade
teacher as stupid a disciplinarian as she was? Bitterness and
revengefulness surge up like a tidal wave.

Moreover, there are even now people, and often our nearest
ones, who misunderstand and misjudge us. Instead of helping us
to grow, they destroy all progress with their criticism and distrust.
Yes, we have forgiven them, consciously, seven times seventy,
but from the depth of the unconscious a hateful voice whispers,
"I wish they would die."

The beatitude says, "The merciful shall find mercy." Look at
the people who offend us; don't they deserve mercy? They are
swayed by egocentric urges and obsessed by unconscious fears.
The same Shadows control them and us. We suffer from the lack
of love, lack of courage, lack of faith, all of us. We are caught
in the same collective guilt, imprisoned in the same debtor's jail,
we and our opponents.

To forgive means to unearth this old inner image, the Shadow,
which we project on friend and foe alike. But how and why does
this monster originate in our unconscious mind? Psychology answers: when first egocentric patterns, pride, irritability of the

parents, hurt the defenseless soul of the baby, the original one-ness between mother and child, the We-feeling, begins to break down. Fear and hostility take hold of the child and his light turns into darkness. His inner security is replaced by egocentric defenses. We poison our children as we have been poisoned by our parents, and we continue poisoning each other. That is why we need mercy, all of us without exception.

THE POWER AND BLESSINGS OF FORGIVENESS. How can we for-give? How is it possible to show mercy? Before we can forgive, we have to discover something that we do not yet know. Take the case of a child neglecting a pet bird until it dies. Here we have to discover that the child was not aware of the value and conditions of animal life; and that we were not aware of the child's unaware-ness. We have to gain insight into our own neglect and ignorance; then, with the new insight, if we repent individually, we will discover that repentance is power.

It is terrible that such a tragedy can happen; but without it, the flame of repentance and its creative power would never have disturbed the smugness of our parental mind. It is terrible that life has to use so dangerous a means to disturb our egocentric peace. But now it has happened; thank God! Now we are aflame. Now we can do something creative. The child's courage and loyalty and truthfulness, and above all his attitude toward death, can be formed and developed, and that will help him for the rest of his life.

Only if we find the creative way out, can we honestly say we have forgiven him, and God has forgiven us. In tribal and feudal life we confess, repent, and feel the "contrition of the heart"; we promise not to do it again and the tribe, or the feudal lord, lets us feel that we are a good child once more, exactly on the same level as we were before. If this pattern is used in individual life, it causes stagnation, hypocrisy and ever-increasing egocentricity. On the individual level, there is no forgiveness without a creative development.

The turning point, where the negative energy of regret changes into the positive energy of new life, is the mysterious point which is described by the word "grace." Something is given to us, not only to compensate for the debt we have incurred; a new capital is added and, together with the new urge to try again and to avoid the old mistake, we now have the chance to do better than ever before. We have learned the power and the blessings of forgive-ness.

Now we can forgive our enemies, our friends, and even our

parents; they are excused because we are all in the same predicament. But that does not help us as long as we cannot forgive
God. The whole problem of forgiveness has to be postponed until
this terrible thing, our lawsuit against fate, can be settled. We
are therefore desperately in need of the next prayer.

"*Hallowed be thy name*" (6:9). If an ambassador speaks "in
the name of my government," he indicates that his government or
his nation with all its dignity and power is symbolically present.
The prophet who preaches "in the name of the Lord" means that
God is present in his prophecy. The "name" in the ancient sense
of the word is not only the definition or essence of a person—it
is his presence.

ACCEPTING GOD'S PAINFUL LESSONS. A child is kidnapped. Where
was God when it happened? The parents say: There is no God.
Or even worse: He punishes us for our sins. If they could honestly apply the words "Hallowed be thy name" to their tragedy,
they would discover that God is present now, and was present in
the fatal moment, too. Creation is going on, through death and
birth alike. Let us try to hold His name holy.

We cannot prove it, but if we accept, tentatively, the hypothesis
that God's will is fulfilled even while the evildoer moves to destroy
creation, we reach for a moment the third point looking at the
destroyer and his victim from a higher plane. We may see vaguely,
as in a fog, how God achieves His ends through His enemies too.
Judas's betrayal served creation. Our suffering is not lessened by
this insight, but it changes its color. Bitterness becomes awe.
Pain, now accepted, though not yet understood, stimulates us to
cooperate in this divine battle which costs us our dearest friends.
There is no acquiescence, no passive submissiveness to the inexorable will of the Lord; on the contrary, it is active, powerful
participation, growing understanding and courageous endurance.
No hardship is too hard if we can win the battle of creation.

There is a spiritual point of view which enables us to accept
(but not to condone) the most inhuman crimes. We have to
reach this point in order to settle our lawsuit with God. To make
use of Judas's crime in the service of the divine purpose Jesus
had to accomplish a task of superhuman proportions. If that is
so, sum up all the errors, faults and crimes that have ever been
committed against you. (Be sure, God is hidden behind every vice,
as He was behind Judas's betrayal.) It is our task to reveal His
presence, and to hallow His name, turning the dark forces of
destruction into bright streams of creativity. If your bitterness

and grief, resulting from all the darkness of all your friends and enemies, would break loose in a blazing flame of mourning, it would melt away your egocentric shell, and the same power and intensity which is present in your suffering would express itself in a creative response.

Did God put us on purpose into our early environment where egocentricity and failure were bound to come? Did He confront us with all our small and medium-sized Judases because He expects us to accomplish our task and to serve creation as He expected Jesus to do when He matched him against his great Judas? We begin to see. The place where we were born foreshadows our later Gethsemane. Our fate, our mission in the battle of darkness and light, becomes comprehensible.

All mourning harbors the possibility of a decisive step forward, and this step is the discovery that God puts us into the place where we are needed. He needs us; He asks for our cooperation, as much as we need His help. Our lawsuit is dismissed. We accept His assignment. We still mourn but we set out to work and to grow. The mourner is blessed. Consenting to his anguish, he admits: Hallowed is His name. Then we are given our commission: to write His name clearly, by making history, however weak and blundering, to learn to read the eternal meaning of reality.

LEARNING TO READ GOD'S NAME IN EVERYTHING. If we could decipher the hieroglyphs of history, we would read His name everywhere, in victory and defeat, in war and peace, in suffering and joy. But we cannot see the whole: therefore we misinterpret the parts. We think we know His name and not finding it in reality we say: It is not there. Actually it is there, but we do not know it; it is a greater name, more comprehensive, more frightening than we expect. Let us learn His name anew. It is holy and whole; therefore it includes the most appalling and incomprehensible facts. We shall try to gain the higher insight from which we can read His name. That is the commitment.

His name is spelled out in creation. We are letters of it. By recognizing His signature everywhere, in evil and evildoers, we could change darkness into light, and destruction into creative growth. To take the helm of creation in our own hands, however weak and blundering—that is our commission.

"Lead us not into temptation" (6:13). Temptation can be described as the danger of going astray, missing the way of spiritual evolution and misusing our energies (the opposite of "hallowing His name"). This danger is evident in the "temptation of plenty";

we have more power than wisdom and therefore might serve our Ego instead of God. Jesus' classic three answers to the tempter show the way out.

However, the opposite situation, the "temptation of want," is equally dangerous, though less recognizable. Outer or inner enemies will assail us. Our props and values are lost, our beloved ones may die. And to avoid this, we escape into wild despair or stupid (pious) acquiescence, shallow sentimentality or suicidal addictions, instead of "hallowing His name."

In all these cases we ascribe our predicament to blind fate or to the devil, or to a cruel divine judge who punishes us for our sins. We misunderstand the dynamics of evolution and therefore regress into childish complaints instead of learning our lesson, discovering the deeper meaning of life and progressing to the next level of reality.

The Creator gave us creative power and freedom to use it as we please. This is temptation. If we use it for the preservation and welfare of our Ego, we hamper our inner development. This causes suffering for us and others. Or we suffer from the egocentricity of others, even before we make them suffer. Suffering is temptation too; it tempts us to become more egocentric, as for instance, feeling sorry for ourselves, and thus replacing the goals of creation by the goals of our Ego-defense.

But it is always God who tests us, stimulating our better insight, expecting us to become of age. Let us commit ourselves to the task of recognizing the creative purpose in every temptation, discovering and using the possibility of growth everywhere. Thus we shall change the temptation into a creative assignment and attain additional freedom, power, and responsibility. We are promoted to a higher rank, faced with the unsolved problems of a larger part of the world.

This deeper understanding presupposes purity of heart; yet, on the other hand, we can cleanse our hearts only by going through the temptation successfully. It is the same vicious circle which we found in the blessedness of the mourners and the holiness of the name of God. Both vicious circles, however, can be dispelled by the discovery of the underlying spiritual situation. The individual would not be caught in his tragic predicament, were he not needed for the evolution of the universe. This is true even to the extent that someone who is not caught in such a predicament and is allowed to live smoothly and serenely, is probably not—or not yet—earmarked for a commission in the army of light. There is "more joy in heaven over one sinner who repents, than over ninety-nine righteous persons who need no repentance" (Luke 15:7). It is the prodigal son who gets the commission first.

"Our Father who art in heaven" (6:9). Our way through temptation, failure, and suffering has shown us that there is nothing on earth on which we can rely. The values we cherished, our natural inheritance and endowment, our traditional philosophy and religion, our membership in family, nation, and church, all these prove to be questionable, futile, perishable, when they are subjected to the test of the final temptation. In the language of the New Testament, when the "great tribulation" begins, all our tribal values, all our boasting that we are children of Abraham (or followers of some other authority), proves utterly useless. We are completely lost, for all our modern education, old-fashioned religion, radical politics, or conservative culture. Our wars and revolutions, our own greed, fear, and pride will certainly destroy us. But the prayer teaches us to say "Our Father in Heaven."

"Father" certainly means protection, guidance, help. There is a Great Father who creates and supports the universe, not a lenient daddy who comforts us when we cry. This inconceivably powerful Creator is supposed to be concerned with each one of us, with every group, with all animals, including the sparrows, and all the stars in the sky. He, then, is definitely superhuman, supernatural. He is "in Heaven," beyond time, space, and number; or better, His existence seems to be in a sort of super-time and super-space, in omnipresence.

Our mind, limited by time and space, can never fathom the qualities of this supreme Being, yet He is "our Father"; somehow there must be some kinship between Him and us. He created us "in His image"; but He is not limited like us nor threatened by errors and failures; we *are* not like Him, but we shall be, we ought to *become* like Him. The words "He created us in His image," then, describe a dynamic process, not a static and remaining *fait accompli*. He created us and is still busy creating us. He is creating His own image, and we are the material, the half-finished work, slowly beginning to show the first traits of His likeness. The great sculptor is hewing his self-portrait out of the marble. We are the marble; we shall be the portrait. Prospective "sons of God," we are in the making. Creation continues.

We now perceive that the beatitude regarding the "poor in spirit" (5:3) implies that we are poor and incomplete portraits; it implies our desire to become better "sons" and our urge to start the spiritual hunger riot which conquers the kingdom. St. Augustine said: "I tremble and I thrill. I tremble because I know that I am unlike Him. I thrill because I feel myself like Him." The paradox disappears in the dynamic growth of unceasing creation.

To co-create means to expose ourselves to the hammer-blows of the great Sculptor and to learn to wield the hammer like Him. Startling, frightening as it may be for us half-finished, only half-conscious creatures, we have to create something new here on earth, whether we like it or not. Under the pretext of being humble and too "poor in spirit," the Christians have refused to create; the power of darkness did it instead, and see where we are now. We should have built the kingdom of heaven, but we are stumbling around at the edges of hell. We have to cry out: "Deliver us from evil!"

"Deliver us from evil" (6:13). The Greek word for "evil" has a form which allows two interpretations: "the evil one," and "the evil thing." Most of us do not believe in devils any more; and "evil things" have become "difficulties which we cannot yet master," such as cancer, economic crises, earthquakes. What kind of evil does the prayer mean? We remember that evil is within ourselves and this we can explore.

All will agree that an action must be called "evil" which causes people, let us say children, to change from a positive and creative attitude to a negative and destructive one. Lack of love and understanding causes a child to withdraw from the group in self-defense, developing distrust, fear, greed, and stubbornness. He becomes egocentric and begins to commit "evil actions" toward other people; he becomes an "evildoer." All our egocentricity is caused in early childhood by egocentric adults. Too much love and too little wisdom on the part of the parents, or too much wisdom and too little love, forestall the creative development of the new generation. In this sense we are evildoers, all of us. Unconsciously, we thwart the purpose of creation, and we deserve to be "cast into the sea" with the "millstone about our necks" (18:6).

Evildoing, then, means to limit or destroy the positive and creative power of other persons through our own negativity. Some people do evil consciously and with purpose; these are the criminals. Most of us, however, try to do good; but our fruits show that we are achieving much more evil than good.

"Deliver us from evil" then means that we want to get rid of our egocentricity and negativity, conscious as well as unconscious. To remove the inner evil means to reconcile the conscious personality with the repressed unconscious. The inner unity, the inner peace is what we are praying for. Let us be peacemakers, first of all, within ourselves. Here again the beatitude and the Prayer coincide.

But as long as repression prevails there is civil war between our egocentric actions and the tribal collective unconscious powers, in the forms of fear, hatred, cruelty, obsession, depression, sleeplessness, anxiety, and the like. As long as we are fighting (unwittingly) against our own unconscious, an outer attack against our Ego strengthens the inner enemy; the Ego feels threatened from outside and inside at once. All "outer evil," enemies, diseases, losses, deaths, are evil only as far as they increase our inner evil like hatred, anxiety and despair.

If we could rid ourselves of the inner evil, we could look at the outer evil with eyes which—like spiritual X-rays—go through the negative substance and discover the divine value behind all wickedness and the creative solution for the most difficult problems.

There is no doubt that God wants us to overcome our inner split and undo the errors of the past, individual as well as collective. He wants us to become creative peacemakers in the outer world and in our inner life as well. He wants us, as the beatitude says, to be "ranked sons of God" (5:7, Moffatt). But as long as we fight the outer world and ourselves, our inner evil increases, and God's creative endeavor appears to us as "organized evil"; God can be seen as Devil, misjudged and fought by Man.

"Deliver us from evil" in the deepest sense means: When the so-called "outer evil" arouses our inner evil to the extent that we see "the evil One" assailing us from every side, may God help us to give up our resistance, to let the ocean of suffering flood our Ego until the "great tribulation" reaches and frees the forgotten center of our soul. There the new creative spark appears like an eye that suddenly opens, and we can see. Then we recognize that it was not the evil One who did this to us; it was God Himself; only our "inner evil" made him appear as an enemy. Now, all the evildoers can be understood as His unknown tools. We can forgive them and help them. The time of creative peacemaking begins.

The more our inner evil is removed, the brighter the Light will shine through our actions; and people, for a short time, may "praise our Father." Soon, however, our Light will provoke their darkness, exactly as some outer evil would do. As long as there is darkness in them, we shall suffer almost as much as if the darkness were within ourselves. Their darkness, as all darkness, is our problem. To feel first our own inner darkness aroused by outer evil (or other people's light), and to face it until it changes into light, then through this new light to provoke the darkness of others and to face it until it changes into light, also—that is our commission.

GROWING IN FAITH

The Greatest Need: Spiritual Growth

The preceding section of the Sermon was a lesson in spiritual mountaineering. Its goal was the towering peak where time and eternity meet, the eternal Presence, the everlasting "now." But even if we reach the mountain peak where for a moment we breathe the air of eternity, the very next minute we find ourselves again in the dust of our earth, worrying about food, shelter, money, and health. This section, therefore, teaches us how to deal with worries and cares, the human variety of animal instincts. Jesus does not tell us to get rid of our natural needs, but to subordinate them to a greater need, the need for spiritual growth. That presupposes faith, and this faith is stated like a huge headline in 6:33: "But seek first his [God's] kingdom and his righteousness, and all these things shall be yours as well."

Choose the Right Values

> "Do not lay up for yourselves treasures on earth, where moth and rust consume and where thieves break in and steal, but lay up for yourselves treasures in heaven, where neither moth nor rust consumes and where thieves do not break in and steal; for where your treasure is, there will your heart be also.
> "The eye is the lamp of the body. So, if your eye is sound, your whole body will be full of light; but if your eye is not sound, your whole body will be full of darkness. If then the light in you is darkness, how great is the darkness!
> "No one can serve two masters; for either he will hate the one and love the other, or he will be devoted to the one and despise the other. You cannot serve God and mammon" (6:19–24).

The treasure means the basis of our security as well as the purpose of our life. If it is mammon, it will fail us; and if it is something more idealistic, health, love, family, patriotism, scientific achievements—everything short of heaven itself—then it must fail us also.

There are two reasons for this. One is obvious for everybody: all earthly values are perishable, moths and rust will destroy them; all attempts to perpetuate human situations are futile. The thieves—including our inner traitors, our unconscious fears and desires—will "break in and steal."

Single-mindedness essential. The second reason is less conspicuous though more destructive. Only a single-minded person can grow; all divided minds go astray, suffer and perish, at first inwardly and later outwardly. That is not a moral law, it is a simple and inexorable fact.

The treasure, the highest value in our life, attracts all our attention and interest. It is tiresome to do things which are not related to the treasure and we can never do them creatively. If a man's treasure is a beautiful woman, he forgets his friends and sacrifices his career, unless he needs his career to satisfy her. Our heart is the emotional source of all our valuations and judgments. It is the channel through which our creative energies flow. This fountainhead lies where our treasure lies. The heart, the source of our vitality, and the treasure, the goal we are striving for, are identical. The future controls, creates, equips us, not the past.

If we are created—as we think we are—to create the kingdom, and if the development of the New Man is our reason for existence—as we think it is—our own future and the future of mankind must be our treasure; it must be the center of gravity where all our thoughts and tendencies converge and where our heart is at home—unless we are deviated, divided by secondary values which blind us to the main purpose of creation.

The division may be conscious; we may see, as it were, with one eye the dynamic goal of evolution, while with the other eye we leer at the false treasure of static self-preservation or static race-preservation. We long for the dangers and adventures of the future but we prefer the security, stability and stagnation of the time being. The inner conflict then forces us sooner or later to make a decision.

However, the conflict might remain unconscious for a long time. Consciously we may serve God while unconscious fears and greed cause us to stumble; or we may consciously choose mammon while our unconscious longing for the higher life prompts us to destroy our earthly happiness by terrible blundering. That is the case of complete darkness in 6:23. Many accidents, physical diseases and nervous disturbances, originate in this conscious or unconscious lack of single-mindedness.

In tribal life the treasure was the self-preservation of the tribe until men like Abraham and Moses discovered the real value of tribal life beyond the tribe. But then the treasure seemed to be lost until Jesus discovered that not the tribe, not the king, not the priesthood, but every single individual now must become a treasurer of eternity. Indeed, if we do not learn to "store up treasures in heaven," all our labor is in vain. But how can we do it? To find "the Beyond Within," to obey God's law of gravity which draws us into the kingdom of heaven, to play an active part in creation—these are big words, but what do they actually and practically mean? Matthew gives us the answer.

Overcome Worries by Trust

> "Therefore I tell you, do not be anxious about your life, what you shall eat or what you shall drink, nor about your body, what you shall put on. Is not life more than food, and the body more than clothing? Look at the birds of the air: they neither sow nor reap nor gather into barns, and yet your heavenly Father feeds them. Are you not of more value than they? And which of you by being anxious can add one cubit to his span of life? And why are you anxious about clothing? Consider the lilies of the field, how they grow; they neither toil nor spin; yet I tell you, even Solomon in all his glory was not arrayed like one of these. But if God so clothes the grass of the field, which today is alive and tomorrow is thrown into the oven, will he not much more clothe you, O men of little faith? Therefore do not be anxious, saying, 'What shall we eat?' or 'What shall we drink?' or 'What shall we wear?' For the Gentiles seek all these things; and your heavenly Father knows that you need them all" (6:25–32).

Matthew wrote for Jewish Christians who lived in the great centers of Hellenistic cultures. They were intellectuals, like us, with a keen sense of independence. When they heard that "no man can serve two masters," their reaction must have been: "Why should we serve a master at all?" It is the same attitude which John records: "We are Abraham's offspring, we have never been slaves to anybody. What do you mean by saying 'You will be free'?" (John 8:33, Moffatt). The old tribal pride of the "select people" has turned into an egocentric feeling of superiority and a corresponding fear of inferiority, exactly as it is in our day.

Matthew knows this from his long experience in teaching and preaching; and he arranges the sayings of his Master accordingly. Consciously we—the students of Matthew and followers of Jesus —are free, we do not serve anybody; but we are egocentric; and now we are asked: "Which of you by taking thought can add one cubit unto his stature?" (6:27, KJV). The great humorist smiles. He does not mean to offend us, but he hits our weakest spot. The

Greek word for stature means also "age." Who can add ten years to his lifetime? Unconsciously, we are slaves of time, of nature, of innumerable needs and fears. We are not free at all. The more egocentric we are, the more we depend on circumstances which we cannot control.

The way up is the way down; to grow mature means to become like children. To become carefree and efficient means to live like birds; to face death with calmness and dignity means to achieve the perfect wisdom and inner equilibrium of flowers and trees. Not the egocentric arrogance of the human mind which stresses our superiority over animals and plants, but humble open-mindedness allowing us to admire, discover, and learn their secrets, is the helpful attitude. "Behold the birds . . . consider the lilies." That means to spend many hours of meditation on the mysteries of animal and vegetal life. We might then discover that we share their mysteries. We are plants; but we are more. We are animals also; but we are still more. The calm beauty of the plant which grows and dies without resentment and the warm eagerness of the animal which works unceasingly for its food, no anxiety for the future—all this should be part of our human nature too. Yet, still we are more than all this: we are conscious individuals, free to choose and to err; and this freedom of ours makes us forget that, in spite of it, animals and plants we remain.

How then can we grow into more individuated personalities, avoiding the conflict between our egocentric goals and our animal and vegetal limitations? How can we live in the infinite and in the finite, in the spiritual and in the earthly world at the same time? The answer is hidden in the last sentence of 6:25: "Is not life more than food, and the body more than clothing?"

In modern language we would say: Is not the whole prior to the part? Does not the goal control the means? And if we solve the central problem of life, does not the solution of all the peripheral problems follow suit? Yes, it does, we know it; but it takes faith to act accordingly.

Animals and plants have their proper place in creation. They follow the will of God. The egocentric person wants to add a cubit unto his stature; he mistakes his place in the universe, wants to serve no master at all, but actually serves two masters and thereby causes his own destruction. If he could find his place as a part of the whole, he would participate according to his individual freedom and his spiritual insight in the great decisions of the evolution of the universe. He would be "of more value than the birds"; and the same carefree enthusiasm with which the sparrows look for food would serve him, the master of the planet Earth, in the solving of his creative task. To provide food and shelter for two billions of his fellowmen would then be one of his minor achievements.

Search for the Kingdom

> "But seek first his kingdom and his righteousness, and all these things shall be yours as well.
> "Therefore do not be anxious about tomorrow, for tomorrow will be anxious for itself. Let the day's own trouble be sufficient for the day" (6:33–34).

We have been told that we need treasures in heaven, and that our new born individuality, proud and independent as it may be, can certainly not defend itself against its hostile environment. Individualism will deteriorate into rigid egocentricity unless it finds a new basis on which to stand and a new home wherein it belongs. All social and material props turn out to be treacherous. There is left only one source of security: the spiritual universe and its spiritual Creator; and this again means faith.

The expression "seeking God's righteousness" is the keyword. We already know that in Matthew's language it does not signify that stable and unchanging quality of virtuousness which we do or do not possess. We cannot learn "righteousness" as we learn spelling and arithmetic, so that it becomes a quality of our minds. Jesus uses the word in a different sense. It is dynamic now and indicates ceaseless change, endeavor, and growth. It refers to our evolution from higher to ever higher levels of being, and implies the hardship, dangers, and trepidations of traveling, experimenting, and discovering.

Then we hear, "Therefore do not be anxious about tomorrow." Most readers may think that this is a mere repetition of verse 31, "Therefore do not be anxious saying, 'What shall we eat?' " But Matthew does not repeat himself unnecessarily. At first sight it is difficult to grasp the particular meaning of this verse, and its relation to verse 33; but if we rid ourselves of our traditional patterns of thought, we shall discover what this special admonition means.

Our entire endeavor should be focused on "seeking God's righteousness," or in more dynamic terms, on our spiritual growth. This goal may cause new difficulties if we project it into the future. We are not yet "righteous." We have to work diligently to reach this goal. If we should die before having achieved righteousness, what would happen to us? Would we be doomed to hell, or at least not admitted to the kingdom of heaven? Even the dynamic concept of righteousness might create fears and anxieties concerning the future. Only a moment ago Jesus told us that we were not to worry about food and clothing; if we "seek the kingdom" he taught, the material things will come to us. Are we now to be harried by fears about our "salvation"?

Matthew is the only one among the four evangelists who boldly applies the imperative, "Take no thought for the morrow" to our spiritual future. He knows that eternity will not begin "tomorrow." Eternity is here already.[3] If we could but rid ourselves of our inner evil today, we would find ourselves in the kingdom this very minute. The entrance therein, though it is to be prepared step by step, does not take place on a given "day of judgment." It comes "like lightning"; it is the discovery of something which exists beyond time and therefore has been here and will be here through all ages past and future.

The kingdom of God is within, it is the "Beyond Within"; it is not a grave concern regarding our future existence; it is a present challenge, a task which can be solved now and here.

---

3. Later we shall study Matthew's special emphasis on this idea in connection with his parables about "watching and praying," Chapter 25.

Chapter 7

SPIRITUAL DECISIONS

Introduction: Our Independence

Jesus does not tell us what the kingdom of heaven is: he only tells us what we might do to find it. He leads us into independence; he teaches us self-responsibility, sending each one of us on his own journey into the unknown. To his disciples this was the hardest of all lessons: they were so happy under his leadership. How could they understand that it was necessary for them to be left alone (John 16:7)? But we, nineteen hundred years later, begin to see what individuation means. Jesus had to die, to withdraw his personal leadership, otherwise the Spirit of the Christ would not have been born in his disciples.

Judge Not

> "Judge not, that you be not judged. For with the judgment you pronounce you will be judged, and the measure you give will be the measure you get. Why do you see the speck that is in your brother's eye, but do not notice the log that is in your own eye? Or how can you say to your brother, 'Let me take the speck out of your eye,' when there is the log in your own eye? You hypocrite, first take the log out of your own eye, and then you will see clearly to take the speck out of your brother's eye.
> "Do not give dogs what is holy; and do not throw your pearls before swine, lest they trample them underfoot and turn to attack you" (7:1-6).

Our insight has increased, our love for humanity is growing. We have found a treasure, or we think we have. Should we not help others to find it too? Our brothers are going astray in the wilderness. Should we not share our new insight, giving alms of wisdom, becoming their teachers?

No! "Judge not!"

Matthew hits here the sorest spot of our still remaining egocentricity. Would *we* like to be considered as sheep and to be shepherded by a friend who was (or thought he was) newly commissioned as the Lord's shepherd dog? We should not do to him what we do not want him to do to us (7:12).

As long as we notice all the motes in other people's eyes, we are likely to project our own unsolved problems onto them; and we certainly have not yet discovered what individuation means. Individuation, among other things, presupposes our independence from each other. Respect your neighbor's own rights; take him seriously even where you think he is wrong. Give him the privilege of making his own mistakes and discoveries. If you are asked for help, help, but remember: the best helper, leader and teacher is the one who soonest becomes superfluous. Let us teach each other to stand on our own feet, spiritually as well as materially.

"Not to judge" then means not to compare our spiritual progress, thinking of ourselves as more advanced or less advanced than the others. The question whom we should or should not invite, hire, ask for service, invest with responsibilities, requires all our judgment and all our wisdom; but the answer should only say what is the right thing for us to do. It should not measure and judge the virtues and values of our fellowmen.

Our tendency to take splinters from other people's eyes indicates immaturity. Even criticising others silently is judging them in an attitude of condemnation. Jesus warns "With the judgment you pronounce, you will be judged." How easily we disregard this caution, in our gossiping, our resentments and our critical attitudes toward family, friends, neighbors, strangers, thus giving ourselves a superior feeling, consciously or unconsciously.

Trying to understand the other without judgment is the new way of Christian living; how can we teach this new wisdom without appearing conceited? Wait. Do not try to convince others forcefully no matter how much you have learned or how enthusiastic you are. Uninvited teaching or preaching is like throwing your pearls before swine and you will only be rebuffed without serving the higher cause. Searching for the kingdom is a voluntary act.

Seek and You Will Find

> "Ask, and it will be given you; seek, and you will find; knock, and it will be opened to you. For every one who asks receives, and he who seeks finds, and to him who knocks it will be opened. Or what man of you, if his son asks him for a loaf, will give him a stone? Or if he asks for a fish, will give him a serpent? If you then, who are evil, know how to give good gifts to your children, how much more will your Father who is in heaven give good things to those who ask

him! So whatever you wish that men would do to you, do so to them; for this is the law and the prophets" (7:7–12).

If we do not help others because they would become dependent on us, others should not help us for the same reason. However, being left alone, we cannot rid ourselves of our egocentricity. We are not equal to the task. How can we find our way? It is our own endeavor on which we have to rely. "Who asks receives": that refers to prayer. "Who seeks finds": that refers to practical experiments. We have to look around, to try many different ways, and sooner or later—it is not stated how soon—we shall find our way. "If we knock, it shall be opened to us": that refers to a door. Finally, it will be the entrance to the kingdom of heaven; but first it is the entrance to the storeroom where the secret sins and treasures, our hidden resentments—the unlived life—are piled in our unconscious mind.

These two doors lead in the same direction. If we enter the storehouse of the unconscious, we shall discover that this weird and forbidding room changes into the greenhouse of creation. It is the antechamber of the entrance to the kingdom itself.

We have to take the steps, to make the decisions, and to run the risk; but we cannot accomplish the whole task alone. "It shall be opened to us." We cannot open the door ourselves. Here the interplay of human activity and grace from above is pictured with amazing precision. If we do not knock, the door will remain closed; yet if we knock, *must* it be opened? Is grace forced to answer our prayer? Is there a mathematical law in the spiritual world, or is God free? Can He refuse His grace? In spite of our asking and seeking and knocking?

Matthew's answer is marvelous. Verses 7 and 8 present the only instance in the whole Gospel where a verbal repetition occurs. Matthew has preserved it from his source, as did Luke (Luke 11:9–10). Why did they not leave out one of the two parallel statements? They must have been impressed by the organic unity of the imperative: "Ask and it shall be given to you," and the following affirmative, "Everyone that asks receives," and by the word "for" linking the two together.

Knock and the Door Will Be Opened

The imperative is clear; but the statement in 7:8 gives the real reason and foundation of the imperative, showing that all our needs are there only in order to make us ask. God wants to open the door but he will not do so unless we knock. He must therefore cause us to knock, which we will do when we have suffered enough. But He will not force us directly to knock at His door, because that would interfere with the highest of all our values, namely freedom, independence, and individuation. Thus He will wait until we knock voluntarily.

The right attitude essential. However, it is not correct to think of the entrance as being just one door. There seem to be several doors between several courts or ante-rooms. It is like a great emperor's palace; the closer we come to the throne, the more power is given to us and the greater is the temptation that we might misuse it. God is eager to help us, if only we find an attitude which enables us to use His help properly. Like hungry children, we should ask for "bread and fish"; then He will not give us "stones and serpents." Usually we ask for stones and serpents, and then are angry if we get what we asked for; or we waste the bread because we cannot appreciate it. A wise father does not give his child bread as long as the child asks for stones. The child should find out what he needs and learn to ask for it; otherwise he will never become mature.

It takes time to learn the diet of evolution and to ask for the right kind of daily bread; but there is no doubt that we shall get it as soon as we discover our need for it. In the meantime, we should try to live according to the Golden Rule. If our valuation is wrong and we treat our fellowmen in the wrong way trying, for instance, to convert them and to inform them about their faults, they will do the same to us; they will defend themselves aggressively. This will enable us to discover our own mistakes and to give new content and new zest to our self-education, until we finally learn for what we should ask and find the right door on which to knock. Then the door will be opened.

Enter by the Narrow Gate

> "Enter by the narrow gate; for the gate is wide and the way is easy, that leads to destruction, and those who enter by it are many. For the gate is narrow and the way is hard, that leads to life, and those who find it are few" (7:13–14).

There are two ways: one leading into Life, spiritual growth, higher consciousness, eternal creativity; the other leading into destruction, loss of consciousness and individuality, reduction to rubbish, dross, raw material for future creation.

The imperative "enter" presupposes our capacity for choosing between the two ways. In fact, our individual freedom is limited to a small margin; the larger part of our activities is controlled by racial instincts, tribal habits, unconscious complexes, and egocentric patterns far stronger than all our good resolutions. But we are not completely fettered by cause and effect; we are not mere automatons. We have enough freedom to take small steps which lead into a little more freedom, then larger steps which lead into a frightening degree of freedom, and finally huge steps which lead up into the blinding light of a superindividual consciousness.

If we do not use our margin of free choice, we shall be pushed by circumstances in the wrong direction. To avoid the conscious decision is an unconscious decision in favor of destruction. We had better take the risk consciously and deliberately.

The narrowness of the right gate does not allow us to carry with us our possessions. All security, all guarantees have to be left behind, not only health, mammon, the old-age pension, and life-insurance, but also reputation, social standing, and religious merit. Moreover, the gate is so narrow that only single individuals can pass through it. The group, the tribe, the community, even the new brotherhood, have to be left behind.

The gate can be found at the end of our physical career, or between two periods of our life; or there may be many fates of different degrees of narrowness. The narrow gate symbolizes rebirth. Almost every person at a given time during his life has dreams where he is forced to crawl through a narrow tunnel or to press forward through locked doors. He is filled with anxiety, alone, hopeless, and helpless; often he fails to emerge from his prison: but ultimately, if his search is positive, he finds himself free, on a green meadow under a blue sky. This is an age-old dream, recorded in ancient myths and fairy tales as well as in modern psychology. Whoever has this dream should know that he is pregnant with the Spirit, and that he could give birth to his own highest reality, if only he could avoid the broad and easy way which leads to spiritual miscarriage.

Know Them by Their Fruits

> "Beware of false prophets who come to you in sheep's clothing but inwardly are ravenous wolves. You will know them by their fruits. Are grapes gathered from thorns, or figs from thistles? So, every sound tree bears good fruit, but the bad tree bears evil fruit. A sound tree cannot bear evil fruit, nor can a bad tree bear good fruit. Every tree that does not bear good fruit is cut down and thrown into the fire. Thus you will know them by their fruits" (7:15–20).

Moreover, the narrow gate forces us to choose our teachers on our own individual responsibility. "Beware of false prophets." The individual is now free to select his spiritual leader and is therefore responsible if he chooses the wrong one. It is not only the pastor who should be chosen by the community; every individual has to choose his teacher, his denomination, his creed, rejecting all authorities which come "in sheep's clothing, but inwardly are ravenous wolves."

The child in his natural development has to live through the period of tribal and feudal consciousness. He needs and wants leadership enforced upon him from without. The adult, however, must have the right to challenge and to test his teacher and to overthrow his authority if it is not creative enough. ("Authority" means "authorship" and presupposes creativity.)

How can we distinguish between the true and the false prophet? Our own sympathy for a special creed or group or leader may be based on unconscious motives which would make us blush if we were aware of them. Jesus gives us the secret in a few words. The contrast of a man's outer appearance and his inner motivation is formulated once and for all by the symbol of the wolf in sheep's clothing. The fact that some people are to some extent conscious of their ravenous selfishness does not exclude the more important fact that all of us are quite unconscious of the tremendous power which our inner wolf exerts through our unconscious actions, choices, blunders and omissions.

It is not difficult to unmask a false prophet who knows that he is an imposter. His insecurity forces him to exaggerate the attitude of the sheep. The more sheeplike he bleats, the more he proves that he is a wolf. The one, however, who honestly believes that he is a sheep, repressing into his unconscious the inner wolf, can successfully use the wolf's power for the wolf's ends in a sheep-like way. He appeals to all the disguised in all his sheeplike hearers, and these will pay him any price if he helps them to repress their inner wolves and to repair the outworn sheep's clothing. They believe in him and fight for him with a fanatical fury which is indicative of all repressed unconscious forces.

In the beginning it is often impossible to distinguish between the genuine, creative power of the Light and the destructive power of darkness which appears as an angel of Light. Jesus, however, gives us the key: "You will know them by their fruits" (7:16). This theme is so important that it is developed at length.

The evidence of the evil fruit is well known in modern psychology as the "vicious spiral." Suppose there is a religious teacher, consciously honest and eager to improve himself as well as his students, though unconsciously a "ravenous wolf." His most creative talents have been repressed into the unconscious from early childhood. Without knowing it, he feels insecure and tries to assert himself consciously by being humble and obeying meticulously the commands of his religion. Unconsciously, however, he is craving for outer successes and spectacular triumphs, dreaming to be the best religious teacher living, the foreman of the Lord's vineyard, though he tells everybody that he is the lowliest of God's servants.

His students will admire him because he teaches them to keep their sheep's clothing well trimmed and combed. Their consciousness and their conscience answer all the requirements of religion. Yet underneath, not by his words but by his attitude, he teaches them to remain, or to become, ravenous wolves, egocentric exploiters or tribal tyrants. The teacher's fruits, his followers, show or conceal the same problem which poisons his own life: buried talents turning into unconscious vices. Thus the teacher's problem is multiplied in the next generation, and the more so the more admirers he has.

It is easy to conceal a single "ravenous wolf" in a large sheepskin; but to keep a hundred of them covered and quiet is difficult. Their egocentric greed is insatiable; unconsciously each one of the students wants to be the master student, envying and defaming his colleagues. Everybody in this fold must of necessity distrust everybody; and if a bone of contention is cast among them, the herd of lambs will throw off their masks and jump at one another's throats, showing what they really are: a pack of hungry wolves.

Do the Will of the Father

> "Not every one who says to me, 'Lord, Lord,' shall enter the kingdom of heaven, but he who does the will of my Father who is in heaven. On that day many will say to me, 'Lord, Lord, did we not prophesy in your name, and cast out demons in your name, and do many mighty works in your name?' And then will I declare to them, 'I never knew you; depart from me, you evildoers'" (7:21–23).

Every human function, eating and sleeping, weeping and laughing, hard work and artistic creativeness, can be misused by the Ego. How can we distinguish between egocentric pseudocreation and genuine creative work? The distinction has to be based on the principle of the part and the whole, or in ancient language, of the many gods of paganism and the one God of monotheism.

A development which is truly creative has no rigid limitations; it serves the Creator, His universe, the whole of creation, and not a select and limited part of it. If what we do is done only for the benefit of our family, the group, the nation, it has as its author the ravening wolf. If it tries to serve Creation itself, and that means the whole of mankind, through the family or nation, it is more likely to be a fruit of the "good tree," though the distinction may not yet be visible at the beginning. Only the final judgment of history or of the spirit beyond history will show whether the fruits of the tree were evil or good.

Build on the Invisible Rock

> "Every one then who hears these words of mine and does them will be like a wise man who built his house upon the rock; and the rain fell, and the floods came, and the winds blew and beat upon that house, but it did not fall, because it had been founded on the rock. And every one who hears these words of mine and does not do them will be like a foolish man who built his house upon the sand; and the rain fell, and the floods came, and the winds blew and beat against that house, and it fell; and great was the fall of it."
>
> And when Jesus finished these sayings, the crowds were astonished at his teaching, for he taught them as one who had authority, and not as their scribes (7:24–29).

The two stories, daring in their simplicity, balance the paradoxes of the Beatitudes. The Sermon on the Mount begins with the statement that heartbreak and hunger are blessings, and it ends with the admonition to build our house upon an invisible rock, on something as safe and tangible as the very foundation-stone of Mother Earth, though this rock remains intangible to our senses and inaccessible to natural science. The complete reversal of values, which is the essence of Christianity, is here shown in all its paradoxical recklessness. The tree of life has its roots in the sky, its branches reaching down to our earth. The goal of history, the endeavor of our life, appears not only as a castle in the air, but as a reversed castle, its roof and battlements pointing downward and its foundation based on rocks which no earthly architect can ever touch. This is either the most foolish idealism of a dreaming poet and should be limited to that or it is the beginning of a new day of creation.

Jesus laid the foundations on the invisible rock. The house is being built. It is up to us whether we help to complete it and learn to live in it, or whether we prefer the sham-security of our earthly house on the shifting sand, that house which is just now breaking down in the rainstorm and gusty winds of rebellion, doubt and disillusionment—and great will be the fall of it.

Part Three

THE WAY

Introduction

The third part of Matthew's Gospel (Chapters 8 to 13) is the practical preparation of the disciples for their service in the creative development. The first half (Chapters 8 to 10) describes the inner experience of the disciple who actually sets out to follow the Master. It may be called the inner way of practical individuation. The second half (Chapters 11 to 13) describes the breadth of the new work, its perilous problems and final victories. It is the outer way of practical individuation. The discourse in Chapter 10 can best be understood as the order of the day issued for the newly enrolled disciples, while the discourse in Chapter 13 is the order of the day for the historians of the kingdom.

Chapter 8

THE INNER JOURNEY

Spiritual Power—Three Healings

> When he came down from the mountain, great crowds followed him; and behold, a leper came to him and knelt before him, saying, "Lord, if you will, you can make me clean." And he stretched out his hand and touched him, saying, "I will; be clean." And immediately his leprosy was cleansed. And Jesus said to him, "See that you say nothing to any one; but go, show yourself to the priest, and offer the gift that Moses commanded, for a proof to the people."
>
> As he entered Capernaum, a centurion came forward to him, beseeching him and saying, "Lord, my servant is lying paralyzed at home, in terrible distress." And he said to him, "I will come and heal him." But the centurion answered him, "Lord, I am not worthy to have you come under my roof; but only say the word, and my servant will be healed. For I am a man under authority, with soldiers under me; and I say to one, 'Go,' and he goes, and to another, 'Come,' and he comes, and to my slave, 'Do this,' and he does it." When Jesus heard him, he marveled, and said to those who followed him, "Truly, I say to you, not even in Israel have I found such faith. I tell you, many will come from east and west and sit at table with Abraham, Isaac, and Jacob in the kingdom of heaven, while the sons of the kingdom will be thrown into the outer darkness; there men will weep and gnash their teeth." And to the centurion Jesus said, "Go; be it done for you as you have believed." And the servant was healed at that very moment.
>
> And when Jesus entered Peter's house, he saw his mother-in-law lying sick with a fever; he touched her hand, and the fever left her, and she rose and served him. That evening they brought to him many who were possessed with demons; and he cast out the spirits with a word, and healed all who were sick. This was to fulfil what was spoken by the prophet Isaiah, "He took our infirmities and bore our diseases" (8:1–17).

The "miraculous" healing of the leper was no miracle at all in the eyes of Jesus' contemporaries; it was simply a "sign" of spiritual power. Things like that happened frequently enough. But

119

what happened to the disciples who followed him and saw his
healing power—that was miracle indeed; for even though they
failed badly in their self-discipline, they became cleaner and
wiser every day. It was not achieved without struggle, but it was
achieved; and his presence made them forget the sting of his
inexorable lessons. That is the value of spiritual feudalism. If we
could follow their Master, our psychological "leprosy" would be
cured. And afterwards, we should think, it would be easy with his
help to rid ourselves of our feudalistic dependence.

There is no doubt that Jesus' capacity to heal and influence the
physical as well as the mental functions of man was developed
to an extent which the natural scientists of our day would refuse
to record, just as they refuse to record certain facts of clairvoyance
and telepathy. This does not mean, however, that Jesus did or
could do anything against the laws of reality. But he applied
higher laws, and the people who did not know these higher laws
could not explain what he did. Jesus' unusual power was evidently
connected with his capacity to meditate and pray for long hours
at a time; but he did not consider this as his unique privilege. He
hoped that many of his followers would one day accomplish even
"greater works" (Matt. 17:20, 21; John 14:12).

Pondering the healing of the leper, we may notice that something of this sort has already appeared in our own lives, years
ago; it was only that we were too blind to see it. In other words,
there is, besides our own endeavor, another power at work which
helps and guides us with or without our knowledge. We might as
well acknowledge this power and try to cooperate with it. Let us
therefore look at it and observe how it works.

In the first story it is the faith of the patient which opens the
way for the healing influence. In the second story it is the faith of
the captain which accounts for the cure of his servant. In the
third case, Peter's mother-in-law, it is faith again, but faith in the
form of personal confidence.

The decisive factor is not the bodily touch nor the spoken word.
It is a spiritual power, conveyed by the healer, and received by
the patient through the channel of confidence. Sometimes, however, this power works without the personal presence of the healer.
Matthew tells of the Roman captain, visualizing his calm and
warlike dignity. Face-to-face with him, infinitely alive, stands
Jesus. Two empires meet; and curiously enough, they are pleased
with one another. Jesus, marveling at the captain's faith, predicts
in his excitement a vast spread of the teaching to "many from
east and west." In this case Jesus needed to do nothing: the heal-

ing was done "as you have believed." The power of the Spirit was not limited to Israel.

Peter's mother-in-law was angry, we may suppose, because Peter neglected his trade while he wandered with a questionable man of Nazareth. When this supplanter of conservative virtues invaded her hometown, Capernaum, the whole town was excited. Would all fishermen run after him? Oh, she would have liked to hear him preach, but he had stolen her son-in-law. It made her sick. She hated him, and still was eager to see him. Then he was there. They looked at each other and she was conquered and convinced by his eyes in less than a minute. Peter was right! This was the Master! Her grudge changed into joy; she got up and made supper.

What is the nature, origin, and purpose of this power? Is it impersonal like electricity, or personal like the power of a hypnotizer, or superpersonal like the creative power which forced fish to evolve into birds and cavemen into civilized personalities? We are forced to explore the spiritual kingdom on our own account. Matthew, and Jesus, want us to come of age.

The Night-Sea-Journey—Test of Faith

> Now when Jesus saw great crowds around him, he gave orders to go over to the other side. And a scribe came up and said to him, "Teacher, I will follow you wherever you go." And Jesus said to him, "Foxes have holes, and birds of the air have nests; but the Son of man has nowhere to lay his head." Another of the disciples said to him, "Lord, let me first go and bury my father." But Jesus said to him, "Follow me, and leave the dead to bury their own dead."
> And when he got into the boat, his disciples followed him. And behold, there arose a great storm on the sea, so that the boat was being swamped by the waves; but he was asleep. And they went and woke him, saying, "Save, Lord; we are perishing." And he said to them, "Why are you afraid, O men of little faith?" Then he rose and rebuked the winds and the sea; and there was a great calm. And the men marveled, saying, "What sort of man is this, that even winds and sea obey him?" (8:18–27).

The Sermon on the Mount gave us the impression that the disciple has to achieve his initiation himself. His admission to the kingdom of heaven seemed to depend on the success of his religious self-education. We wondered where the beginner could find the strength to carry out such a difficult undertaking. In response, Matthew told us about the help which came to the earliest Christians through the Master's divine power. Who then does the work, we or he? Is it his energy or ours which has to be mobilized?

Moreover, if Jesus' personal help was necessary to the disciples, who will help us, since he is no longer with us?

These questions were as urgent for Matthew's students as they are for us. Is there an omnipresent "Spirit of Christ"? Is our relationship to it the same as was the relationship of the disciples to Jesus? What is the relationship between this "Spirit of Christ" and the man Jesus? The two ensuing stories are the first part of his reply.

The Sermon on the Mount and the healings have aroused the enthusiasm of the multitudes, and new disciples throng around the Master. Jesus withdraws, however, taking with him but a handful of men; and this handful is carefully sifted. The admission is limited to those who accept two different conditions; and the two conditions are related to two opposite ways of life.

The recruits who come from the upper layer and have already developed a great deal of sophistication are represented by the scribe. These have to submit to the most difficult test which could be devised for them. Their social standing and financial security will be replaced by a life where they will have no security whatsoever. "The foxes have holes, and the birds of the air have nests; but the Son of man has nowhere to lay his head." "Son of man?" we ask; and we learn that Matthew used this expression here "casually" because it was in one of his documents. It means "the human one" and refers to Ezekiel (2:3) who was called by the Spirit "thou human being" in the sense of "thou little man." Jesus liked this title; he might have had a similar experience as Ezekiel. "Is that all?" "Yes, for the moment. Later we shall learn more about it."

The other recruits who come from the countryside are accustomed to such insecurity. These, therefore, have to fulfill another requirement. Rooted as they still are in tribal habits and traditions, they are asked to sever their ties. If they neglect the most natural of ritual duties (to "bury their father"), they will be outcasts forever in the eyes of the tribe. The war is on; no private sorrows must interfere with the call to colors.

In modern language, Jesus tells the villager that he has to relinquish his tribal habits. He tells the intellectual his egocentric pattern of rugged individualism has to find its spiritual form. It is safe to assume that only a small percentage of both groups were willing to pay this price for their admission. We, however, if we wish to proceed with our inner development have to pay this price too. Neither artistically nor psychologically nor religiously can we expect to find the right understanding of Matthew's work, if we do not consider ourselves as disciples, or at least as aspirants of discipleship.

Those who enter the boat will be confronted instantly with a more dangerous test. "Behold, a great tempest!" The best interpreters have understood this story as the description of one of the seeker's central experiences. Similar stories have been recorded many times in non-Christian religions. The Old Testament has two such tales: Noah, with his household, delivered from the great flood (Gen. 6–8), and Jonah, saved from drowning by a fish (Jon. 1:17). The New Testament mentions two more events of this kind: Peter walking on the waves (Matt. 14:28–31) and Paul shipwrecked on the Mediterranean (Acts 27:9–45).

The tempest and the waves are age-old symbols for the "perils of the soul" during a time of crisis and that means of possible initiation. Mythologists have termed this inner experience "the Night-Sea-Journey."[1] The hero is usually rescued by a miracle and the tempest or flood often turns out to be the purposeful arrangement of a god for the benefit of the hero's development.

Our present story, however, comes nearer to the truth than all poems and myths. Jesus forces his disciples to face a storm; he takes away their security; then leaves them alone in the danger. He wishes them to try out the power of their own faith. But he does not desert them; he is ready to help if need be. He is only asleep. He acts like a good teacher who gives his students just as much independence as they can sustain.

The disciples fail. They cannot extricate themselves from their predicament without him, and he has to come to their rescue. As soon as he arises, their fear disappears, and they see that the lake is serene. When he "rebuked" the winds and the sea, did he speak to the elements in the outer world, or did he speak to the violent waves of anxiety within the disciples' hearts? The inner and the outer world coincide. "O ye of little faith!" This is not primarily the story of a great miracle, but of a great failure. The disciples were not yet individuated at all.

Jesus did not mind. He knew the difficulties of spiritual evolution; but then he did something which we should not expect from a human teacher. The task had proved to be too frightening, yet he proceeded to another of greater danger. This seems to answer a general law of the spiritual world. We find the same process in our decisive dreams. We fail in one part of the dream, and the next part grows more dangerous. It is as if a guide were trying to

---

1. Cf. C. G. Jung's analysis of Longfellow's *Hiawatha* in *Psychology of the Unconscious*, Ch. VII.

awaken us, first calling us in a low voice, then louder, and finally shaking us vigorously.

Jesus formed the second part of this nightmare, however, not as a new test; for there was no doubt that the disciples would fail again. This time he taught them the lesson through his own example. He showed them what can and must be achieved if mankind is to evolve.

The Madmen—a Teaching Demonstration

> And when he came to the other side, to the country of the Gadarenes, two demoniacs [madmen] met him, coming out of the tombs, so fierce that no one could pass that way. And behold, they cried out, "What have you to do with us, O Son of God? Have you come here to torment us before the time?" Now a herd of many swine was feeding at some distance from them. And the demons begged him, "If you cast us out, send us away into the herd of swine." And he said to them, "Go." So they came out and went into the swine; and behold, the whole herd rushed down the steep bank into the sea, and perished in the waters. The herdsmen fled, and going into the city they told everything, and what had happened to the demoniacs. And behold, all the city came out to meet Jesus; and when they saw him, they begged him to leave their neighborhood (8:28–34).

Beyond the lake there is a strange country called Gadara, the land of the Gentiles, a region of darkness and horror. This weird landscape exists within every human being because once upon a time our ancestors were cavemen, and (seen from the standpoint of incipient Christianity) demon-worshipers, evildoers, and addicts to all kinds of filthy practices. Psychologically, they groped their way through the mist of tribal consciousness. Moreover, every one of us, as a newborn infant, lived innocently and lustily in a similar world, a smelling world of unclean diapers and primordial urges. This whole world has been forgotten, left behind, repressed, but not yet fully outlived. Our vital roots reach down as deeply into the nether world as our spiritual functions strain up into the higher world of what we call the divine. The imagined split between our so-called "lower life" (our animal and vegetal existence) and the higher life which we ascribe to spiritual developments has to be overcome; the two halves of the universe have to be welded together.

The man who was able to integrate the two opposites, to unify matter and spirit, and to reconcile the disparate layers of creation, was Jesus of Nazareth. He had to go to the depths of humanity, carrying the light of the Spirit through the very heart of the abysmal night. This journey to Gadara was neither his first nor his last adventure in this direction; but it was the first lesson of this sort which he dared to impart to his followers. Later, they would have to go the same way, each one alone, through his own individual "valley of the shadow of death." He wanted them to know what to expect when that moment came. If each would remember then in his own Gethsemane what the Master had done for them all at Gadara, the temptation would be less powerful and the likelihood of failure would be diminished.

The abyss, the valley of the shadow, always exists in the outer world and in the inner world as well. The parallelism between the outer and the inner reality is never more clearly experienced than in the great and dangerous moment when physical danger from without and mental danger.from within coincide so that we do not know whether we are threatened with inner madness because of the unbearable pressure from without, or if the outer danger is so overwhelming only because our inner resourcefulness and courage fail us so thoroughly.

The madmen of Gadara characterize the final test of our voyage toward initiation. Jesus is not the first one to lead this way, but he is the only one who enabled mankind to solve the problem.

Dante's *Purgatorio* is the best example of a Christian version of this theme, but few readers are aware of the failure of medieval Christianity as shown in Dante's great poem. He neither dares to help the sufferers, nor does he propagate a crusade for their rescue; he only teaches an uncreative morality. The dynamics of ceaseless evolution is replaced by a static pattern of heaven and hell.

Protestantism has found a more active attitude toward the nether world. It has rediscovered the fact that the country of Shadows exists within every individual as well as within every community and every nation, and that this dark power can and must be redeemed and changed into new creativity, lest mankind destroy itself in revolutions and wars.

These dark powers turn out to be creative forces in disguise; they can be redeemed by endurance, understanding, and love. Here again the devil is God's devil. But there are some cases where the evil is more deeply rooted and the split more complete. The deepest point of horror we can reach is no longer one point; it appears as two points. The two madmen represent complete madness, the madness of the split itself. The rift between the conscious and the unconscious mind, between the individual and the group, between the world and God, is present in the two madmen who are mad because they are two. As long as they are two, they will act without correlation, each one in his separate insane way; nobody can induce them to cooperate. They will destroy everything and finally themselves.

That Jesus is able to cure the two madmen is a simple expression of the fact that the central light is able to redeem all darkness and that the oneness of redeemed creation overcomes the duality of destruction.

When redemption takes place, the negative powers turn positive. The split is replaced by wholeness. Why, then, do the demons rush into the swine and the swine into the lake? If the redemptive process would reach ideal completion, such a thing would not happen; but nothing on earth is complete. Even Jesus could not convert the Pharisees. He had to leave them to the "eternal fire" (Matt. 23). Here he can only save the two madmen, which in the deeper meaning of the event, is a superhuman achievement.

Chapter 9

THE NEW WINE

Steps to Maturity

When the disciples returned to Capernaum, they had not yet fully reached an independent state of mind, the presupposition for the new life. But their former life, and their reliance on conventional religion and traditional values were gone forever. For the time being, however, they depended on their new leader as if they were his children. Jesus to them was Abraham, Moses, David, the Messiah, and almost God.

Matthew takes care to describe this feudalistic religion as the normal introduction into mature Christianity. The inner development of his students, which, according to our hypothesis, parallels the development of Jesus' disciples, does not reach the final goal of mature Christianity before the final chapter of the Gospel. It is the Christian's encounter with the glorified Christ which enables him to face a world of enemies, but this encounter is possible only after his feudalistic dependence is destroyed in the dark night of Golgotha. Up to that time he is the childlike follower of his Master, utterly unable to think and act creatively without his most minute instructions. We wonder what Jesus will teach his disciples (and us) in order to prepare them (and us) for the last and most painful step toward spiritual maturity.

Who Is He Who Can Forgive Sins?

> And getting into a boat he crossed over and came to his own city. And behold, they brought to him a paralytic, lying on his bed; and when Jesus saw their faith he said to the paralytic, "Take heart, my son; your sins are forgiven." And behold, some of the scribes said to themselves, "This man is blaspheming." But Jesus, knowing their thoughts, said, "Why do you think evil in your hearts? For which is easier, to say, 'Your sins are forgiven,' or to say, 'Rise and walk'? But that you may know that the Son of man has authority on earth to forgive sins"—he then said to the paralytic—"Rise, take up your bed and go home." And he rose and went home. When

the crowds saw it, they were afraid, and they glorified God,
who had given such authority to men (9:1–8).

The cure of the palsied man is similar to the cure of the captain's servant. In both cases the "miracle" is based on the faith of
the proxy. Collective responsibility and collective guarantees were
acceptable to Jesus when he was dealing with people on the level
of tribal life. The decisive difference between the first three healings in Chapter 8 and the first three healings of Chapter 9 is the
environment. In Chapter 8 the bystanders are friendly or even
enthusiastic. In Chapter 9 there are some friendly witnesses, too,
but there are also dangerous critics and malevolent enemies.
"The scribes," the conscience of Israel, the censorship of Mosaic
religion, enter the scene.

Most commentators agree that Matthew (in parallelism to
Mark) wished to describe "the rising tide of opposition." This is
true, but it is not a sufficient explanation. Indeed, the battle lines
in the outer field of action begin to shape up. The new religion
and the old must meet sooner or later for a showdown of utmost
historical importance, but the decisive battle takes place not only
in the outer world. It is at the same time an inner crisis within
the psyche of contemporary man, within each of Matthew's students, and in each of Jesus' disciples. Since we studied the nightmare of Gadara, we know that all decisive events take place in the
outer and the inner world at the same time.

The disciples had learned not only theoretically in the Sermon
on the Mount but also practically during the night-sea-journey and
the experience of Gadara that the new life was breaking through
the old dams like a wild flood; but now, returning to the old
familiar ground of Galilee, they could not help looking at the new
life from the standpoint of their own past. When Jesus cures the
palsied man, his disciples (and we) are not identified with the
sick but with the critic. They (and we) raise questions: What
happens here? This is a ground-shaking innovation! Jesus is not
simply a miracle-working rabbi. We already know that he leads
us into earthquake, tempest, and madness.

Who is he? Does he dare to forgive sins? Is he stronger than
the laws of our old religion? Is he God? We simply admired and
loved him when he cured the captain's servant by telepathy; now
we look at him with startled and fearful eyes. Will he destroy all
our former convictions, all tradition, all reasonable ways of life?

Calm and with utmost determination, Jesus answers the scribes'
and our own hidden thoughts. "That you may know that the Son
of man has authority on earth to forgive sins . . . Rise. . . ."

The sick is cured; his sins are forgiven, we have to accept the fact; this man is able to forgive sins.

We are paralyzed with amazement, doubt, skepticism. We are not cured. On the contrary, now we are the paralyzed man and the skeptic scribe at the same time. Matthew forces us to understand that the two opposite attitudes, skepticism and paralysis, belong together. We never find one without the other, though often the scribe does not know he is paralyzed and the paralytic does not know he is a skeptic. Now we know we are both; we are one because we are the other. That is progress.

Who, then, is "the Son of man" who can forgive sins; this bridegroom who invites us to the wedding feast? His place must be between or above the two opposites. He can reconcile them, restoring the lost balance, reaching a new and more creative form of consciousness. In the outer drama, it is Jesus standing between the scribes and the palsied man. In our inner drama it seems to be some creative power which arises in the very heart of our heart as soon as we become conscious of the opposite attitudes which separate the conscious and unconscious parts of our mind. We begin to see that we need the Lord Jesus, the Lord of spiritual feudalism, the forgiver of sins, as long as we do not yet discover the creative Lord within, "the riches of the glory of this mystery which is Christ in you" (Col. 1:27).

Breaking Away from Social Prejudices

> As Jesus passed on from there, he saw a man called Matthew sitting at the tax office; and he said to him, "Follow me." And he rose and followed him.
>
> And as he sat at table in the house, behold, many tax collectors and sinners came and sat down with Jesus and his disciples. And when the Pharisees saw this, they said to his disciples, "Why does your teacher eat with tax collectors and sinners?" But when he heard it, he said, "Those who are well have no need of a physician, but those who are sick. Go and learn what this means, 'I desire mercy, and not sacrifice.' For I came not to call the righteous, but sinners" (9:9–13).

The danger is that we remain identified either with our sins or with our righteousness. Jesus summons Matthew, the publican; and instantly the dramatic triangle leaps into action. How can the creative force carouse and feast with evildoers? Should it not prefer the respectable citizens? But the creative center, the Son of man, wants to help the sick. Who needs help? Who is sick? The publicans? The Pharisees? Or both? The dignitaries look rather blank.

Again, the merciless self-righteous Pharisee and the seeking unstable publican represent complementary attitudes of our inner life. If we are consciously the one we must be unconsciously the other. The opposites presuppose each other. Recognizing them, we are forced to search for the third point, the creative power which supports and transcends them.

The Power over Death

> Then the disciples of John came to him, saying, "Why do we and the Pharisees fast, but your disciples do not fast?" And Jesus said to them, "Can the wedding guests mourn as long as the bridegroom is with them? The days will come, when the bridegroom is taken away from them, and then they will fast. And no one puts a piece of unshrunk cloth on an old garment, for the patch tears away from the garment, and a worse tear is made. Neither is new wine put into old wineskins; if it is, the skins burst, and the wine is spilled, and the skins are destroyed; but new wine is put into fresh wineskins, and so both are preserved."
>
> While he was thus speaking to them, behold, a ruler came in and knelt before him, saying, "My daughter has just died; but come and lay your hand on her, and she will live." And Jesus rose and followed him, with his disciples. And behold, a woman who had suffered from a hemorrhage for twelve years came up behind him and touched the fringe of his garment; for she said to herself, "If I only touch his garment, I shall be made well." Jesus turned, and seeing her he said, "Take heart, daughter; your faith has made you well." And instantly the woman was made well. And when Jesus came to the ruler's house, and saw the flute players, and the crowd making a tumult, he said, "Depart; for the girl is not dead but sleeping." And they laughed at him. But when the crowd had been put outside, he went in and took her by the hand, and the girl arose. And the report of this went through all that district (9:14–26).

The parables of the garment and the wine form the center of this chapter, expressing its theme, "the old and the new." A distinction is drawn between the old egocentric (and partly still tribal) and new individuated consciousness. Chapter 9, as a whole, sketches the future battlefronts between the armies of the past, which now become the armies of darkness because they attempt to arrest history, and the armies of the future, which are definitely on the side of the Light, although the Light is still so dazzling that few people can bear it. The presence of the "bridegroom" is intoxicating.

The state of mind which we have described as "spiritual feudalism" is a necessary transition between tribal and individuated consciousness. Its characteristic is the disciples' (and our) fascination by the personality of Jesus. It gives them (and us) the opportunity to learn gradually two lessons: First, in face of outer and inner difficulties, they learn more and more to resort to their own inner light instead of the light in Jesus; and second, they learn to use the power of this light in the right way without Jesus' personal guidance. But the method of learning is trial and error.

"A certain ruler" asks for help because his daughter is dead. Jesus is in no hurry. He stops to speak with a poor woman who, as it were, had stolen some of his healing power. He does not favor the ruling class to the disadvantage of the underprivileged. This seems to be the outstanding feature in the interesting envelopment of the healing of the woman by the healing of the young girl.

We see how, in the opinion of the disciples, the personality of the Master begins to grow to superhuman proportions; he can raise the dead. Miracle-working rabbis, as we said, were no rarity in Jewish tradition; but the power to raise the dead was a quality not expected even of the Messiah himself. Yet the disciples, being close to Jesus, seeing with their own eyes, and reacting with wonder and ecstasy, accepted the miracle with awe. We also may share the understanding that this is possible, and this means that our faith in the creative power of evolution is growing.

Jesus, as the messenger and guarantor of this evolution, then becomes all-important. The desire to go with him through all the necessary crises until our unlived life is redeemed becomes so urgent that he appears as a symbol of creation and redemption itself.

The Creative Silence

> And as Jesus passed on from there, two blind men followed him, crying aloud, "Have mercy on us, Son of David." When he entered the house, the blind men came to him; and Jesus said to them, "Do you believe that I am able to do this?" They said to him, "Yes, Lord." Then he touched their eyes, saying, "According to your faith, be it done to you." And their eyes were opened. And Jesus sternly charged them, "See that no one knows it." But they went away and spread his fame through all that district.
>
> As they were going away, behold, a dumb demoniac was brought to him. And when the demon had been cast out, the dumb man spoke; and the crowds marveled, saying, "Never was anything like this seen in Israel." But the Pharisees said, "He casts out demons by the prince of demons" (9:27–34).

We are truly, all of us, dumb, as far as spiritual language is concerned. All our writing and preaching is useless and perhaps harmful, going around in circles on the egocentric level. If our eyes would see, we should at least recognize our spiritual muteness and stop our emotional or intellectual verbosity. This is what Jesus accomplished with his disciples, what Matthew tried to achieve with his students, and what we ourselves hope we can attain through self-education. None of us could do it, however, had not Jesus opened the way, and had not Matthew preserved the map.

Two men learn to see; only one learns to speak. We have two eyes, and only one mouth. We should say less than we see. Let us look twice before we talk.

In this chapter the first passage (9:1–13) introduces the dramatic triangle, the two opposites and the center. The last passage tells of two blind and one dumb man. The opposites, at the beginning as far apart as possible—a poor believer and the influential skeptics—are at the end replaced by two blind men; distance and difference have disappeared. At the beginning the Son of man speaks with authority. At the end the ability to speak is given to a mute man while the two blind (the former opposites) are forbidden to talk. The authority and power of "the word" is handed over from Jesus to the unknown person, the common man, who stands between the reconciled opposites.

When Jesus cured the paralytic, the people, according to Matthew, "glorified God who had given such authority unto men" (9:8, KJV). To men? Not only to Jesus; to the common man, to you and me! The creative power is waiting for us in our center, between the opposites; the question is how we can balance the opposites in order to reach the center.[2]

One thing has become clear: Matthew's stories of miraculous healings correspond to definite steps of spiritual evolution within the reader—if he is able to read dynamically. The sum total of cured diseases may represent the complete transition from tribal to individuated consciousness, including the development of new functions (spiritual seeing, hearing, and speaking) as well as the correction of relapses (doubt, skepticism). The resuscitation of the dead girl, then, is the passive, feudalistic, experience of evolution in the same sense as Paul later described this experience as an active achievement on the level of individuation: "Awake, O sleeper, and arise from the dead, and Christ shall give you light" (Eph. 5:14).

---

2. The task of discovering and overcoming the pairs of opposites is as old as religion itself. Cf. C. G. Jung, *Psychological Types*, pp. 234–336.

DISCOVERY BY TEACHING

Introduction

Chapter 10 of Matthew can be considered as an instruction for practical exercises which lead the initiates to the experience of the "coming of the Son of man." The "coming of the Son of man" is the central idea; verses 23–25 are the chapter's keystone. The chapter is also an attempt to make us see why and how the "Son" emerges in the human soul from the welter of fears and hopes that we have to face. But we do not learn what or who this "Son of man" actually is. The full answer to the deepest of all our questions can be found only through our own spiritual growth.

The last four verses of Chapter 9, together with the first four verses of Chapter 10, form a transition of great beauty. These eight verses can be understood as a unit in themselves, which, in its center, shows the gap of silence; that gap which indicates the breakthrough of the eternal into our world of space and time.

The Mission

> And Jesus went about all the cities and villages, teaching in their synagogues and preaching the gospel of the kingdom, and healing every disease and every infirmity. When he saw the crowds, he had compassion for them, because they were harassed and helpless, like sheep without a shepherd. Then he said to his disciples, "The harvest is plentiful, but the laborers are few; pray therefore the Lord of the harvest to send out laborers into his harvest."
>
> And he called to him his twelve disciples and gave them authority over unclean spirits, to cast them out, and to heal every disease and every infirmity. The names of the twelve apostles are these: first, Simon, who is called Peter, and Andrew his brother; James the son of Zebedee, and John his brother; Philip and Bartholomew; Thomas and Matthew the tax collector; James the son of Alphaeus, and Thaddaeus; Simon the Cananaean, and Judas Iscariot, who betrayed him (9:35–38; 10:1–4).

The last verses of Chapter 9 describe Jesus' resolve to expand his one-man warfare by the commission of more or less independent helpers. The old system of religious leadership has failed. The people are like sheep without a shepherd. One day they will no longer need a shepherd, but will be self-reliant and free; that will be the harvest day of the kingdom of heaven.

Early Christians were aware of the spiritual independence of the mature individual. "I will put my laws into their mind, and write them in their hearts: and I will be to them a God, and they shall be to me a people: And they shall not teach every man his neighbour, and every man his brother, saying, Know the Lord: for all shall know me, from the least to the greatest" (Heb. 8:10–11, KJV). The religious aspect of individuation can hardly be stressed more boldly. During the Middle Ages this maturity was lost so completely that even now, four hundred years after the Reformation, many of us prefer the childlike safety of spiritual feudalism to the perilous responsibility of individuation.

Today we still need guidance. Many laborers have to work before the harvest is secured. Everything is ready for the decisive mutation. The old form of life has broken down; the new form is about to begin. The task of finding the laborers remains.

The disciples pray that laborers may be sent—then the gap of silence—then Jesus gives them power over evil spirits, urging them to preach the good news of the kingdom. Their prayer has been answered. By praying, they themselves have become the laborers they are praying for. A fresh step of initiation is achieved; they are apostles now, and ready to receive the new instructions for the new task.

Practice Teaching: "The Kingdom Is at Hand"

These twelve Jesus sent out, charging them, "Go nowhere among the Gentiles, and enter no town of the Samaritans, but go rather to the lost sheep of the house of Israel. And preach as you go, saying, 'The kingdom of heaven is at hand.' Heal the sick, raise the dead, cleanse lepers, cast out demons. You received without pay, give without pay. Take no gold, nor silver, nor copper in your belts, no bag for your journey, nor two tunics, nor sandals, nor a staff; for the laborer deserves his food. And whatever town or village you enter, find out who is worthy in it and stay with him until you depart. As you enter the house, salute it. And if the house is worthy, let your peace come upon it; but if it is not worthy, let your peace return to you. And if any one will not receive you or listen to your words, shake off the dust from your feet as you leave that house or town. Truly, I say to you, it shall be more tolerable on the day of judgment for the land of Sodom and Gomorrah than for that town.

"Behold, I send you out as sheep in the midst of wolves; so

be wise as serpents and innocent as doves. Beware of men; for they will deliver you up to councils, and flog you in their synagogues, and you will be dragged before governors and kings for my sake, to bear testimony before them and the Gentiles. When they deliver you up, do not be anxious how you are to speak or what you are to say; for what you are to say will be given to you in that hour; for it is not you who speak, but the Spirit of your Father speaking through you. Brother will deliver up brother to death, and the father his child, and children will rise against parents and have them put to death; and you will be hated by all for my name's sake. But he who endures to the end will be saved" (10:5–22).

Jesus tells his disciples to heal the sick and raise the dead, while their preaching should be limited to the old slogan of John the Baptist, "The kingdom of heaven is at hand," without even mentioning repentance. The disciples are told to help as many people as they can and to preach as little as possible. This is the "good works," the only thing which makes Christianity real.

However, the most dynamic influence in the training of the new missionaries was the next point of the commission, "Freely ye have received; freely give" (KJV). Without funds or provisions, they had to be supported by newly won followers. On the other hand, as the whole discourse shows, their message would meet with much more criticism and resistance than approval. If they still would rely on the fact that "the laborer deserves his food," this was really the application of the great principles of faith, "Do not be anxious about your life, what you shall eat" (6:25). The disciples—and we with them—need practical experiments in this field in order to convince themselves and others. We are taught, therefore, to learn our lesson silently, and to teach others silently by letting them see how we learn.

Coming for peace. It is a peculiar task to "find out who is worthy" to give hospitality to the disciple. Jesus himself preferred the sinners to the "just," and ate with the publicans as readily as with the Pharisees. The word "worthy," therefore, cannot refer to good reputation or social standing. From the psychological point of view, it should mean "close enough to a spiritual crisis," so that the disciple during his visit can help the person to take a decisive step on the way of spiritual evolution. The coming of the missionary, then, meant the beginning of a new development; but it also meant much suffering, the outbreak of the crisis, new decisions, sacrifice of old connections, and possibly disrepute and persecution. The inner peace of the household will be upset for a long time. It is important, therefore, to state that we "come for

the sake of peace!" in spite of all the turmoil that we bring
(10:12–13).

The verdict that those who do not listen will share the destiny
of Sodom and Gomorrah does not mean a moral judgment or the
interference of a divine judge. It simply describes what happens
if a crisis starts and miscarries. In the positive case, the novice
participates in a new evolution; in the negative case, he destroys
the artificial equilibrium, and the result is Sodom and Gomorrah.

Thus, Jesus sends his disciples, Matthew sends his students,
and we should go by ourselves "as sheep in the midst of wolves."
The more light we carry, the more darkness we shall provoke in
our opponents.

Inspired speech. Yet the more we understand the laws of
creation, the less we are afraid. "Never trouble yourselves about
how to speak or what to say . . . for you are not the speakers,
it is the Spirit of your Father that is speaking through you"
(10:19–20, Moffatt). Many people have undergone this experience; innumerable others have come close enough to it to
know what the words mean. The individual is moved to speak
or to act, not in the service of his Ego, but regardless of his
egocentric interest; not for the sake of some instinct or collective
unconscious power, but on the contrary, often enough against all
instincts and collective tendencies. The new idea, the unpredictable creative action, takes place within the human being; he
becomes the tool of creation itself. But only as long as we are
stewards to something greater than we do we remain creative.
The very moment that someone thinks "I am creative," he is
sterile again.

The powerful new message of such genuine creativity disrupts
the accepted order of things and makes all reactionary forces
feel the necessity of rallying "in order to prevent chaos." Brother
will fear his converted brother, the father will resent the new
ideas of his child, but most of all they will hate the teachers
of the new Way. To balance these predictions, Jesus states again
and again the rewards for endurance: safety, value, and most of
all, eternal life.

The struggles will temper and sharpen the inner spirituality
of the disciples until they have really identified with "the Son
of man" who is Jesus.

The Son of Man

"When they persecute you in one town, flee to the next; for
truly, I say to you, you will not have gone through all the
towns of Israel, before the Son of man comes.

"A disciple is not above his teacher, nor a servant above his master; it is enough for the disciple to be like his teacher, and the servant like his master. If they have called the master of the house Beelzebul, how much more will they malign those of his household" (10:23–25).

As our own creative center. Things happen first in the outer world to provoke the inner event; the tempest (8:23–24) causes a new religious experience (8:25–26). If the inner event can be worked out without the physical stimulus, the result is the same; the encounter with the two madmen might be a completely internal experience. But if the flow of inner evolution begins to stagnate, outer stimuli such as sickness, failure, and persecution will become necessary again. If nobody chases us from city to city in the outer world, we should do this to ourselves, inwardly— or else it will happen externally in a form which we do not expect at all.

Here is a sick man, half eaten up by the cancer of his unlived life. He turns to the Christian because he heard him say the kingdom is at hand. Where is it? Give it to him! The sick one wants to believe, but the Christian cannot help him because his own faith is not powerful enough. Should not this make the Christian flee to another city? However, there it will be the same: promises and failure, words without deeds. So our conscience chases us, or should chase us, from city to city within ourselves, from denomination to denomination, from creed to creed, from the feudalistic "Our Lord Jesus" to the humanitarian "Reformer of Nazareth" or the "divine Scientist," and before we are through with all the creeds, the "Son of man" will arrive.

As the light to be kindled within. The "Son of man" in 10:23 cannot refer to Jesus "in the flesh"; here it does not simply mean "I" as it might be interpreted in 8:20: "(I) have nowhere to lay my head." Rather it may signify the superhuman Spirit, the "glorified Christ," the power which is able and willing to forgive sins. The Aramaic word "Barnasha," which Jesus used, means "son of man, mankind, human being, man."[1] It covers not only the original idea (as in Ezek. 2:1) "the human one," and the Danielic concept of a divine power assuming temporarily a man's outer appearance (Dan. 7:13), but also the universal idea of the "real man," or, as we would say nowadays, the Platonic idea of man. Which one of these possibilities did Matthew actually mean? Which one did Jesus mean? Was the dynamic word "Barnasha"

1. George M. Lamsa, *The New Testament According to the Eastern Text*, p. XXIV.

chosen because it could mean different things to seekers on different levels?

A glance at the writings of St. John and St. Paul convinces us that the early Christians had great difficulty in clarifying and formulating their extraordinary experiences. No language was adequate, no symbol powerful enough. And if we study the confessions of modern converts, we find them struggling with the same problem. The direct religious experience is beyond language. If it is genuine, it cannot be expressed by traditional words which once were dynamic but have become static by theological usage. Indeed, it must not be expressed in theological terms at all. The later development of the convert is seriously endangered if the great dynamic experience is described in traditional static concepts. The experience should break through the shell of our egocentricity like lava, forcing its own way into the future.[2]

The next paragraph illustrates Matthew's conviction that no theoretical learning can replace the practical discoveries of religious growth: "A scholar is not above his teacher" (10:24, Moffatt). Jesus had to learn his lesson the hard way; so have we; and our students, too. There is much vicarious suffering in the world, but we cannot and must not help other people to enter the kingdom without undergoing the trials of their own rebirth. Jesus found the perilous trail through the mountains, but he did not build a highway for our comfortable cars. We are not above him; we have to walk as he did, with bleeding feet. We shall be called Beelzebul, and we might call ourselves even worse; our inner sheep has to face our inner wolf. Between the fighting opposites the "peacemaker" will be born.

As the inner voice

> "So have no fear of them; for nothing is covered that will not be revealed, or hidden that will not be known. What I tell you in the dark, utter in the light; and what you hear whispered, proclaim upon the housetops. And do not fear those who kill the body but cannot kill the soul; rather fear him who can destroy both soul and body in hell. Are not two sparrows sold for a penny? And not one of them will fall to the ground without your Father's will. But even the hairs of your head are all numbered. Fear not, therefore, you are of more value than many sparrows. So every one who acknowledges me before men, I also will acknowledge before my Father who is in heaven; but whoever denies me before men, I also will deny before my Father who is in heaven" (10:26–33).

---

2. Compare C. G. Jung's study of the "immediate experience" in *Psychology and Religion,* Part II, with the confessions of modern converts in William James, *Varieties of Religious Experience,* Lectures IX and X.

If the reader cannot accept Matthew's expression "the Son of man" as a reference to the divine and creative Light which is to be kindled within the individual, he will meet with great difficulty in his interpretation of "Have no fear of them" (10:26). Matthew gives the reason for our courage: "For nothing is covered that will not be revealed." What kind of secret does he mean? When and how shall it be revealed? And why should such a final revelation of the secrets prevent our being afraid?

If we accept the "inner" interpretation of the Son of man, it is clear that the two parallel sentences of 10:26 refer to the growth of our spiritual power and creativity. We may then transcribe 10:26–27 as follows: "Do not be afraid of outer enemies; for all the creative power of the Spirit will be revealed within yourself as well as within others. What the inner voice, the Son of man, your creative center, tells you to do, that do, and the world will recognize what creativity is."

On the other hand, this promise of creative evolution does not mean the guarantee of physical welfare. Many of us might be killed in action; but to lose one's life while giving birth to a new creative development is not a loss at all. The value of individuation cannot be experienced and its spiritual power will not be realized if success or reward is limited to space and time.

The omnipresence of the Eternal excludes all accidents. This is the unquestionable significance of 10:29–31. It is amazing how few Christians are able to accept this view. But if they would listen to the voice within, the "Son of man" would convince them that they underestimate God's presence, and that their philosophy is still fettered by physics and chemistry.

The power of the voice within is described in classic terseness in 10:32–33. If we believe in spiritual feudalism, the "I" who will confess us before his Father if we confess him before men is Jesus of Nazareth. If we have outgrown feudalism, and reached individuation, this "I" is the inner "Son of man," the Spirit of Christ within us; and Jesus is the man through whom we have discovered this eternal treasure. Matthew does not tell us in so many words the difference between Jesus and the Spirit of Christ because he wants to see to it that experience comes first. In due time he will give his students the exact name for a definite inner event. For the time being he pictures Jesus still as the feudal lord, a superhuman prince in a spiritual kingdom; but he wishes us to realize that this kingdom is truly and solely spiritual.

As the bringer of the sword

> "Do not think that I have come to bring peace on earth; I have not come to bring peace, but a sword. For I have come to set a man against his father, and a daughter against her mother, and a daughter-in-law against her mother-in-law; and a man's foes will be those of his own household. He who loves father or mother more than me is not worthy of me; and he who loves son or daughter more than me is not worthy of me; and he who does not take his cross and follow me is not worthy of me. He who finds his life will lose it, and he who loses his life for my sake will find it" (10:34–39).

The "peacemaker" has entered the "worthy house," and instantly the son rebels against his father and the daughter against her mother. Those who wield the sword are the members of the household; yet the one who causes them to draw the sword is not the evil one, but a messenger of the Light. Do the disciples distribute Jesus' swords by the thousands?

The one who came to bring a sword is more than the carpenter of Nazareth; he is the Son of man; he is more than a human individual. This Son of man, this creative spark, is present not only within Jesus but within his disciples as well, if they deserve the name of disciple at all. It is the creative Spirit of the Creator Himself which causes men to outgrow tribal life. Then, not equal to the new task, men disintegrate; egocentricity develops entailing distrust and enmity of everybody against everybody until mankind finds itself at the very brink of destruction. The price of evolution is appallingly high. Luke expresses it even more forcibly. We have to hate not only our parents and children, but our brothers, sisters, wives, and our own lives (Luke 14:26).

Wherever the Spirit of Christ appears, the historical situation becomes clear, the unconscious relationship between relatives and friends is brought to consciousness; sham love is recognized as hatred, and sham morality is unmasked as selfishness. Invisible weapons become visible; where we expected the kiss of allegiance, we get the snarl of an enemy. Primitive confidence and childlike faith break down. The crisis is there and for a moment we wish that the messengers of the Light had never come to show us the truth—until experience reveals that it is this very truth that sets us free.

This dangerous kind of teaching forces the teacher to grow. By helping others, he helps himself, and when he fails, even his failure should help him to discover new treasures. Thus Matthew leads us up to the core of Christianity: the paradox that "he who finds his life will lose it, and he who loses his life for my sake will find it" (10:39).

The Hidden Reward

> "He who receives you receives me, and he who receives me receives him who sent me. He who receives a prophet because he is a prophet shall receive a prophet's reward, and he who receives a righteous man because he is a righteous man shall receive a righteous man's reward. And whoever gives to one of these little ones even a cup of cold water because he is a disciple, truly, I say to you, he shall not lose his reward" (10:40–42).

The disciple is sent as a materially poor messenger to bring his spiritual wealth to the people who are materially richer but spiritually poorer than he. If a person "receives" the disciple as what he is—and this means "in the name of a prophet" (10:41, KJV)—he shall receive a prophet's reward.

If the disciple, his creative center wide awake, be received by an average man whose center is asleep, the latter will either be awakened and recognize the disciple as "a prophet" or he will be irked and offended by him so that the disciple has to leave and to shake the dust from his feet. If the host only recognizes and tends the physical needs, he "shall not lose his reward": physical welfare. If he understands that the guest is righteous, his own righteousness will grow. If he is sensitive enough to discover that he harbors a prophet, he will become a prophet himself; and if he is receptive to the light of the creative center, the inner light will be kindled in his own center too. One candle kindles the other, but the candle is only the tool. The fire does not originate in the candle; it comes from a higher world. Whoever receives the Son of man receives Him that sent him.

All this takes place between the disciples and Jesus. Thus it explains the former's inner turmoil as described in **Chapters 8 and 9.**

Chapter 11

THE COMING ONE

Inner Gain from Outer Experiences

Jesus aroused great expectations. The peasants and fishermen in Galilee expected him to lighten their economic burden, be it by a political revolution or by a cosmic miracle. The scholars and leaders of the Jewish nation, in spite of their rising suspicion, still hoped to understand that the kingdom of heaven was to be different from what they thought it would be, but their expectations were not lowered by this uncertainty.

When Matthew conveyed all this to his students, he found that through his narrative he (or Jesus) had stimulated already in his new hearers the same gamut of expectations, hopes, questions, doubts, criticisms, and fears which swept all Palestine while Jesus lived and the whole Mediterranean world when he had died.

Almost two thousand years later, going through Matthew's record once more, we feel the same disquieting stir. Our expectations have grown even higher. Political and economic changes, in our thinking, are carefully separated from religion, and yet, if Christianity would really and thoroughly come to life, wars, revolutions, and economic miseries would certainly disappear. The individual, each one of us, would reach spiritual maturity and mankind as a whole would turn into a new race. It would be a new step of creation.

To keep our hopes from evaporating into idealistic dreams or emotional revivalism, we need clear understanding, definite evidence in the outer world, and unmistakable experiences within ourselves. Our situation is almost the same as that of Matthew's students. We understand, and occasionally feel, that a new phase of creation, the kingdom of heaven, is waiting for us. It wants to come to life within every individual. That is the "coming of the Son of man."

This new power was apparently present in Jesus, who therefore may be called the prototype of all Sons of man. But many ques-

tions remain unanswered: What made him the Son of man? Was
he born on a higher level than the average person? Or did he
become what he was by his own effort, or by special guidance, or
grace? Did he go through different crises and phases in a gradual
development, or was the new power bestowed on him suddenly
at his baptism?

Matthew does not describe the details of Jesus' inner life. He
wants us to find out what Peter's and John's experience was when
they grew up into spiritual maturity. His principle of initiation
is simple and clear: intellectual information prior to complete
inner realization delays and possibly deviates the whole process;
so he leads us through experiences and experiments to a better
vantage point; he tries to improve our eyesight rather than to
change the picture that he shows. To train our eyes on the religious
development of the human mind and especially our own mind,
he chooses from his documents the story of the Baptist's doubt
(which is our own doubt) about Jesus' Messiahship.

The New Leader—The Christ?

> And when Jesus had finished instructing his twelve disci-
> ples, he went on from there to teach and preach in their cities.
> Now when John heard in prison about the deeds of the
> Christ, he sent word by his disciples and said to him, "Are
> you he who is to come, or shall we look for another?" And
> Jesus answered them, "Go and tell John what you hear and
> see: the blind receive their sight and the lame walk, lepers
> are cleansed and the deaf hear, and the dead are raised up,
> and the poor have good news preached to them. And blessed is
> he who takes no offense at me."
> As they went away, Jesus began to speak to the crowds con-
> cerning John: "What did you go out into the wilderness to
> behold? A reed shaken by the wind? Why then did you go out?
> To see a man clothed in soft raiment? Behold, those who wear
> soft raiment are in king's houses. Why then did you go out?
> To see a prophet? Yes, I tell you, and more than a prophet.
> This is he of whom it is written,
>   'Behold, I send my messenger before thy face,
>   who shall prepare thy way before thee.'
> Truly, I say to you, among those born of women there has
> risen no one greater than John the Baptist; yet he who is
> least in the kingdom of heaven is greater than he. From the
> days of John the Baptist until now the kingdom of heaven has
> suffered violence, and men of violence take it by force. For all
> the prophets and the law prophesied until John; and if you are
> willing to accept it, he is Elijah who is to come" (11:1–14).

Whether we expect the kingdom of heaven or the classless
society or even the restoration of the good old times, we harbor

rather definite ideas as to what the future ought to be. Those of us who consciously refrain from rigid valuations still find ourselves conditioned by unconscious hopes and limitations. If a new philosopher or politician answers our conscious or unconscious conditions, we make him our "Messiah," but as soon as he tries to lead us beyond our expectations, we disown him; and if he is too powerful, we "take offense" and crucify him, if we can.

We ask with the Baptist: "Are you he who is to come, or shall we look for another?" The Baptist is stirred, and so are we, by "what the Christ was doing" (KJV). Some old manuscripts read, "what Jesus was doing," but Matthew wrote "the Christ," using this word for the first time since his "legendary" chapters one and two. The expression "the deeds of the Christ" must have been significant for Matthew's first readers. Jesus was gone, but there remained this miraculous Power which cured the sick and enabled the people to die for Christianity. Did Matthew mean this Power when he referred to "the deeds of the Christ"?

The same Power is still alive among us, curing the sick. Is this Power the beginning of the kingdom, or shall we wait for something else? It is John the Baptist within us, the representative of the past, our conservatism, who raises this question. Were it not for our inner rigidity, our narrow-minded expectations, and egocentric fears, we would not have to ask this question at all. We would recognize the coming one, accept him, and follow him, though he may be quite different from what we had anticipated. But our minds are fettered by religious or political convictions; we are "taking oaths" regarding the future, telling God what he ought to do and what he must not do with his creation.

Jesus answers the Baptist, and Matthew answers us, by referring to the only thing which can dissolve our human rigidity: the experience of the creative power itself. "The blind see, the lame walk, the lepers are cleansed, the deaf hear, the dead are raised, and the poor have the gospel preached to them." The realization of the first slight beginning of creative processes within ourselves is the decisive influence which overcomes our resistance.

Let us not blame the Baptist. He is all right in his place. We have to preserve the values of the past, but "he who is least in the kingdom of heaven is greater than he." A new phase of evolution has begun. "They are pressing into the realm of heaven —these eager souls are storming it!" (11:12, Moffatt). The aggressiveness and the courage with which our inner Baptist used to defend the values of the past turn out to be the weapons which conquer the kingdom, we have only to turn from the past to the future.

The Gap of Silence

"He who has ears to hear, let him hear" (11:15).

This phrase corresponds in Matthew's style, and probably in Jesus' own style also, to the "selah" of the Psalms. We should stop to listen to the inner voice. We have reached the exact center of Chapter 11. Our skeptical question has been answered by a fanfare of encouragement: Go ahead, your own experience will convince you. Your deafness and blindness will disappear. You will feel like a dead man who comes to life.

But how can the Baptist be Elijah? The greatest prophet of the Old Testament supposedly ascended into heaven; the Baptist lies in prison and soon will be beheaded. It is a new kind of truth which we are taught; it is a new insight into the meaning and purposiveness of reality which we have to achieve. From the old point of view, all progress is proved by historical success. From the new point of view, inner success may coincide with outer failure; spiritual evolution may express itself in physical suffering. A blind man may learn to see with his inner eye, though his physical eyes remain sightless. Someone may enter spiritual life by dying physically. Our experiences begin to transcend the finite realm of time and space. No wonder the creative power which achieves this evolution is bound to meet with skepticism and resistance within ourselves and within the majority of mankind.

However, it is clear now that this new Power is not identical with Jesus the carpenter. It is more than he. It was within him but transcended him. He overflowed with it, as it were, pouring it into his disciples. They became channels of it, pouring it into their students, and so it came down to us, still the same creative power which initiates the next step of creation.

If we listen to the stirring of this Power within us, we at first hear the confused voices of "the multitudes." Our reactions are contradictory and noisy like children in the marketplace. But if we keep listening, we hear more distinct utterances from a deeper layer of our human nature: the deviated authorities begin to speak. However, we should not be discouraged. Let us face our mistakes and errors. Let us listen again and again. Finally we will hear the answer from the center of creation; the Son of man will speak.

Victory in Defeat

"But to what shall I compare this generation? It is like children sitting in the market places and calling to their playmates,

'We piped to you, and you did not dance;
we wailed, and you did not mourn.'

For John came neither eating nor drinking, and they say, 'He has a demon'; the Son of man came eating and drinking, and they say, 'Behold, a glutton and a drunkard, a friend of tax collectors and sinners!' Yet wisdom is justified by her deeds."

Then he began to upbraid the cities where most of his mighty works had been done, because they did not repent. "Woe to you, Chorazin! woe to you, Bethsaida! for if the mighty works done in you had been done in Tyre and Sidon, they would have repented long ago in sackcloth and ashes. But I tell you, it shall be more tolerable on the day of judgment for Tyre and Sidon than for you. And you, Capernaum, will you be exalted to heaven? You shall be brought down to Hades. For if the mighty works done in you had been done in Sodom, it would have remained until this day. But I tell you that it shall be more tolerable on the day of judgment for the land of Sodom than for you."

At that time Jesus declared, "I thank thee, Father, Lord of heaven and earth, that thou hast hidden these things from the wise and understanding and revealed them to babes; yea, Father, for such was thy gracious will. All things have been delivered to me by my Father; and no one knows the Son except the Father, and no one knows the Father except the Son and any one to whom the Son chooses to reveal him. Come to me, all who labor and are heavy-laden, and I will give you rest. Take my yoke upon you, and learn from me; for I am gentle and lowly in heart, and you will find rest for your souls. For my yoke is easy, and my burden is light" (11:16–30).

The kingdom is at hand. Its power unfolds, but people are not aware of it. They discuss and criticize the creeds and philosophies of their leaders and are like children in the marketplace. There is no hope that the new evolution can begin with the masses.

The "cities" as distinguished from the masses, refer to the organized communities of small towns or even to the ruling classes which are responsible for those communities. They see the evidence of the new power. They have a chance to play an important part in the spiritual revolution of mankind. But they fail. The organized groups and their leaders are not aware of "the signs of the times." Who, then, will be the bearer of the new light? Who are those "eager souls who storm the kingdom"? This is our question as well as the question of Matthew's students, of Matthew, and of Jesus himself. We see the answer already shaping up in history. Matthew's students did not see it though they were sure that there was an answer. Jesus himself must have had the impression that his problem was completely unsolvable. Neither the multitudes nor the small communities would respond to his message. Neither the common man nor the leaders were aware of the impending change in human history. Jesus no doubt brought this question before his heavenly Father. And the answer came immediately, not God speaking to Jesus but Jesus speaking to God: "I thank thee, Father . . ." Now it was clear: Not the prudent and satisfied ones, not the "wise," but the "babes," the poor in spirit, the hungry ones, and the seekers, could enter the kingdom. Failure, defeat, and suffering are the price of admittance.

Only when our old securities and props break down do we learn the lesson that we cannot rely on the past, on the finite world, on our fellowmen, or on ourselves. We are pried loose from our environment; we are lonely and helpless, newborn babes in the newly discovered universe. In this moment of utmost detachment and solitude, the Son reveals himself within us (11:27). It is the same Power which made Jesus the Son of God. It is the "Christ" within us, the inner voice and the spiritual light of the mystics. Nobody can ever understand what this power is and what its appearance means unless he has experienced it within himself.

Do we have to wait, then, until we are utterly crushed? Shall we hope for suffering in order to be comforted? We look at Matthew in bewilderment. Does he teach us an active and courageous way of life or does he want us to acquiesce and suffer until we are saved?

Matthew answers our question by the continuation of Jesus' words: "Come to me, all who labor and are heavy-laden" (11:28). We can prepare ourselves for the trial; we can replace the impending blows of destiny by purposeful steps and daring experiments. "Taking his yoke" means to follow Jesus' instructions and to obey the voice of the inner babe, the Christ Child within us. The two outstanding authorities of our life, Jesus of Nazareth and "the Beyond Within," are identical. This is Matthew's answer to our question whether Jesus is the Christ or whether we shall wait for someone else: Wait until you feel like a babe in the outer world; then, if the inner babe, the Son of man, appears within you, his identity with the spirit of Christ will be beyond any doubt.

Chapter 12

THE NEW SABBATH

Creative Introversion

At first sight the twelfth chapter of Matthew's Gospel appears as an incoherent collection of stories and discussions, arranged in a strange way.

We have to accuse Matthew of an unusual carelessness or we have to look for deeper reasons which prompted him to write as he did. As soon as we begin to read dynamically, identifying ourselves with the whole cast of the drama, we discover that all the "confusions" which impair the outer story are indispensable features of an inner development. Matthew accompanies us through a decisive battle of our civil war; and the battle fought with all the modern equipment of our civilization proves to be the same old conflict which Matthew's students had to settle in Antioch and which was raging already in our caveman ancestors more than ten thousand years ago. It is the struggle for the evolution of mankind.

Matthew's students in Antioch may still have felt a sentimental loyalty to the old laws concerning the Sabbath. We are free from their prejudices and see more clearly the deeper value of the Sabbath as the symbol of introversion.

According to the Old Testament, God "worked" six days and appointed the seventh day for rest (Exod. 20:11). His people had to limit their toil to the six weekdays. According to the new religion, creation does not stop (John 5:17). The Creator works during the Sabbath, too, and He wants us to work like Him. The Sabbath, the time of introversion, becomes the real working day for the new phase of creation. Physical evolution has ended. We do not develop new bodily organs. But spiritual evolution began when physical evolution came to a standstill; and spiritual evolution takes place on the Sabbath. It is a result of hard work, in quietude and introversion.

Mankind has conquered the earth and organized the resources of nature. Now the six working days can be shortened. The forty-hour week may soon be replaced by that of thirty hours. The Sabbath will increase. What shall we do with so much spare time? From now on we have to conquer our inner world and organize the resources of our own nature. The works of the Sabbath, introversion, meditation, inner growth, expanding consciousness, have become the decisive tasks of mankind. All creative work now is Sabbath work.

Spiritual Growth Breaks with Tradition

At that time Jesus went through the grainfields on the sabbath; his disciples were hungry, and they began to pluck ears of grain and to eat. But when the Pharisees saw it, they said to him, "Look, your disciples are doing what is not lawful to do on the sabbath." He said to them, "Have you not read what David did, when he was hungry, and those who were with him: how he entered the house of God and ate the bread of the Presence, which it was not lawful for him to eat nor for those who were with him, but only for the priests? Or have you not read in the law how on the sabbath the priests in the temple profane the sabbath, and are guiltless? I tell you, something greater than the temple is here. And if you had known what this means, 'I desire mercy, and not sacrifice,' you would not have condemned the guiltless. For the Son of man is lord of the sabbath."
And he went on from there, and entered their synagogue. And behold, there was a man with a withered hand. And they asked him, "Is it lawful to heal on the sabbath?" so that they might accuse him. He said to them, "What man of you, if he has one sheep and it falls into a pit on the sabbath, will not lay hold of it and lift it out? Of how much more value is a man than a sheep! So it is lawful to do good on the sabbath." Then he said to the man, "Stretch out your hand." And the man stretched it out, and it was restored, whole like the other. But the Pharisees went out and took counsel against him, how to destroy him.
Jesus, aware of this, withdrew from there. And many followed him, and he healed them all, and ordered them not to make him known. This was to fulfil what was spoken by the prophet Isaiah:
"Behold, my servant whom I have chosen,
  my beloved with whom my soul is well pleased.
I will put my Spirit upon him,
  and he shall proclaim justice to the Gentiles.
He will not wrangle or cry aloud,
  nor will any one hear his voice in the streets;
he will not break a bruised reed
  or quench a smoldering wick,
till he brings justice to victory;
  and in his name will the Gentiles hope"
(12:1–21).

Matthew's outer drama has three scenes: the field, the synagogue, and the desert. The disciples eat the grains in the field;
Jesus cures someone in the synagogue; then he withdraws into
the desert and there has a long debate with the Pharisees.

The inner drama begins with our spiritual hunger. We are the
disciples. We follow the master, and the more we watch him, the
more we are eager for our own development. Soon we learn to
find our own food. Without him we would not dare to do so.
We would remain in the narrow limits of our tradition. But his
presence encourages us to overstep the old boundaries. However,
the authority of the past is still alive within us. Our conscious
liberalism does not free us from the reactionary narrowness and
rigidity of our unconscious mind. A feeling of guilt and insecurity
surges up within us; our inner Pharisee begins to blame us. We
are identified with the progressive disciples as well as with the
regressive Pharisees; the inner conflict is on.

Jesus tells us that the feudal lords, the kings and the high
priests, always have satisfied their spiritual hunger on the Sabbath. To them the temple was the place of introversion and
individual development. Only the common man, the multitudes,
had to avoid progress and to remain in the narrow precinct of the
tribal law. But the new religion teaches us to find the spiritual
nourishment everywhere. Here is something greater than the
temple (12:6). Here is individual mercy instead of the old tribal
sacrifice. Now the Sabbath is the means; and the future of mankind, the Son of man, is the goal (12:8).

The disciple has overcome the Pharisee; but we want to win
him, not to defeat him. So we follow him into his synagogue. We
comply with the tribal law. But "it is lawful to do good on the
sabbath" (12:12). Let us remove the inner obstacles; let us
develop and use the limbs of the spirit. That is the task of the new
Sabbath. The dead hand of the past comes to life; we are different
from what we were an hour ago. We are healed.

Our first reactions are contradictory. There is the joy of unexpected growth and horror in the face of the unknown. Our
revolutionary courage seems to lead into disaster. We must
destroy this new religion, this Son of man, or he will destroy us!
Once more we are identified with the Pharisees. The inner battle
is rising toward a climax.

Again it is Jesus who helps us. Feudalism is necessary as the
background of individuation. Let us withdraw to the desert where
we can explore and assimilate the creative power without disturbing the inner peace of our fellowmen.

Here the introversion reaches a deeper layer. We discover that the new creative Power is not quite so new as we thought it was. Isaiah has already described it clearly enough (Isa. 41:1–4). The Son of man is the friend and helper who turns human suffering into new creation. Our inner conflict makes us feel like a bruised reed or a smoldering wick. We are not able to find the way out alone. We are identified with the possessed man who was blind and dumb.

Integration of the New Power

> Then a blind and dumb demoniac was brought to him, and he healed him, so that the dumb man spoke and saw. And all the people were amazed, and said, "Can this be the Son of David?" But when the Pharisees heard it they said, "It is only by Beelzebul, the prince of demons, that this man casts out demons." Knowing their thoughts, he said to them, "Every kingdom divided against itself is laid waste, and no city or house divided against itself will stand; and if Satan casts out Satan, he is divided against himself; how then will his kingdom stand? And if I cast out demons by Beelzebul, by whom do your sons cast them out? Therefore they shall be your judges. But if it is by the Spirit of God that I cast out demons, then the kingdom of God has come upon you. Or how can one enter a strong man's house and plunder his goods, unless he first binds the strong man? Then indeed he may plunder his house. He who is not with me is against me, and he who does not gather with me scatters. Therefore I tell you, every sin and blasphemy will be forgiven men, but the blasphemy against the Spirit will not be forgiven. And whoever says a word against the Son of man will be forgiven; but whoever speaks against the Holy Spirit will not be forgiven, either in this age or in the age to come.
>
> "Either make the tree good, and its fruit good; or make the tree bad, and its fruit bad; for the tree is known by its fruit. You brood of vipers! How can you speak good, when you are evil? For out of the abundance of the heart the mouth speaks. The good man out of his good treasure brings forth good, and the evil man out of his evil treasure brings forth evil. I tell you, on the day of judgment men will render account for every careless word they utter; for by your words you will be justified, and by your words you will be condemned" (12:22–37).

The inner drama can develop its full energy only if we recognize within ourselves some unexpected progress or growth. Otherwise, our identification with the cured madman would not be justified. Actually we all have had experiences like this but we do not yet see them and cannot discuss them because we are still blind and dumb. In this case it may be enough to identify ourselves with "the people," watching the cure of someone else. The question which stimulates our new development is the same, only its intensity is much greater if it concerns our own case. The question is: What kind of power causes our growth?

Primitive people ascribe all astonishing events to demons or spirits. The enlightened people of our civilization ascribe everything to cause and effect. Growth is "nothing but" the blind energy of whirling molecules which, "by coincidence" of many factors, have formed human brains. Causality is for us "the prince of demons." His other titles are determinism, fatalism, and absence of responsibility.

Causality argues: The universe is one. We cannot believe in any kind of dualism. Your monism is "free." Your Creator is a miracle worker. Our monism is materialistic, we believe in cause and effect only. Your monism is spiritualistic. You believe in nothing but freedom.

Matthew's argument translated into modern language would run somewhat like this: Yes, it is one universe. It is all God's. There is no dualism. Causality has its place. It is the human aspect of reality but it is not its only aspect. Humans can and should outgrow it. The universe is one, but you can look at it from two different points of view. The intellect sees only causality and determinism; the spirit sees freedom and creativeness, using causality as the architect uses his material.

The argument, of course, does not lead to a stringent conclusion. It ends with an "if." There is, however, the possibility of understanding the whole universe from the spiritual point of view. "The Reign of God has reached you already" (12:28, Moffatt).

Yes, we see the two possibilities, but we are still undecided. The old and the new, the Pharisee and the disciple, are in abeyance. Philosophy does not help us, but there is something alluring and persuasive in Jesus' personality, not an argument but an experience. He has found a foothold within us.

Matthew smiles. Causality, like Beelzebub, the prince of demons, is a very "strong man." There will always be such a strong man within each individual, defending the house of the Ego. But there seems to be a stronger one who slips in almost without a struggle, binding the strong man and spoiling his goods. This is the power of creation which changes us against our will.

Is this cause and effect again? Are we conquered by the stronger force? Have we simply to accept what happens to us? No. We have to make the decision. "He who is not with me is against me." The opposite forces are fighting about us and within us. But we have to make up our own mind. The result of the battle is our responsibility. We may be mistaken regarding the Son of man. Not knowing him in advance, we may look for him in the wrong direction. But we cannot be mistaken regarding the simple decision between evolution and regression. If we deny the spirit of creation, we are lost. The seeker can believe false doctrines; but as soon as he discovers his mistake, he will correct it if he be still a seeker. But if he considers himself already a "finder," he does not seek further. He allows of no doubt, and his mistake cannot be redeemed. He is lost because he has lost the seeker's spirit.

There are theories which take into consideration all the different standpoints and all the ifs and buts of the human mind. However, no philosophy can help us unless it comes out of the "good treasure" of the heart and brings forth good things. "He that gathereth not with me scattereth abroad" (12:30, KJV). The most brilliant theory is useless unless it helps us to overcome our fear of an unknown evolution and our longing for an impossible security.

From Isolation to Brotherhood

> Then some of the scribes and Pharisees said to him, "Teacher, we wish to see a sign from you." But he answered them, "An evil and adulterous generation seeks for a sign; but no sign shall be given to it except the sign of the prophet Jonah. For as Jonah was three days and three nights in the belly of the whale, so will the Son of man be three days and three nights in the heart of the earth. The men of Nineveh will arise at the judgment with this generation and condemn it; for they repented at the preaching of Jonah, and behold, something greater than Jonah is here. The queen of the South will arise at the judgment with this generation and condemn it; for she came from the ends of the earth to hear the wisdom of Solomon, and behold, something greater than Solomon is here.
>
> "When the unclean spirit has gone out of a man, he passes through waterless places seeking rest, but he finds none. Then he says, 'I will return to my house from which I came.' And when he comes he finds it empty, swept, and put in order. Then he goes and brings with him seven other spirits more evil than himself, and they enter and dwell there; and the last state of that man becomes worse than the first. So shall it be also with this evil generation."
>
> While he was still speaking to the people, behold, his mother and his brothers stood outside, asking to speak to him. But he replied to the man who told him, "Who is my mother, and who are my brothers?" And stretching out his hand toward

his disciples, he said, "Here are my mother and my brothers! For whoever does the will of my Father in heaven is my brother, and sister, and mother" (12:38–50).

Resistance against spiritual evolution is the unforgivable sin. As often as the Pharisee prevails within us, we come perilously close to the edge of this abyss. We need a definite and unmistakable proof that creation continues and that the kingdom is coming. Matthew, or Jesus, should give us a "sign" which reminds us of the truth in case we forget it. But this need for a sign, natural and human as it is, again identifies us with the "adulterous generation" of the Pharisees. The outer sign, the objective evidence, would relieve us from the inner work of the Sabbath. We would not have to struggle for a decision; the inner achievement would be replaced by outer necessity. Fortunately, this will never happen. We always will be free to choose. The only help which will be given to us will be "the night-sea-journey." The subjective experience of the inner crisis will confront us with the necessity of spiritual decisions, time and again, until we finally take sides with creation. We shall be with Jonah in the stomach of the great fish. The Son of man, the divine spark which we saw already at the horizon, will disappear again. We shall be dead and buried with him in the "heart of the earth."

The more we lack the longing for the light and the readiness to sacrifice our security for the adventure of a new development, the more we shall have to suffer in the darkness of despair. Primitive people, like the men of Nineveh, and adventurous souls, like the queen of the South, can teach us a better way; if we could find within ourselves a tendency or an attitude which would allow us to imitate them, we would find the way out.

At the moment we seem to be completely identified with the Pharisee. We were confronted with the most important decision of our life. We felt insecure. We asked for a "sign," and we recognized that our insecurity was identical with the wrong decision. How did this come about? We thought we had got rid of our "unclean spirit."

The reason for our relapse is simple enough: The house was empty. The miraculous power had bound the strong man, the former master of the house. But the power of creation evidently did not remain in our house. It wanted us to take over and to use the house in the service of creation. We did not recognize our new responsibility, thinking that the new power would rule us and tell us what to do exactly as the old "strong man" had done.

Now the house is empty and seven evil spirits take possession of it. How can we get rid of them again?

Matthew's answer is clear and practical, though clothed in the indirect form of a simile. Jesus renounces his relatives, replacing the old tribal family by the new brotherhood of the spirit.

Withdrawal and introversion are the first presuppositions for the work of the new Sabbath. If, however, meditation only leads to meditation, and withdrawal engenders further withdrawal, our house remains empty and we are bound to relapse into some kind of obsession. The work of the new Sabbath does not succeed unless we replace our solitude at the right time by new contacts and new responsibilities. The new inhabitants of our house are the brotherhood of the common man, that is, of those who do the will of our Father in heaven.

PARABLES OF THE KINGDOM

Introduction

The seven parables of Chapter 13 are surrounded by a frame, which, like a fence, excludes strangers. But the strangers are former relatives and countrymen. Chapter 13 itself is skillfully arranged. The size of the parables gradually decreases while their importance and depth grow. The first four parables are told publicly; the last three are given to the disciples alone. We notice the difference between the outer exoteric circle of the many followers and the small, esoteric circle of the disciples. Matthew frames the four exoteric parables by special remarks concerning the "great crowds," making the publicity of this part of Jesus' teaching as impressive as possible: Jesus "went out of the house, and sat beside the sea" (13:1).

The Soil and the Seed

That same day Jesus went out of the house and sat beside the sea. And great crowds gathered about him, so that he got into a boat and sat there; and the whole crowd stood on the beach. And he told them many things in parables, saying: "A sower went out to sow. And as he sowed, some seeds fell along the path, and the birds came and devoured them. Other seeds fell on rocky ground, where they had not much soil, and immediately they sprang up, since they had no depth of soil, but when the sun rose they were scorched; and since they had no root they withered away. Other seeds fell upon thorns, and the thorns grew up and choked them. Other seeds fell on good soil and brought forth grain, some a hundredfold, some sixty, some thirty. He who has ears, let him hear."

Then the disciples came and said to him, "Why do you speak to them in parables?" And he answered them, "To you it has been given to know the secrets of the kingdom of heaven, but to them it has not been given. For to him who has will more be given, and he will have abundance; but from him who has not, even what he has will be taken away. This is why I speak to them in parables, because seeing they do not see, and hearing they do not hear, nor do they understand.

With them indeed is fulfilled the prophecy of Isaiah which says:

'You shall indeed hear but never understand,
and you shall indeed see but never perceive.
For this people's heart has grown dull,
and their ears are heavy of hearing,
and their eyes they have closed,
lest they should perceive with their eyes,
and hear with their ears,
and understand with their heart,
and turn for me to heal them.'

"But blessed are your eyes, for they see, and your ears, for they hear. Truly, I say to you, many prophets and righteous men longed to see what you see, and did not see it, and to hear what you hear, and did not hear it.

"Hear then the parable of the sower. When any one hears the word of the kingdom and does not understand it, the evil one comes and snatches away what is sown in his heart; this is what was sown along the path. As for what was sown on rocky ground, this is he who hears the word and immediately receives it with joy; yet he has no root in himself, but endures for a while, and when tribulation or persecution arises on account of the word, immediately he falls away. As for what was sown among thorns, this is he who hears the word, but the cares of the world and the delight in riches choke the word, and it proves unfruitful. As for what was sown on good soil, this is he who hears the word and understands it; he indeed bears fruit, and yields, in one case a hundredfold, in another sixty, and in another thirty" (13:1–23).

The important aspect of the first story is not the disappointment of the preacher whose words fall on poor soil, but the experience of the hearer who asks himself: "What kind of soil am I?"

There are creative words which can change lives, redeem the past, and create a better future. Time and again people have heard such words. Why do we not hear them? Jeremiah knew them: "Let the prophet who has a dream, tell the dream, but let him who has my word speak my word faithfully. What has straw in common with wheat? says the Lord" (Jer. 23:28).

A ceaseless stream of discoveries, new activities and deeper experiences can be started by a single word; but the result depends on the ear that hears the word, on the soil that receives the seed, on our inner life which responds or does not respond to the stimulus.

Jesus distinguishes between people who hear the parables with understanding and those who hear them without understanding. He does not say that the parables represent the inferior method of teaching for inferior people, while the superior hearers, the

disciples, would be informed in a more abstract, intellectual way.
The simple mind of the average hearer can receive the parable
only as an interesting story; whether he will subsequently forget
it or will realize in later years its hidden meaning is not yet
decided.

The interpretation, intellectual and unsatisfactory as it is,
probably does not come from Jesus himself. But it opens the
door for our meditation. The problem, of course, is not the
understanding of the four groups of hearers; it is the understanding of our own inner situation. If our mind is a "stony place," we
do not have to trouble about the three other groups; our only
concern is to rid ourselves of the stones. The simple question,
"What are the stones in our soul?" may start a self-analysis which
will occupy us for weeks and lead to extremely disagreeable
though helpful discoveries. Old grudges and grievances, old fears
and inhibitions which we considered stifled years ago, might come
to light again, and it takes hard work to dig up and carry away
these stones from our field.[1]

If we decide that thorns are in the way, we shall have to
clear the soil, like pioneers who settle in a new land; and if our
soul is like the "wayside," we simply have to plow, and to build
a new path skirting the field.

In all three cases the soil can be prepared by human effort.
The result of the parable, therefore, is a new impulse to religious
self-education; and the discovery which prompted this impulse
proves to be the beginning of the process itself. The pessimistic
question, "How can I educate myself? How shall I know the
methods and the means?" is answered by the experience of this
meditation. The very fact that the new impulse arises shows the
dynamics of the seed-word, and the discovery that we are not yet
able to "hear the word" leads us to the discovery of the obstacles
which prevented our hearing it; and this in turn will lead to the
discovery of new means and ways to remove them. There is no
end to our discoveries, if the creative meditation has been started
by the first vague hearing of the word.

Seeds—Good and Bad

> Another parable he put before them saying, "The kingdom
> of heaven may be compared to a man who sowed good seed in
> his field; but while men were sleeping, his enemy came and
> sowed weeds among the wheat, and went away. So when the
> plants came up and bore grain, then the weeds appeared also.
> And the servants of the householder came and said to him,

---

1. See Fritz Kunkel, *In Search of Maturity*, Part III, Chapter 4.

'Sir, did you not sow good seed in your field? How then has it weeds?' He said to them, 'An enemy has done this.' The servants said to him, 'Then do you want us to go and gather them?' But he said, 'No; lest in gathering the weeds you root up the wheat along with them. Let both grow together until the harvest; and at harvest time I will tell the reapers, Gather the weeds first and bind them in bundles to be burned, but gather the wheat into my barn.' "

Another parable he put before them, saying, "The kingdom of heaven is like a grain of mustard seed which a man took and sowed in his field; it is the smallest of all seeds, but when it has grown it is the greatest of shrubs and becomes a tree, so that the birds of the air come and make nests in its branches."

He told them another parable, "The kingdom of heaven is like leaven which a woman took and hid in three measures of meal, till it was all leavened."

All this Jesus said to the crowds in parables; indeed he said nothing to them without a parable. This was to fulfil what was spoken by the prophet:

"I will open my mouth in parables,
I will utter what has been hidden since the
foundation of the world"

(13:24–35).

Some seeds in the foregoing parable "fell upon thorns." This time they are mingled with weeds. But these weeds were not there in advance; they were sown later by an enemy. A flood of questions surges up in our minds. The essence of our religious life is brought into focus. If we could understand this parable thoroughly, we would know why some trees are good and some are unfruitful.

Did Jesus mean to say that we should watch and not sleep, that the enemy will have his way anyhow, or that the "wicked ones" will be punished whatever we do? All these difficulties disappear if we turn from intellectual interpretation to introverted, and that means a more comprehensive, study. We see then that the underlying symbol, the seed, is the same in the first three parables of Matthew's collection, though it is observed from three different angles.

The symbol of the plant is as old as religion itself. The tree of life is found not only in Genesis (2:9) but also at the outset of many other pre-Christian religions. We saw how John the Baptist used the tree as a figure of speech and how Jesus illustrated the relationship between a person's character and his actions by the tree and its fruit. The distinction between the good and the corrupt tree was a familiar thought to him. Now he goes down to the roots. The question why some trees are good and some corrupt leads to the meditation about seeds. The bad tree

cannot produce good fruit; it must produce bad seeds and they
will produce a new generation of bad trees.

We know that once upon a time someone sowed extremely
dangerous words into the ears of the Master (4:3). Could the
same enemy have sown the tares in our own field?

We can almost hear the words: "Why explore the unknown?
Why set yourself at odds with your friends and neighbors? It is
foolishness to disturb the peace of the world." Or, "You are strong
enough. Conquer the world for yourself." The enemy is the egocentric form of our own free will which has deteriorated into the
will to power or the will to security.

Shall we wait quietly, letting both wheat and tares grow, finally
suffering the punishment for this acquiescence? This time it
looks as if we had caught old Matthew in an impasse. He must
allow us to use fire and sword at least against our own inner
vices, or he cannot tell us that we shall be punished afterwards.
But he laughs: "Listen! Another parable he put before them
. . . " and he tells the parables of the mustard seed and of the
leaven.

The conflict between good and evil is in full swing. The thorns
are choking the wheat. But the power of the mustard seed is
much greater than we should have expected. Symbols are growing
like trees; words may fertilize our minds and enable us to receive the "Son of man" within our own innermost being. The
mustard plant outgrows all herbs, though its seed is the smallest.
There seems to be no point in our attempt to purify and discipline
ourselves; grace seems to come regardless of merit. However,
Matthew continues: "The kingdom of heaven is like leaven"
(13:33).

Acquiescence? Trust in grace? Yes, endurance, fortitude, courage in unspeakable pain! This time it is "a woman" who takes
the place of the sower. How many of us have felt her hands
kneading the dough, penetrating the very core and substance of
our life? Whenever we suffer and ache from outer or inner pain,
whenever nightmares from within or evil actions from without
disturb our peace, we can be sure that these are the hands of the
woman who prepares us for the leaven of the Kingdom. While
we are suffering by her hands, it is important to know that without her work the leaven would never permeate the dough.

The Treasure and the Pearl

"The kingdom of heaven is like treasure hidden in a field,
which a man found and covered up; then in his joy he goes
and sells all that he has and buys that field.

> "Again, the kingdom of heaven is like a merchant in search of fine pearls, who, on finding one pearl of great value, went and sold all that he had and bought it" (13:44–46).

Matthew wishes to convey some difficult and important truth to his students. He leads them, so to speak, into the private council of the Master with his intimate friends. We enter with them, knowing that Matthew will make us pay the price for his treasure by hard mental work and long meditations.

The parables of the Treasure and the Pearl are often considered as parallel illustrations of the same fact. The text says, however, that in spite of their parallelism, they point in opposite directions. The kingdom of heaven, like a treasure, is hid in a field. We have no doubt that this field is our soul. It is our task to find the treasure and to buy the field. In modern language, we have to integrate the hidden powers of the unconscious, to discover our real center, and to make it the center of gravity for our conscious as well as our unconscious life. But the price is high. We have to sever the moorings which bind us to the past, to give up the security on which we have learned to rely, and to sacrifice our social prestige.

If we do not want to "sell all," we have an excellent excuse: to buy the field without telling the owner about the treasure means to cheat him. Moral conduct becomes an alibi for rejecting the kingdom. Only when our longing for the treasure grows so overwhelming that we are ready to sacrifice literally anything, including our moral self-esteem, we finally discover that we do not cheat anybody. The field and the treasure were ours from the beginning. We buy ourselves from ourselves for ourselves. We are seller, buyer, and price at the same time. It is our own unconscious that we integrate into our future personality, and it is our egocentric past which we pay as the price.

We are confronted with the transition from the old static pattern of life with its firm conventional valuations to a new patternless dynamic life with apparently no rational orientation. It is a superhuman task and the danger of error is so grave that we can hardly expect any sensible person to take such a risk. Matthew, therefore, tells us that our situation in the universe has another aspect which shows the whole picture in reverse. Matthew makes us, as it were, peer over the edge of space and time, allowing us for a second to glance at the metaphysical hinterland of our lives.

We are not only hunting for the treasure, sacrificing the past for the future: we are also sought from beyond. Someone is looking for us, ready to pay whatever is required, in order to rescue us. Each one of us is the "pearl of high price" (13:46, Moffatt). Without this metaphysical aid, we should not be able to fulfill our task. Without being bought by the kingdom, we could not buy it. To find here means to be found, and to decide, to be decided upon.

The wrong interpretation that the pearl, like the treasure, represents the kingdom (against the clear statement of the text that the kingdom is the merchant) is caused by the difficulty that we can hardly expect the government of the universe to sell everything in order to save a lost soul. Fortunately, we have another parable where precisely this unbelievable fact is ascertained. It is the parable of the Lost Sheep (18:11–14). The strange behavior of the "good shepherd" who leaves ninety-nine sheep to the hazards of the desert, concentrating his whole endeavor upon the rescue of the one who went astray, would make him a very bad shepherd in reality. In super-time and super-space, our categories and our logic do not apply. We can see only flashes of light here and there.

The Esoteric Aspect of Christianity

> Then he left the crowds and went into the house. And his disciples came to him, saying, "Explain to us the parable of the weeds of the field." He answered, "He who sows the good seed is the Son of man; the field is the world, and the good seed means the sons of the kingdom; the weeds are the sons of the evil one, and the enemy who sowed them is the devil; the harvest is the close of the age, and the reapers are angels. Just as the weeds are gathered and burned with fire, so will it be at the close of the age. The Son of man will send his angels, and they will gather out of his kingdom all causes of sin and all evildoers, and throw them into the furnace of fire; there men will weep and gnash their teeth. Then the righteous will shine like the sun in the kingdom of their Father. He who has ears, let him hear. . . .
>
> "Again, the kingdom of heaven is like a net which was thrown into the sea and gathered fish of every kind; when it was full, men drew it ashore and sat down and sorted the good into vessels but threw away the bad. So it will be at the close of the age. The angels will come out and separate the evil from the righteous, and throw them into the furnace of fire; there men will weep and gnash their teeth.
>
> "Have you understood all this?" They said to him, "Yes." And he said to them, "Therefore every scribe who has been trained for the kingdom of heaven is like a householder who brings out of his treasure what is new and what is old" (13: 36–43; 47–52).

The explanation of the parable of the Tares is almost unanimously considered unauthentic. The main reasons for this condemnation are the stilted style, the mechanical interpretation of the successive details, and the fact that a decisive part of the parable, namely the tolerance towards the tares until the time of harvest, is not interpreted at all.[2] In Matthew's structure, however, this passage takes an important place, and it must have been the piece of material which fitted his purpose best. If he had found another parable which would have conveyed the same metaphysical idea, he probably would have preferred it.

The title, "Son of man" is used here in a superindividual sense, describing the judge, the deputy of God at the last judgment. This is the final step of a long development. First we learned that "Son of man" was a title by which Jesus indicated his physical poverty (8:20) and his spiritual power (9:6). Then it dawned on us that this expression refers to a creative quality which was present in Jesus but might come to life within his followers, too (10:23). This Spirit of Christ within (Gal. 4:6) brings us joy when he comes (11:19). He is the goal of our religious training (12:8); but he has to undergo a strange development (12:40) which gives him a definitely superindividual and almost metaphysical aspect. He is to appear at the judgment day as a witness (12:41). Now we hear that he will be the judge.

This seems to bring back John the Baptist's ideas about the one "whose fan is in his hands . . . and he will burn the chaff with unquenchable fire" (3:12, KJV). A short time ago Matthew stressed the opposite aspect. The Son of man "shall not strive nor cry . . . a bruised reed shall he not break" (12:19, 20, KJV). How shall we reconcile the two opposing views?

The answer is simpler than we might expect. Not all individuals will enter the kingdom of heaven. During our world age the loss of souls must be understood as a failure on the part of "the Son of man." He is limited by the powers of darkness; his work is imperiled by them. Every help is needed. We are able, and therefore obligated, to help him with all the forces we have; and by helping him, we share his creative power and serve our own evolution.

Who is the "enemy"? The "Devil" seems to be equal to "the Son of man." The two constitute a pair of opposites. Christ, the "Spirit of individuation," accounts for our evolution into personal consciousness and personal responsibility. He is opposed by a pseudo-spirit which accounts for regression, laziness, and relapse

---

2. *Abingdon Bible Commentary,* p. 977, and H. B. Sharman, *Son of Man,* pp. 25–54.

into obsolete mechanical patterns. The devil's exact name is: Anti-Christ.

This corresponds to the findings of depth-psychology. Within the individual, as well as within groups, there is a positive, creative center, the source of power and growth.[3] If it remains hidden, like the treasure in the field, some other "value" takes its place. The person or the group then revolves around the wrong center; an idol is deified and creativity turns into destructiveness.

There is no doubt Jesus himself believed in the last judgment and the throwing away of the "bad fish." But the parable corroborates the impression that he did not condemn morally. He saw all mankind subject to the law of the spiritual survival of the spiritually fit. The unfit were to be burned with "aeonean fire," where they have to serve other purposes beyond the scope of our human understanding. It must be stressed, however, that the fire where "there shall be wailing and gnashing of teeth" is not "everlasting." It is beyond time, between the aeons, as it were, and therefore it does not last at all. It is, like all metaphysical things, incomprehensible.

At the end of this difficult lesson Jesus says, "Have you understood all this?" The disciples answer: "Yes, Lord." We may question the truth of this "Yes." Mark's "Do you not yet perceive or understand . . . do you not see?" (Mark 8:17–18) seems to be more appropriate. We can be certain that Matthew's students honestly said, "No, we do not understand. We are not yet able to appreciate the esoteric aspect of Christianity." More work, more meditation, more instructions are needed for Matthew's earlier students as well as for us.

The metaphysical aspect of the Son of man remains bewildering. The "Son," now, has become a divine being, judging all mankind and commanding the angels. Is the coming of the "Son" identical with the coming of the kingdom and the last judgment? Could the same Son of man become an integral part of our life? May such a transcendent entity be the treasure in our field, and can the field and the treasure become our property?

Creation Is Unlimited

> And when Jesus had finished these parables, he went away from there, and coming to his own country he taught them in their synagogue, so that they were astonished, and said, "Where did this man get this wisdom and these mighty works? Is not this the carpenter's son? Is not his mother called Mary? And

---

3. See Fritz Kunkel, *In Search of Maturity*, pp. 76–80, 162–68. Analogous to Carl Jung's "Self."

are not his brothers James and Joseph and Simon and Judas? And are not all his sisters with us? Where then did this man get all this?" And they took offense at him. But Jesus said to them, "A prophet is not without honor except in his own country and in his own house." And he did not do many mighty works there, because of their unbelief (13:53–58).

By now we know Matthew's method. His next story answers the question. We are the people of Nazareth, narrow-minded and petty (and we thought we were the esoteric enlightened ones!). Jesus, for us, is the carpenter, our cousin; he is human, and by this we mean he is limited by fear and greed as we are. Can anything creative, metaphysical, transcendent, grow out of our common fear and greed and pettiness? Matthew answers: "Yes, it can."

Part Four

THE CROSSROADS

The Turning Point

The fourth part of Matthew's Gospel comprises five chapters. The central chapter (16) contains the turning point of Jesus' way as well as of the way of initiation for Matthew's students. We shall learn the most difficult of all lessons: The way up in the spiritual world coincides with the way down in our world of space and time. Outer success turns out to be inner failure; spiritual growth looks like physical decay.

Theoretically this paradox is well known as the core of Christianity. Matthew's goal is not to explain it or to prove its truth. He mobilizes all his art and skill to make us discover this paradox within ourselves.

Conscious Search for "The Christ"

The sequence of the stories in Chapters 14–17 is to be found, with a few though significant variations, in Mark as well as in Matthew. It can be traced to the earliest documents. This is the more interesting because the arrangement is as confused as it was in Chapter 12. In the outer confusion, the inner development of the disciples is described clearly and consistently. The stories are stations on the disciples' spiritual journey. The sequence of the stories is determined by their psychological usefulness.

We have to assume, therefore, that this material was recorded from the very beginning for the inner need of the early Christians rather than for the sake of a chronological biography of Jesus. Matthew was not the inventor of this method of initiation, but he was the master who developed it into perfection.

The inner need of the novice does not call for theoretical or intellectual information: though consciously this may be his main concern. What he really needs is the new point of view, the new eyes and ears to perceive the new truth. From here on, Matthew tries to answer the question, "What is 'the Christ'?" But he re-

frains from theological and philosophical discussions, forcing us
instead to consider the different answers which different people
give from different viewpoints. Thus he invites us to share
tentatively a number of contradictory opinions and to recognize
once more how far we are Herod, or Peter, or the Pharisees.

It is as if the instructions of the Sermon on the Mount were
forgotten, and the emotional experiences which followed had been
in vain. We begin from scratch again. Only the disquieting urgency of the question "Who is this Jesus?" indicates that something has been stirred up in our inner life and that we cannot
come to rest without an adequate answer. This is good psychology.
Religious evolution like childbirth always proceeds in waves;
there are innumerable relapses followed by new throes and new
progress. The early Christians were conscious of this fact. Paul
wrote: "My little children, with whom I am again in travail until
Christ be formed in you" (Gal. 4:19). Now Matthew is in travail
with us, until "the Son of man" takes shape inside ourselves.

Chapter 14

THE NEW START

Herodism

> At that time Herod the tetrarch heard about the fame of Jesus; and he said to his servants, "This is John the Baptist, he has been raised from the dead; that is why these powers are at work in him." For Herod had seized John and bound him and put him in prison, for the sake of Herodias, his brother Philip's wife; because John said to him, "It is not lawful for you to have her." And though he wanted to put him to death, he feared the people, because they held him to be a prophet. But when Herod's birthday came, the daughter of Herodias danced before the company, and pleased Herod, so that he promised with an oath to give her whatever she might ask. Prompted by her mother, she said, "Give me the head of John the Baptist here on a platter." And the king was sorry; but because of his oaths and his guests he commanded it to be given; he sent and had John beheaded in the prison, and his head was brought on a platter and given to the girl, and she brought it to her mother. And his disciples came and took the body and buried it; and they went and told Jesus (14:1–12).

Sometimes we feel like the people of Nazareth: Jesus is only a wise carpenter: his words and actions are quite natural. All the miracles and mysteries of his life are due to the wild imagination of the oriental mind. It is comforting to deny the possibilities of transcendent developments within Jesus as well as within ourselves. But there appear disconcerting facts, in the past and in the present. Some prayers are answered. A few moribund people are cured "by faith" to the greatest embarrassment of their physicians. Their number may be small but one case suffices to overthrow our whole philosophy. What is this unpredictable, unexplorable power which upsets our materialistic vision of life?

Herod thinks John the Baptist has risen from the dead. Jesus, the messenger of the future, appears to him as the representative of the past, the Baptist. The reason is that Herod cut himself off from the past, from his tribal tradition, when he beheaded the Baptist. He broke with the past because its voice became his conscience, telling him that he must not steal his brother's wife. His egocentric tragedy, as usual, expressed itself in sexual entanglements. But by killing his conscience he also destroyed the source of vitality, the straight red-blooded courage which enables primitive men to conquer the world. The result was insecurity, bloodshed, and superstition. Cut off from the past, Herod could not recognize the future. John and Jesus represented to him the same weird authority which he feared without fully admitting its reality.

The question is: How much do we harbor a Herod within us?

If we do not find our Herodism at first sight, we may proceed in the opposite direction, from the effect to the causes: loss of contact with our tribal inheritance, and subsequent loss of creative trust in the future. Jesus appears as the reincarnated Baptist. We murdered him in the past, now the boomerang comes back. Karma clamps down on us. Is there still a way to redeem the past and to use our inherited potentialities in the service of new creation? Herod does not see the way. But Matthew takes us with Jesus "by boat to a desert place in private" (14:13, Moffatt). It is a secret mission to which Herod cannot be admitted.

The New Food

> Now when Jesus heard this, he withdrew from there in a boat to a lonely place apart. But when the crowds heard it, they followed him on foot from the towns. As he went ashore he saw a great throng; and he had compassion on them, and healed their sick. When it was evening, the disciples came to him and said, "This is a lonely place, and the day is now over; send the crowds away to go into the villages and buy food for themselves." Jesus said, "They need not go away; you give them something to eat." They said to him, "We have only five loaves here and two fish." And he said, "Bring them here to me." Then he ordered the crowds to sit down on the grass; and taking the five loaves and the two fish he looked up to heaven, and blessed, and broke and gave the loaves to the disciples, and the disciples gave them to the crowds. And they all ate and were satisfied. And they took up twelve baskets full of the broken pieces left over. And those who ate were about five thousand men, besides women and children (14:13–21).

The sinister birthday banquet in Herod's palace and Jesus' miracle at his beggar's banquet in the desert form a significant contrast. The past ends with crime and anguish, in a setting of purple and gold; the future begins with joy and love and mutual confidence in a setting of rags, bare feet and unwashed hands.

Some time ago, when the Baptist was arrested, Jesus began to teach in his place. Now that the old teacher is dead, what will his great pupil do? Jesus was confronted with a decision and a responsibility which we can understand only gradually while going through the ensuing developments. He tried to be alone, praying, meditating, asking the Eternal what he should do. Then his contemplation was interrupted by an appalling answer. Was it a vision, an insight, a real event? It does not matter. St. John has recorded Jesus' inner experience: "I am the bread" (John 6:35). Jesus decided to give himself, to satisfy the hunger of mankind. The old temptation is reversed: now he does not change stones into bread; he becomes bread himself, thus making good his promise that the hungry shall be satisfied.

The Baptist, too, had given himself for the cause, but nobody was helped by his sacrifice. Jesus had to discover a new kind of giving. We must learn to give more than we have, and more than we are, or we remain in the past, on the level of the Baptist, and creation cannot go on.

Jesus was teaching: the crowds were eating his words. There was no hunger except the spiritual hunger of the listeners. Then the disciples remembered their materialistic responsibility: "Send off the crowds to buy food" (14:15, Moffatt). Jesus laughed: "You give them something to eat." We are identified with the disciples, careworn and troubled. How can we give more than we have? Herod promised more than he could give: we try not to be Herod.

Jesus "looked up to heaven." He saw the situation from a higher level. Should he change stones into bread? or multiply the five loaves into five thousand? He is already beyond the temptation of material miracles.

The disciples distribute what they have. There is hardly one crumb for each person. Jesus gives more than he has, distributing freely the treasures of his Father. All are looking at him, with the crumbs in their hands. He gives and gives, saying that all this comes to them from Beyond. They know it is true; God supports him; God supports them too; they feel it in body and soul. They eat, some even drop their crumbs from trembling hands. All are satisfied, their hunger is gone. The joy of their new faith sways them in rhythmical waves while they give thanks.

Joy makes us see clearly. We understand that Herod, the center of egoism, fails; he promises more than he can give (someone else's life) and destroys himself, because he cuts himself off from his source which is in the past. Jesus, the center of love, gives more than he has, using the inexhaustible resources of creation.

He does not cut himself off from the past but is supplied, guided, and supported by the future.

To live does not only mean to eat but to be eaten, also. We give ourselves or we are devoured against our will. To give ourselves as the Baptist did is not enough: it might even be a waste of material. Jesus gave himself, and more than himself. He gave the Beyond which he carried within. Before we can learn to give ourselves as he did, we must acquire the Beyond Within. We must carry it as he did. How can we find it?

Matthew gives us the first glimpse of a new answer to our old question. Jesus gives to the five thousand in the desert a unique experience. They learn to eat as they never ate before. The crumb of physical substance becomes unimportant. What matters is the giving and taking, the flow of energy through our bodies and minds, the miracle of transmutation of one form of energy into another. We, our thoughts, our growth, are the result of this unending miracle. The more we learn from Jesus how to eat, the more we shall be able to be eaten properly, giving more than ourselves.

The New Night-Sea-Journey

> Then he made the disciples get into the boat and go before him to the other side, while he dismissed the crowds. And after he had dismissed the crowds, he went up into the hills by himself to pray. When evening came, he was there alone, but the boat by this time was many furlongs distant from the land, beaten by the waves; for the wind was against them. And in the fourth watch of the night he came to them, walking on the sea. But when the disciples saw him walking on the sea, they were terrified, saying, "It is a ghost!" And they cried out for fear. But immediately he spoke to them, saying, "Take heart, it is I; have no fear."
>
> And Peter answered him, "Lord, if it is you, bid me come to you on the water." He said, "Come." So Peter got out of the boat and walked on the water and came to Jesus; but when he saw the wind, he was afraid, and beginning to sink he cried out, "Lord, save me." Jesus immediately reached out his hand and caught him, saying to him, "O man of little faith, why did you doubt?" And when they got into the boat, the wind ceased. And those in the boat worshiped him, saying, "Truly you are the Son of God."
>
> And when they had crossed over, they came to land at Gennesaret. And when the men of that place recognized him, they sent round to all that region and brought to him all that were sick, and besought him that they might only touch the fringe of his garment; and as many as touched it were made well (14:22–36).

Jesus is ready to give himself; but first he withdraws, spending the night in seclusion. We may presume that he is looking for food also, his kind of food, which he once described, saying, "My food is to do the will of him who sent me, and to accomplish his work" (John 4:34, Moffatt). He is confronted with one of the greatest decisions of his life.

The disciples, in the meantime, are alone. If they have eaten and assimilated the food that Jesus gave them in the desert, they are and remain in contact with the Beyond, individually, each one of them carrying the eternal spark within himself. Jesus, the man, then can be absent; the spirit, the Christ, like a flame which Jesus kindled, remains alive.

Once more the fishermen in their boat are tested. Their second night-sea-journey is more frightening than the first (8:23–27), because in addition to the wind and the waves this time they are haunted by a "ghost." Then the ghost turns out to be Jesus. Are they alone or with him? Is it the man Jesus in the outer world or the inner experience of the Spirit, this contact with the Eternal which he imparted to them? The text seems to imply that they are as much afraid of his presence as of his absence.

The disciples are still in the feudalistic state of mind. They need the physical presence of their Lord; and he comes. Matthew wants his students to outgrow feudalism. By the careful wording of his text, he wants to say: "Remain feudalists as long as you can. To become individuated means to discover the Spirit within; if you make this discovery, you will see the real meaning of my text." When the disciples, during their second night-sea-journey, experienced a new and unknown power, they were as frightened as Herod; then they called this power "Jesus" since they had to locate it somewhere in their frame of reference. This was a relapse into feudalism, it is true, but it helped.

Peter was so elated that he dared to put his own faith to a test; and he almost succeeded. During the night-sea-journey, as in every serious crisis, we are so close to the Beyond that the reality of matter becomes questionable. The difference between the boat and the water almost disappears; both are equally unreliable. Only faith can keep us alive, and if it cannot yet be the individual faith of tomorrow, it has to be the feudalistic faith of yesterday. Both kinds of faith, if strong enough, enable us to live in this world and at the same time look through it as if it were a mist. The rock then turns into thin air and truth becomes a rock; you can stand on it while people think you are walking on water.

If Peter's feudalistic faith were complete, he soon would out-grow it. But it is weak, it collapses, and he relapses into fears and doubts. He feels Jesus' hand support him physically.

Jesus' attempt to teach his disciples, and Matthew's attempt to teach his students the distinction between Jesus the man and Christ the creative power has utterly failed. The failure is stated in the same words as after the first night-sea-journey: "O man of little faith."

Chapter 15

THE HEART AND THE WHOLE

The Beginning of Spiritual Revolution

> Then Pharisees and scribes came to Jesus from Jerusalem and said, "Why do your disciples transgress the tradition of the elders? For they do not wash their hands when they eat." He answered them, "And why do you transgress the commandment of God for the sake of your tradition? For God commanded, 'Honor your father and your mother,' and 'He who speaks evil of father or mother, let him surely die.' But you say, 'If any one tells his father or his mother, What you would have gained from me is given to God, he need not honor his father.' So, for the sake of your tradition, you have made void the word of God. You hypocrites! Well did Isaiah prophesy of you, when he said:
> 'This people honors me with their lips,
> but their heart is far from me;
> in vain do they worship me,
> teaching as doctrine the precepts of men.'"
> And he called the people to him and said to them, "Hear and understand: not what goes into the mouth defiles a man, but what comes out of the mouth, this defiles a man." Then the disciples came and said to him, "Do you know that the Pharisees were offended when they heard this saying?" He answered, "Every plant which my heavenly Father has not planted will be rooted up. Let them alone; they are blind guides. And if a blind man leads a blind man, both will fall into a pit." But Peter said to him, "Explain the parable to us." And he said, "Are you also still without understanding? Do you not see that whatever goes into the mouth passes into the stomach, and so passes on? But what comes out of the mouth proceeds from the heart, and this defiles a man. For out of the heart come evil thoughts, murder, adultery, fornication, theft, false witness, slander. These are what defile a man; but to eat with unwashed hands does not defile a man" (15:1–20).

Jesus did not blame his disciples when they failed; Matthew did not blame his students; we should not blame ourselves nor each other. Spiritual evolution is difficult; errors and relapses are bound to occur. No coercion can help us; each individual must

177

find the way into the new freedom on his own account, voluntarily. The teacher, therefore, tries to teach us that soon we shall not need a teacher any more, that is, a teacher in the outer world. We shall discover the best of all teachers, the voice of guidance, within our own heart.

The outer drama enters a new and dangerous stage. So far Jesus had to do only with local authorities (12:10, 38); now the government sends its experts from Jerusalem. At first they raise a minor point, about washing hands, probing his position. He could easily divert their attack into one of the endless debates which are the delight of scholars and scribes, but he immediately hits back with his strongest weapon: "Why do you transgress the commandment of God for the sake of your tradition?" This is a declaration of war. He has lost all common ground with his opponents; and to show this clearly, he does something unbelievable: he appeals to the "multitudes" (15:10-11). The academic prizefight is replaced by the fanfare of the beginning spiritual revolution. Jerusalem can never forgive him this unacademic procedure.

The inner drama is still our conflict between progress and regression, represented by the disciples and the Pharisees. This conflict, however, makes us able and willing to listen. The voice of true authority speaks, the Center between the opposites may appear any moment, reconciling them on a higher level. There is no need to relinquish the past if only we recognize the voice of the Center which spoke in the past as it speaks today. Moses and Christ do not contradict each other.

As long as we cannot yet hear the "Spirit of Christ" speaking in our own conscience, we have to listen to the man of Nazareth who was a clearer instrument of the creative Voice and a cleaner channel of creative Power than we can hope to be. But soon he will leave us alone, compelling us to develop our own receiving set and our own channels of Power.

In the outer drama, Jesus withdraws, rallying his forces, reassuring his men: The enemies "shall fall into the ditch" (15:14, KJV); they are not "planted" by his Father. That is encouraging as far as it refers to the Pharisees and Sadducees. But what about our inner traditionalism and conservatism? Even the most extravagant leftist harbors a reactionary tendency in his unconscious, otherwise he would not be a radical. Whether we identify ourselves with the inner trend of inherited authority, or try to fight against it, its destruction would destroy an important part of ourselves. We remember the "bad tree" of the Sermon on the

Mount and we feel the axe at our roots. Are we plants that our Father in heaven did not plant?

Fortunately Peter does not give up. He remembers Jesus defending the disciples against the scribes and his turning from the authorities to the crowds, calling them to his colors. There must be some hope.

Peter is right. But Jesus' answer, more exactly Matthew's record of Jesus' answer, is given step by step, like a strong medicine in small doses. This is part of the great strategy. Within Peter and within each one of us the battle is raging between darkness and light, cowardice and faith, egocentricity and creativity. If we lose courage, we see the fatal array of destructive rigidity versus equally destructive ecstasies and chaos. There seems to be no way out. But when we are courageous, the creative Center appears, the opposites are reconciled as coordinated organs of a greater whole.

"Out of the heart come evil designs" (15:19, Moffatt) if the heart is bad, like the tree not planted by the Father. If the heart were good, planted by the Father, it would produce creative thoughts and deeds, even if it were hurt and injured from outside. Nobody in the outer world can poison a good heart, neither we ourselves, with our unwashed hands, nor anybody else with hatred, persecution and torture.

What, then, is a bad tree; what makes the heart evil? The answer is clear theoretically, though it will take Peter and us a long time to experience its practical truth: the tree is rotten if and because it is cut off from its healthy root; the heart is evil if and because it is severed from the Father who created it. If we can let the power of God work in our hearts, love will flow and evil thoughts will disappear. How, then, can we reestablish the lost contact with the Creator?

Relating the Parts to the Whole

> And Jesus went away from there and withdrew to the district of Tyre and Sidon. And behold, a Canaanite woman from that region came out and cried, "Have mercy on me, O Lord, Son of David; my daughter is severely possessed by a demon." But he did not answer her a word. And his disciples came and begged him, saying, "Send her away, for she is crying after us." He answered, "I was sent only to the lost sheep of the house of Israel." But she came and knelt before him, saying, "Lord, help me." And he answered, "It is not fair to take the children's bread and throw it to the dogs." She said, "Yes, Lord, yet even the dogs eat the crumbs that fall from their master's table." Then Jesus answered her, "O woman, great is

your faith! Be it done for you as you desire." And her daughter
was healed instantly (15:21–28).

Jesus' withdrawal (15:21) can be read as the beginning of
the next section, but we can understand it also as the subject of
our meditation which Matthew wants us to insert between the
discussions of the spiritual revolution in the heart, and the whole.

The Pharisees and Sadducees get a respite. Our doubts and
fears are suspended. Peter, symbolizing our conscious personality,
has ample time to wonder about the new phase of creation which
lures and frightens him at the same time.

The future will be chaos if it cuts itself off from the past. The
past will become evil if it refuses to change and grow into the
future. The heart, our center, is evil if it is cut off from the whole,
and even a whole such as a nation with its infinite spiritual potentialities, turns out to be a "bad tree" if it is cut off from the
rest of the world. Our problem therefore is: the whole and its
parts. What is the whole; what is the part; and what is their
relationship?

Jesus came to destroy the old loyal ties, setting "a man at
variance against his father . . . and a man's foes shall be they
of his own household" (10:35–36, KJV). But God's command,
"Honor your father and your mother" (15:4) remains valid. The
new loyalty, after a painful and turbulent time of transition, will
include our family, our nation, together with all the other families
and nations of the earth. In psychological language: individuation
is inseparably connected with integration. The new life is not
possible without the new love. What integration means, the nature
of this new relationship between the independent individual and
the larger wholes, Christianity and mankind, will be taught in
the second half of the gospel.

Overcoming Racial Prejudice

Jesus withdraws to the north into the country of the gentiles
in order to find the new whole. His disciples, Matthew's students,
and we follow him; his quest is ours. When he went to Gadara, we
understood that his journey into the pagan country was identical
with an expedition into the darkness of our own heart. There we
met the two madmen. Whom shall we meet at Tyre and Sidon?
Is there anything in the lonely heart beyond darkness, despair,
and madness?

A gentile woman comes wailing, "My daughter is severely possessed by a demon." We are not afraid, this time there seems to be

no danger. The question is whether we should bother to help her. We want to meditate; we are on a mission of utmost importance; we want to find the good heart behind the evil heart, the good root under the rotten tree, the center where we can come in contact with the Son of man. This woman should be silenced; we must not be disturbed in our search for the kingdom.

However, the woman is tenacious. She needs the food that Jesus can give; and she knows the words which Jesus recognizes as his own language. She is one of the many gentiles who "will come from east and west" replacing the children of Israel (8:11–12).

The two madmen of Gadara symbolize the anxiety of the egocentric heart when it destroys itself in the antagonism of unreconciled opposites. The two Phoenician women, mother and daughter, do not represent madness; they are the victims of madness. They are two not because of a central split, but because they do not pretend to be the center. It is the absence of the center which makes them suffer. To them, therefore, Jesus is like food for starving people, the central value which was lacking in their lives.

Each of us harbors in the depth of his soul the madness of Gadara, which will explode with insane fury when the light of the new consciousness reaches the "evil heart." But even the evil heart is a heart and has not been evil forever. It is the victim of darkness, longing for the light, and therefore eager to accept the light if the opportunity comes. But this dark heart has lived for many years in the "pagan country," in the dungeon of our soul together with all our underprivileged functions and repressed potentialities. We cannot yet recognize it as part of ourselves. We must integrate what we hate and fear, accept outcasts, embrace former rebels, and make peace with enemies, or we cannot become whole.

Thus we learn that the foreign woman is our sister. We overcome an age-old prejudice, transgressing the tradition of our tribal authorities. The dark inner image of the inferior race has to change its color. The new sister in Phoenicia has to be accepted as a child of our Father exactly as good or bad as our own sister at home.

This is an inner earthquake. The center of gravity suddenly shifts from our hometown to—where? to Phoenicia? No, to everywhere. No inner image is excluded from the light; none, therefore, remains completely negative, and that means no person in the outer world is excluded from our sympathy. The disturbance of our meditation has become the answer to our question. We found our heart when we allowed it to act from love.

The Redemptive Power Within

> And Jesus went on from there and passed along the Sea of Galilee. And he went up into the hills, and sat down there. And great crowds came to him, bringing with them the lame, the maimed, the blind, the dumb, and many others, and they put them at his feet, and he healed them, so that the throng wondered, when they saw the dumb speaking, the maimed whole, the lame walking, and the blind seeing; and they glorified the God of Israel.
>
> Then Jesus called his disciples to him and said, "I have compassion on the crowd, because they have been with me now three days, and have nothing to eat; and I am unwilling to send them away hungry, lest they faint on the way." And the disciples said to him, "Where are we to get bread enough in the desert to feed so great a crowd?" And Jesus said to them, "How many loaves have you?" They said, "Seven, and a few small fish." And commanding the crowd to sit down on the ground, he took the seven loaves and the fish, and having given thanks he broke them and gave them to the disciples, and the disciples gave them to the crowds. And they all ate and were satisfied; and they took up seven baskets full of the broken pieces left over. Those who ate were four thousand men, besides women and children. And sending away the crowds, he got into the boat and went to the region of Magadan (15:29–39).

In the outer drama, Jesus is still in pagan territory, though he returned to the Sea of Galilee, evidently on the eastern shore. The large crowds were gentiles, including presumably some people of Gadara. Jesus feels free to teach and heal this motley crowd as if they were all Jews; thanks to the Phoenician woman, he has completely outgrown his own racial prejudice.

Matthew shows this inner development of the Master, though it is at variance with the eternal perfection of a "divine Lord Jesus." Matthew sacrifices theological consistency for psychological efficiency. At this moment, he could help his students best by an exact parallelism between the outer story of Jesus' life and the inner story of the students' religious experience.

In the inner drama, our conflict forces us to search for a synthesis, a point of reconciliation which can be found only on a higher level of consciousness. This new center of gravity, however, must have existed long before we were able to face the inner conflict. Our progress should not be described as the creation, but as the discovery of the new center. Once recognized and accepted as the source of redemptive and creative power, this center spreads its influence through our inner and outer life until a new "whole," a double sphere is created: the ever-growing consciousness inside, and the ever-growing brotherhood outside. If we do not like to say that the center itself is growing, at least we have to admit that its redemptive influence, power, and radiance are growing. This is what Matthew describes in the feeding of the four thousand.

With the five thousand, the disciples were stirred by the materialistic fear of starvation; this time Jesus sees the people's need for spiritual food and gives them the experience of a "Lord's Supper."

Why do the disciples in the second case not remember what happened the first time? Mark probably recorded faithfully and blindly the doublet because it was there in oral tradition. Matthew would have omitted or changed it had he not needed it exactly as it stands.

Jesus' later remark about the disciples' forgetfulness (16:9) gives us the clue. We always forget the lessons of life which could help us to overcome our egocentricity. In this respect we are almost morons. But we remember well what suits our Ego: there we are ingenious and alert. That is why the lessons of the night-sea-journey and of the feeding have to be repeated.

Chapter 16

THE DISCOVERY

Looking for Proof

> And the Pharisees and Sadducees came, and to test him
> they asked him to show them a sign from heaven. He answered
> them, "When it is evening, you say, 'It will be fair weather;
> for the sky is red.' And in the morning, 'It will be stormy
> today, for the sky is red and threatening.' You know how to
> interpret the appearance of the sky, but you cannot interpret
> the signs of the times. An evil and adulterous generation seeks
> for a sign, but no sign shall be given to it except the sign of
> Jonah." So he left them and departed (16:1–4).

There must have been a lack of conspicuous evidence of Jesus'
messiahship. The Pharisees and Sadducees were not convinced at
all by the wild rumors of miraculous healings and feedings. Some
people were changed and "reborn" by the inner experience which
Jesus provoked; others questioned the outer and the inner events
alike.

Let us take sides with the skeptics. Their need for scientific
proof seems to be justified. On the other hand, we know quite
well: if Jesus convinces us by miracles, he enslaves us in spiritual
feudalism instead of developing our maturity and independence.
By asking for evidence, we prove that we do not yet understand
"the signs of the time." Otherwise we should look for the sign
within ourselves; the sign of Jonah, the crisis; we should then
recognize that we are actually swallowed and carried away by the
great fish. Indeed, we are still in the grip of unconscious powers,
doubt, fear, passion and greed. The fish has us, though we think
we have the fish. The discovery of our true situation makes us
cry out for help. We are on our third night-sea-journey.

The Third Night-Sea-Journey

> When the disciples reached the other side, they had forgotten
> to bring any bread. Jesus said to them, "Take heed and be-
> ware of the leaven of the Pharisees and Sadducees." And they
> discussed it among themselves, saying, "We brought no bread."

> But Jesus, aware of this, said, "O men of little faith, why do
> you discuss among yourselves the fact that you have no bread?
> Do you not yet perceive? Do you not remember the five loaves
> of the five thousand, and how many baskets you gathered? Or
> the seven loaves of the four thousand, and how many baskets
> you gathered? How is it that you fail to perceive that I did
> not speak about bread? Beware of the leaven of the Pharisees
> and Sadducees." Then they understood that he did not tell
> them to beware of the leaven of bread, but of the teaching of
> the Pharisees and Sadducees (16:5–12).

Now Jesus takes a new step. He speaks about the "leaven of
the Pharisees and Sadducees," evidently contrasting it with the
leaven of the kingdom, "which a woman took and buried in three
pecks of flour, till all of it was leavened" (13:33, Moffatt). Later
he explains he is speaking of philosophy. Both the legalistic doctrine of the Pharisees and the materialistic view of the Sadducees
are equally dangerous.[1] From the standpoint of psychology, they
are equally egocentric, less consciously in the former, more consciously in the latter, case. All the forms of individualism are
symbolized by leaven, the leaven of the kingdom standing for
individuation.

The disciples are even more materialistic than the Sadducees.
They think of the physical bread, which they forgot in their at-
tempt to become more spiritual. Once more they disappoint the
Master. Again he calls them "O men of little faith."

Who Is the Son of Man?

> Now when Jesus came into the district of Caesarea Philippi,
> he asked his disciples, "Who do men say that the Son of man
> is?" And they said, "Some say John the Baptist, others say
> Elijah, and others Jeremiah or one of the prophets." He said
> to them, "But who do you say that I am?" Simon Peter replied,
> "You are the Christ, the Son of the living God" (16:13–16).

Jesus does not give up on his disciples. As in earlier cases, he
goes straight forward. He asks them who people say the Son of
man is. The disciples are still feudalists. Their answer is naïve:
John the Baptist, Elijah, Jeremiah, or some other prophet. Jesus,
and Matthew, step down to their level. "And who do you say that *I*
am?" (16:15, Moffatt). Jesus looks at his disciples with keen expectation. Matthew looks at us in the same way. Between the lines

---

1. The Pharisees insisted upon the observance of the oral as well as the
written law, and believed in future life, angels and demonology. The Sadducees were priests mainly concerned with politics and the wealthy. Written
law (Pentateuch) was authoritative but not the oral law and they denied the
resurrection of the body. W. O. E. Oesterley in *A New Commentary on the
Bible,* pp. 18 ff.

of Matthew's text looms a secret. "Who is the Son of man?" and "Who is Jesus?" These are two different questions.

Peter answers for us. "You are the Christ, the Son of the living God."

This is the turning point of human history. In spite of all his failures and relapses, suddenly the disciple is able to see the truth. His eyes, for a great and blissful moment, penetrate the physical world like spiritual X-rays. Peter gazes through Jesus into the infinite. Where Jesus stood, there is now a new consciousness, able to face the eternal essence of the human soul. The Beyond looks at the Beyond recognizing its identity. Two humans, teacher and pupil, suddenly meet on a higher level, experiencing their encounter as the outburst of the Beyond Within. This experience is as real as a rock. Single ecstasy is unreal; it may be insanity. The meeting of two people on the higher plane is creation: it is sound evolution even if it lasts only a second. And it is love.

That it happened was neither Jesus' nor Peter's merit. The Creator took the creative step as soon as His creatures were prepared. But why does Peter say, "You are the Son of God," instead of "We are the Sons of God"? Does the feudalistic pattern still interfere with his spiritual evolution?

The Son of man is alive within Jesus: his adult sonship is beyond doubt. Within Peter, the Son of man stirs and moves him as if he were waking from a deathlike sleep; then he sinks back into unconsciousness; he stands where he saw Jesus standing before. And he recognizes that Jesus again is a step ahead of him, on a still higher level, in much closer contact with eternity: "the Son of the living God."

Trying to express his unspeakable experience, Peter uses the word "Christ," the new name, beyond all the expectations and traditions of the Old Testament. It comes to Peter spontaneously and unexpectedly.[2]

Silence

Here is the climax of the Gospel, the culmination of history, and the crossroads for the individual reader. A fully mature person looks at you: you look at the first human being who is completely free from tribal bondage and egocentric fear. He sees you as you are. Do you see him as he is? He asks you: "Who do

---

2. The word "Christ" appears five times in Matthew's text (1:1, 16, 17; 2:4; 11:2) before this use, but only in the narrative, used retrospectively. It never occurs in any conversation prior to this passage.

you say I am?" Peter's answer lingers in our ears, breathless, in utter sincerity: "You are the Christ . . ." We cannot repeat it. It has been repeated too frequently. We are not asked about our belief or creed. The question is what we actually see, what we discover while looking at this man—and any man—who is as he ought to be: mature and free. What our eyes can see in this moment will decide what we shall do from now on. We stand at the crossroads of our life.

The Keys of the Kingdom

> And Jesus answered him, "Blessed are you, Simon Bar-Jona! For flesh and blood has not revealed this to you, but my Father who is in heaven. And I tell you, you are Peter, and on this rock I will build my church, and the powers of death shall not prevail against it. I will give you the keys of the kingdom of heaven, and whatever you bind on earth shall be bound in heaven, and whatever you loose on earth shall be loosed in heaven." Then he strictly charged the disciples to tell no one that he was the Christ (16:17–20).

Jesus had "known" his disciple for a long time; now he solemnly repeats his "secret name," Peter. It is Peter's baptism: he is christened. Thus far the word Peter, meaning a little stone, has had the humorous connotation of a nickname much as the sons of Zebedee were called "Sons of Thunder" (Mark 3:17). Now the pun becomes a paradox and an awe-inspiring prophecy: "You are Peter, the little stone, and upon this huge boulder I will gather my assembly."

The Greek word *ekklesia* literally means a "meeting," without any reference to purpose or organization. Most translations render it by "church," some even with a capital C. This is a misinterpretation based on the tendency of the Roman Catholic Church to find the justification of its own existence in the Gospel. The rock which Jesus had in mind was something infinitely stronger than any human organization can be. It was the fact that Peter, transcending his own limitations, had experienced the very principle of evolution. Peter was courageous enough to conceive and express the sacrilegious idea that a man, a carpenter, could actually be a "Son of the living God."

The old-fashioned title "Son of God" (14:33), meaning "the divine one," which occasionally was given to judges and priests, is suddenly charged with the high voltage of a new consciousness. Mankind enters a new phase of evolution. The man Jesus achieves this "sonship"; he becomes Christ, the spiritual man, the man of the future; and another man, Peter, is able to recognize this event. This experience is the boulder on which all Christianity is built. But each Christian, if he deserves this name, must find this boulder within himself. It is the rock on which the wise man builds his house.

Peter experiences the creative power of the kingdom to come. He is not yet a Son of the living God, but his servant or friend; the Son of man within him is still a babe. His power, however, is strong enough to evoke the same development in other people; he is now the light of the world and the salt of the earth. If he influences the others in the right way, helping them to see the "sign of Jonah" and to work through their crises, they will find the same rock of spiritual certainty within themselves. He will be in charge of "the keys of the kingdom of heaven."

The Spiritual We-Experience

All men and women are Peter's brothers and sisters, because they are prospective citizens of the kingdom. Their suffering is his, because it is the suffering of the kingdom. He discovers the oneness of all men, the new brotherhood, the new unlimited love.

We can repeat Peter's discoveries; indeed we must do so if we want to become Christians. Then we shall see that the two discoveries—that Jesus is the son of God and that all men are brothers—are two different aspects of one and the same truth.

Peter's (and our) way seems to soar high up. We have looked into eternity; soon we shall carry the keys of the kingdom. But how can we take the responsibility for all the others whom we left behind? If they fail, our success is useless. Mankind fails or succeeds as a whole. Up to this point, our goal was individuation, the emergence of the individual from tribal consciousness. Now we recognize the collective responsibility of all mankind. There is no individuation without integration. Integration means the experience that everybody is an integral part of everybody else. The "spiritual We-experience" unites us with friends and enemies alike. Therefore the sins of mankind are our sins. We are liable for the debts of all nations. How can we bear this terrifying burden?

The Way Down Is the Way Up

> From that time Jesus began to show his disciples that he must go to Jerusalem and suffer many things from the elders and chief priests and scribes, and be killed, and on the third day be raised. And Peter took him and began to rebuke him, saying, "God forbid, Lord! This shall never happen to you." But he turned and said to Peter, "Get behind me, Satan!

You are a hindrance to me; for you are not on the side of God, but of men."

Then Jesus told his disciples, "If any man would come after me, let him deny himself and take up his cross and follow me. For whoever would save his life will lose it, and whoever loses his life for my sake will find it. For what will it profit a man, if he gains the whole world and forfeits his life? Or what shall a man give in return for his life? For the Son of man is to come with his angels in the glory of his Father, and then he will repay every man for what he has done. Truly, I say to you, there are some standing here who will not taste death before they see the Son of man coming in his kingdom" (16:21–28).

The silence of our helpless bewilderment is broken by Jesus' voice. He tells us that he is going to Jerusalem and that he will be tortured and executed. Is this the answer? Is this the way of paying the debts of history? We are startled. Peter does not even hear Jesus' last words, "and be raised on the third day."

The Master's way leads down into misery and defeat. Can we not find a better solution for him? Let us use the power of our keys, trying to open a wider gate into the kingdom. We take an oath regarding the future: "God forbid!" We were baptized, as Jesus was; now we are tempted, as he was; but we fail where he succeeded.

Jesus, with unusual violence, turns against us: "Satan, get behind me!" He is completely human; our temptation is his temptation. We realize that his resolve to face torture and death, though we do not yet understand his full motivation, is a human experiment, a heroic adventure, not a divine blueprint carried out by a slave. Peter, the little pebble, lies on the sands once more, and the huge boulder of eternity hangs over him as an incomprehensible danger.

The two systems of values clash and all the teachings of the Sermon on the Mount come to life: the narrow and the wide gates, the treasure in heaven, and the "taking thought for tomorrow." When it comes to a test, our "outlook is not God's but man's" (16:23, Moffatt). The Beyond Within has disappeared. Where is Christ, the Son of man, whom we believed to find within ourselves? Where is Christ, the Son of God, whom we thought we saw before us? Only the empty words remain, like a dry river bed. The living water is gone. Our way up was our way down.

Jesus' way down might well be the way up. The mourners are blessed and those who give their earthly possessions away store up treasures in heaven. The reversal of values becomes frightening:

the torture of evolution begins to squeeze us. We hold the keys of the kingdom in our hands, but we do not dare to open the gate, the narrow gate, because it leads us downhill and we do not yet see that the way down is the way up.

The Greek words translated "behind" ("Get behind me") and "after" ("come after me"—16:24) are identical. Peter is not told to leave Jesus, but to follow him. Our attempt to act independently as individuated stewards of the kingdom broke down in our first temptation. We are sent back to the training school. We have to learn from our "divine Lord Jesus" how to replace our earthly valuation by something better.

From the standpoint of eternity it may be a simple and clear truth; from our standpoint in space and time it is a paradox: "Whoever wants to save his life will lose it, and whoever loses his life for my sake will find it" (16:25, Moffatt). Only by sacrificing the temporal values (which will be destroyed by rust and moths anyhow—6:19) can we attain the eternal values. Only by selling all can we buy the infinite treasure (13:44). But all these big words have become static laws which may induce us to repress our desires and to bury our talents rather than to develop them into something better. Mere moralistic training is even worse than mere intellectual teaching. We have to go with Jesus down (or up) to Jerusalem, to Gethsemane and Golgotha. There we shall learn the great lesson.

His way leads into earthly disaster and at the same time into the kingdom of heaven. He is the pioneer who finds for us the way through the impenetrable valley of darkness; he and many of his followers will be killed while entering the kingdom. Some of us, however, shall discover the Son of man and enter the kingdom before dying physically. The road soon will be open for dying and living people alike.

A new paradox appears. If we have to die in order to live, how can we live without "tasting death" (16:28, Moffatt)? Can we die without dying? Theoretically we have learned that it is our egocentricity which has to be destroyed in order to make room for a God-centered life. But how it is done in reality, we do not yet know. Therefore we have to go to Jerusalem taking the risk of being destroyed altogether. The paradox has to be explored and experienced practically.

Chapter 17

SPIRIT AND MATTER

Spirit

> And after six days Jesus took with him Peter and James and John his brother, and led them up a high mountain apart. And he was transfigured before them, and his face shone like the sun, and his garments became white as light. And behold, there appeared to them Moses and Elijah, talking with him. And Peter said to Jesus, "Lord, it is well that we are here; if you wish, I will make three booths here, one for you and one for Moses and one for Elijah." He was still speaking, when lo, a bright cloud overshadowed them, and a voice from the cloud said, "This is my beloved Son, with whom I am well pleased; listen to him." When the disciples heard this, they fell on their faces, and were filled with awe. But Jesus came and touched them, saying, "Rise, and have no fear." And when they lifted up their eyes, they saw no one but Jesus only (17:1-8).

We cannot rise into the spiritual world without diving into the world of matter. If we accept spiritual power, the keys of the kingdom, without assuming the responsibility for the collective sorrows of mankind, we shall be blown away like a kite detached from its string. On the other hand, if we recognize our task, trying to clear the slums and to feed the hungry, our new love may drown us in gloom and despair. How can the way down become the way up?

Jesus needed six days to prepare his best disciples for the new lesson. Matthew may have spent much more time with his students before they were ready to take the next step. We cannot expect our development to proceed faster. We should reread and rethink Chapter 16 for more than a week. Then, if we dare to count ourselves among the few initiates who formed the innermost circle, we may climb with Jesus to the mountaintop, in solitude.

This mountain in the center of the Gospel—commentators think it was Mount Hermon—together with the mount of the

Sermon at the beginning and the Mount of Olives at the end, marks the architecture of the whole narrative. It is the highest of the three peaks, reaching up into the strata of spiritual experiences, while the other two reach only to the height of inspired words. This spiritual reality is beyond space. The mountain peak is, as it were, nowhere. Matthew does not give its name. And it is beyond time. The past is present. The law and the prophets, the history of Israel condensed in the two leading characters, Moses and Elijah, become visible even to the dull eyes of the disciples.

Peter is intoxicated by the glory of super-time and super-space. He will make three huts, the practical quartermaster, earthly huts beyond space and time! If he were allowed to do so he would live for the rest of his life in a kind of spiritual illusion, enjoying himself, founding a cult, and impressing his followers with his marvelous visions. He would accept and propagate half of the truth, namely "spiritualization," the way up; and he would forget and deny the other half, namely the way down into the valley of death, Gethsemane and Golgotha. He would die in glorious self-deceptions instead of using the keys of the kingdom.

Peter, however, has no chance to develop such a pseudo-religion. On the mountain peak beyond space and time, not only is the past present with Moses and Elijah, but also the future, the Spirit, the Creator himself. The disciples are "overshadowed" by a bright cloud. The blazing light from beyond petrifies Peter. It paralyzes those who shun the valley of darkness. And the voice says, "This is my son . . ."

The disciples hear now what Jesus heard when he was baptized (3:17). This time Matthew, Mark, and Luke write unanimously, "This is my son." At Jesus' baptism only Matthew had "this is"; the others wrote, "Thou art my son." Oral tradition was feudalistic: the feudal king dubs the feudal prince addressing him directly. Matthew knows better. According to him, God tells Jesus the name of the power which, like a dove, comes down upon him. Its name is "My son." Now the voice again explains the terrifying event, but we remain free either to understand that "the Son" is the spiritual power which permeates Jesus, or to assume that the carpenter, the man of flesh and blood, is called "my beloved Son."[1]

---

1. The wording "Thou art my son" is quoted from Psalm 2:7. It refers to the coronation of a Jewish king who by his ascension to the throne became "divine." The quoted text therefore continues, "this day have I begotten thee." The words "in whom I am well pleased" are from Isa. 42:1; and "hear ye him" from Deut. 18:15. But the formula "This is my son" does not occur anywhere else. What the disciples hear is a mixture of well-known quotations, all related to the long-expected Messiah, but reshaped to fit the

Peter's subjective discovery "You are . . . the son of the living God" (16:16) is answered by the objective assertion, "This is my beloved Son" (17:5). At Caesarea one man, Peter, looked at one man, Jesus; it was the experience of Individuation. Now three men, Peter, James, and John, look at three men, Jesus, Moses, and Elijah; it is the experience of Integration. In both cases, the Here and Now is face to face with the Beyond, and the framework of space and time disappears for a moment. In the first case, Jesus answers, "Thou art Peter . . . " In the second case, the Eternal himself answers, "This is my Son . . . " The two events are the two decisive steps in Peter's initiation. Jesus' initiation is recorded in two verses (3:16, 17). Peter's is elaborately explained in two full chapters (16 and 17).

At Caesarea Jesus was to Peter, so to speak, a window through which the latter could see into eternity. On the mountaintop Jesus becomes a door and through it comes eternity to visit the three disciples. Jesus himself seems to be on the other side, for a short time, and then to come back. He is equally familiar with the different strata of reality. But this does not yet make him a god; it only shows what true initiation can achieve. He is reborn, adopted by the Father: "Today I have begotten you" (Ps. 2:7).

Assimilation of the Great Experience

> And as they were coming down the mountain, Jesus commanded them, "Tell no one the vision, until the Son of man is raised from the dead." And the disciples asked him, "Then why do the scribes say that first Elijah must come?" He replied, "Elijah does come, and he is to restore all things; but I tell you that Elijah has already come, and they did not know him, but did to him whatever they pleased. So also the Son of man will suffer at their hands." Then the disciples understood that he was speaking to them of John the Baptist (17:9–13).

Jesus' next concern is that on coming down into their accustomed environment they should not speak about their experience on the higher level. For the second time we hear that the "mystery of Jesus the Christ" has to be kept secret. The strata of reality must not be confused. Only the adepts of the higher level, those who are capable of seeing the Christ—which means the true Christians—will know when and how much they should reveal of this mystery.

---

present situation ("this is" instead of "thou art"). A Veda-student under the same circumstances would have heard the corresponding words from the Upanishads. At the Pentecost, "when this sound was heard . . . each heard them speaking in his own language" (Acts 2:6, Moffatt).

The disciples, if they had been sent into the world at this time —before Jesus died—would have been blind leaders of the blind. Their initiation so far has been a deeply disturbing experience which they do not understand. They are excited, ecstatic, but not enlightened. They have to assimilate their startling experience, connecting it with their former categories and ideas, without depriving it of its meaning. This is possible only if they develop their categories and ideas, indeed their whole frame of reference, into something greater, more comprehensive, more adequate to the new phase of creation.

The new frame of reference is given in the reversal of values as described in the paradox self-preservation is death; and death for the sake of creation is new life. We, nowadays, learn the philosophical formula first and its practical application later. Jesus' disciples, more fortunately, had to learn it the opposite way.

How Spirit Conquers Matter

> And when they came to the crowd, a man came up to him and kneeling before him said, "Lord, have mercy on my son, for he is an epileptic and he suffers terribly; for often he falls into the fire, and often into the water. And I brought him to your disciples, and they could not heal him." And Jesus answered, "O faithless and perverse generation, how long am I to be with you? How long am I to bear with you? Bring him here to me." And Jesus rebuked him, and the demon came out of him, and the boy was cured instantly. Then the disciples came to Jesus privately and said, "Why could we not cast it out?" He said to them, "Because of your little faith. For truly, I say to you, if you have faith as a grain of mustard seed, you will say to this mountain, 'Move hence to yonder place,' and it will move; and nothing will be impossible to you."
>
> As they were gathering in Galilee, Jesus said to them, "The Son of man is to be delivered into the hands of men, and they will kill him, and he will be raised on the third day." And they were greatly distressed.
>
> When they came to Capernaum, the collectors of the half-shekel tax went up to Peter and said, "Does not your teacher pay the tax?" He said, "Yes." And when he came home, Jesus spoke to him first, saying, "What do you think, Simon? From whom do kings of the earth take toll or tribute? From their sons or from others?" And when he said, "From others," Jesus said to him, "Then the sons are free. However, not to give offense to them, go to the sea and cast a hook, and take the first fish that comes up, and when you open its mouth you will find a shekel; take that and give it to them for me and for yourself" (17:14–27).

Mark says the disciples who failed to cure the epileptic boy were those who remained in the valley while Jesus with Peter, James, and John went to the mountaintop (Mark 9:14–29). Luke gives us the impression that the three favorite disciples failed as well as the others (Luke 9:37–43). Matthew leaves it to us whether we feel identified with the nine who failed because they were not yet illuminated, or with the three who failed in spite of their new contact with the Eternal. We certainly cannot cure epilepsy. Matter, some physical "demon," subdues the spirit of the boy, and our spiritual power is not sufficient to rescue him from his material entanglement.

The demon, as Mark puts it, often casts the boy "into the fire and into the water, to destroy him." Jesus, for the sake of our spiritual evolution, has helped us to face the stormy waves of the night-sea-journey. And he gave us the first glimpse of the eternal fire: His face shone like the sun. The boy is on the same way with us, but he is blind, stumbling at random. He is we, minus the Son of man. Why can we not become the Son of man to him? We have the key of the kingdom, but it does not yet unlock the prison doors of the material world. Why can we not cure epileptics?

The early Christians were as embarrassed by this question as we are. From the fifth century on, the manuscripts insert 17:21. "But this kind never comes out except by prayer and fasting," borrowing Mark's 9:29 and disturbing badly Matthew's magnificent structure. Matthew, too, has an answer for our question, but it is more appalling than "prayer and fasting." The answer is: "The Son of man is to be delivered into the hands of men; and they will kill him; and on the third day he will be raised."

There is no other way. If the Spirit wants to conquer matter, it has to go into it, accept it, love it, share its fate, permeate, revitalize, and redeem it. We have to suffer and die in order to grow and live, dying not only our own death but everybody's death. We have to undergo the destruction of our physical body before we can master it. "It is sown a natural body; it is raised a spiritual body" (1 Cor. 15:44, KJV). The epileptic boy is going through death in every seizure of his sickness. He dies daily in anguish and horror. In this respect he is far ahead of us. Jesus has decided to go to Jerusalem, knowing that he will be tortured and killed. Since this resolve, he, too, dies daily; but he knows why he chooses to do so. His anguish and horror are lined with calm courage and surrounded by the aurora borealis of new creation. He is equally far ahead of the epileptic boy and of us.

The answer is clear: To cure mankind, we must conquer matter; to conquer matter, we need faith; to get faith, we must learn to die daily. And to learn this, we must go with Jesus through his crucifixion.

The story about the tribute money seems to interrupt the flow of the narrative. How can this little miracle balance the great picture of the Transfiguration? But the discrepancy between the first and the last part of this chapter reveals the deeper meaning of the "miracle" and the money in the mouth of the fish.

Matter is transparent and permeable to Jesus. He can remove mountains. To Peter the material world looks like a mountain of unsurpassable difficulties. The tax collectors presume that Jesus does not consider himself any longer a "son of Abraham" and therefore does not pay the temple tribute. Peter, half-heartedly, pretends to stay in the tribal precinct of Israel. He is and is not a loyal Jew. But the material world requires clean decisions—pay or do not pay; no compromise is possible.

Jesus is amused. The loyalty of the "sons" is proven by the payment of their taxes? No, the sons are free; only the strangers pay. What a confusion! We cannot settle this question in terms of tribes and nations. But in terms of matter and Spirit the issue is clear. We are aliens in the world of matter; our home is in the spiritual world. As guests we should not offend our hosts. We must observe the laws of this world more cleanly and correctly than anybody else. Our spiritual task must not be mixed up with lawsuits for tax evasion or petty theft. But then we have to earn money, to do business—we are caught in mountains of material difficulties.

Peter's, and our, Transfiguration begins. We learn to remove our inner mountain of care, concern, and taking thought. The name of the first mountain is "fear of failure." Jesus, still laughing, tells the fisherman Simon (not calling him Peter) to catch a fish. It can be a real fish in the real lake; or it can be a new convert, since Peter has become a fisher of men; or it can be another creative idea turning up from the unconscious like a fish from the water. There are innumerable ways of earning money if you have the power of the Spirit at your disposal. The Transfiguration of matter into Spirit begins by catching fish and paying taxes. Simon tries and succeeds. He pays the tribute money; and he is Peter again. He is on his way to his own Transfiguration.

Chapter 18

THE WE-EXPERIENCE

Introduction

The structure of Chapter 18 confronts us with a difficult problem. There seem to be three major sections, yet without any balance between sections one and three (18:1–10 and 21–35). However, the third section, the parable of the debtor, can be understood as a conclusion for the whole fourth part of the Gospel, balanced by the story of the Baptist's execution (14:1–12). Powerful pictures of guilt and forgiveness form the proper frame of these five chapters (14–18).

That leaves us 18:1–20. At first sight this material is a collection of scattered sayings rather than a discourse; but it becomes a source of profound wisdom as soon as we understand its elaborate architecture. Matthew has worked painstakingly to achieve the greatest possible success through the smallest possible number of words.

The center gives us the clue: "For the Son of man came to save the lost" (18:11). But, curiously enough, this sentence is not in the original manuscripts; it was inserted as late as about 500 A.D. The modern translators therefore omit it. But without it our understanding is greatly hampered. Thus, the interpolation was justified.

It has been said that the discussion in 18:12–20 must have been a late addition. And it is almost certain that Jesus himself never gave the advice of verses 15–17. The repetition of earlier passages in verses 8, 9, and 18 seems to indicate also that the material here is compiled for the sake of the early community— but so is Matthew's whole Gospel.

Accept the Child in You

> At that time the disciples came to Jesus, saying, "Who is the greatest in the kingdom of heaven?" And calling to him a child, he put him in the midst of them, and said, "Truly, I say to you, unless you turn and become like children, you will

never enter the kingdom of heaven. Whoever humbles himself
like this child, he is the greatest in the kingdom of heaven.
"Whoever receives one such child in my name receives me"
(18:1–5).

The valuations of ancient cultures were based on visible success, victories, earthly possessions, and fame. The result was
egocentricity. "Who is the greatest . . ." is a typical egocentric
question. Jesus overthrows all our traditional values together
with our egocentricity. What he wants to teach us is so new and
so difficult that no adequate words are available. Like an Old Testament prophet, therefore, he preaches through action. He puts a
child in the midst of the disciples. It is a real child, undiscouraged,
without any self-consciousness. Such a child has no inferiority
feelings and therefore no aggressiveness; he is alert, creative, and
willing to cooperate if you ask his help. Matthew's expression
"whoever humbles himself" still allows the misunderstanding
that the wrong kind of "meekness," the fawning sugar-coated fear-
fulness of the appeaser could be recommended. But the peasant
child of the Galilean hills with his indomitable vitality, his spar-
kling eyes, and his carefree laughter excludes such an error.

How can we get rid of our egocentric fears and ambitions? How
can we find the way back to the innocence and creativity of our
early years? How can we undo repressions and compensations, re-
establishing the fearless equilibrium of the "primitive We-experience"? The way out is stated at the very beginning: "Whoever
receives a little child like this for my sake receives me" (18:5,
Moffatt). To be able "to receive him" is the very goal of our
spiritual evolution. Why is it so amazingly difficult?

Cause Not the Child to Stumble

". . . but whoever causes one of these little ones who believe
in me to sin, it would be better for him to have a great millstone fastened round his neck and to be drowned in the depth
of the sea.

"Woe to the world for temptations to sin! For it is necessary
that temptations come, but woe to the man by whom the temptation comes! And if your hand or your foot causes you to sin,
cut it off and throw it from you; it is better for you to enter
life maimed or lame than with two hands or two feet to be
thrown into the eternal fire. And if your eye causes you to sin,
pluck it out and throw it from you; it is better for you to enter
life with one eye than with two eyes to be thrown into the hell of
fire.

"See that you do not despise one of these little ones; for I tell you that in heaven their angels always behold the face of my Father who is in heaven" (18:6–10).

All the little ones, including ourselves when we were little, are "offended," wounded, discouraged, deviated by the lack of love or lack of wisdom on the part of their educators. And why do all the educators destroy the courage and creativeness of all their children? Because they have been offended, wounded, discouraged, deviated themselves when they were defenseless and confident babies. Now we are all murderers of souls, manufacturers of egocentricity on a large scale. We are all doing the devil's job. Would it not be better to be drowned in the sea with millstones around our necks?

But "offences" (KJV), "hindrances" (Moffatt and Goodspeed), "causes of stumbling" (Weymouth) have to come. The "scandalons," to use the Greek root, are unavoidable. Otherwise the primitive We-experience would last forever, consciousness would never reach a higher level, and spiritual evolution would be impossible. We must learn to choose and to take responsibility. Therefore we shall make mistakes, lose our way, and cause others to go astray and die in the wilderness. "It is necessary that *scandalons* come, but woe to the man by whom the *scandalon* comes." This negative paradox is exactly as deep and essential to Christianity as its positive counterpart "whoever loses his life for my sake will find it" (16:25). Indeed the positive paradox presupposes the negative. Without the mystery of deviation, the mystery of redemption would be useless, and the mystery of spiritual evolution, the "coming of Christ," would be impossible were not the primitive We-experience destroyed by the "scandalon."

Are we forced, then, to inflict on our children the evil which we recognize as the source of all human suffering and as the main obstacle in our own development? No, there is another way. Matthew repeats the advice to cut off hand and foot and to put out the eye if they offend us. To eliminate the epidemic of egocentricity from our communities, we have to eliminate it from within ourselves. If we have no inferiority feeling and subsequently no striving for superiority, our neighbors will stop competing and envying. Fear and greed disappear around us if they disappear within us. Most of us know from casual experiences that this is so, but we also know how extremely difficult it is to redeem our egocentric urges.

Silence

> "The Son of man came to save the lost" (18:11, RSV footnote).

The "scandalon" is bound to come. How can we undo the evil consequences of our and our ancestors' errors? Can we undo the curse that seems to be inherent in human history? If evil is unavoidable, it is so in order to make the new evolution possible. Baffled, as St. Paul, we stand before the mystery of life: are we "to 'remain on in sin, so that there may be all the more grace'" (Rom. 6.1, Moffatt)? What shall we do? Out of the silence comes the answer: "The Son of man came to save that which was lost." This reversal of values causes our former philosophy to collapse. The appearance of the new phase of creation, the Son of man, gives us a new point of view which removes all contradictions and reveals the simple meaning of the most complicated paradox. The Son of man gives us the answer, and the answer is the Son of man.

Rescue the Little Ones

> "What do you think? If a man has a hundred sheep, and one of them has gone astray, does he not leave the ninety-nine on the hills and go in search of the one that went astray? And if he finds it, truly, I say to you, he rejoices over it more than over the ninety-nine that never went astray. So it is not the will of my Father who is in heaven that one of these little ones should perish" (18:12–14).

We have heard many statements about the Son of man. This time we feel that his coming—whatever that means—would achieve the same result, and better, and with less suffering, as we could attain by tearing out our eye or cutting off our hand. Matthew should say more about this "coming of the Son of man."

Instead, he tells us the story of the lost sheep and the shepherd who finds it. If we are the lost sheep, we are the "little ones." We feel helpless enough to accept this description. But a minute ago the "little ones" were our children. That puts us in the position of the shepherd. We have to rescue them. The saving power, the Son of man, approaches them through us, in us, and we remember that the keys of the kingdom are in our hands. This time Matthew does not say much about the Son of man, but he tells us what to do in order to find him within us; rescue the little ones, instead of "offending" them.

Here we stand, endowed with the power to loose and bind in

this world and the next, and this power seems to be almost identical with the Son of man himself. But we are utterly helpless in the face of the lost sheep, the little ones whom we have wounded, discouraged, and almost murdered in our families, churches, and business organizations. We are lost sheep ourselves; how can we function as shepherds? We cannot cure epilepsy, nor juvenile delinquency, nor can we prevent wars or revolutions.

The Reconciling Power

> "If your brother sins against you, go and tell him his fault, between you and him alone. If he listens to you, you have gained your brother. But if he does not listen, take one or two others along with you, that every word may be confirmed by the evidence of two or three witnesses. If he refuses to listen to them, tell it to the church; and if he refuses to listen even to the church, let him be to you as a Gentile and a tax collector. Truly, I say to you, whatever you bind on earth shall be bound in heaven, and whatever you loose on earth shall be loosed in heaven. Again I say to you, if two of you agree on earth about anything they ask, it will be done for them by my Father in heaven. For where two or three are gathered in my name, there am I in the midst of them" (18:15–20).

Matthew advises us to settle our grievances first between two, then in a small group, and finally before the whole community. This would be a good way, were it not onesided. There is no case where "our brother sins against us." We always do as much wrong to him as he does to us. Matthew's "ecclesiastical court" must be understood as our inner court of self-discovery and self-education. It must be experienced in the inner drama before it can be helpful in the outer world.

We should understand that one member of our group has to do what we all abhor, and therefore repress, within ourselves. He does openly what we unconsciously desire. His deed is the confession of our secret sin. Only by facing this unconscious desire within our own soul, recognizing and verifying it as part of our being, can we learn what he does for us: he carries vicariously our burden. He is the scapegoat, and he becomes our mirror; he teaches us what we really are.

We have to solve his problem within ourselves. If he commits a sexual crime, our sexual needs, even within the cleanest members of our group, are not settled. If we open the doors of our unconscious, we shall find a welter of filthy desires, repressed fantasies and deviated creativity. We must use the keys of the kingdom first to unlock our own inner prison doors, accepting and redeeming our inner shadow, removing the beam from our eye; otherwise the keys will become a curse, leading into self-righteousness, power-politics, and inquisition.

Self-analysis is a long and painful process. It takes a lifetime and, unless the Son of man interferes with his creative power, it has to be paid for with cut off hands and torn out eyes. In the meantime the little ones, who are entrusted to us, will perish under the impact of our egocentricity. We need a shortcut, or we shall end in chaos.

Jesus answers our need: "Again I say to you . . ." One person alone, encumbered by his egocentricity, can hardly find the right way. If two cooperate, their blind spots differ, they can make each other see more clearly. The group spirit, seeing through two people as if they were two eyes, discerns the truth and knows what they should pray for. Single prayer may go astray. Though it remains the main source of creative power, its results have to be compared with the results of the solitary prayer of others. One person may misunderstand the Son of man. Two or three will find him. And even if they—like the disciples at Emmaus—do not recognize him, he will be there.

The "I" who says that he will be in our midst when we are gathered in his name, is the Son of man, speaking through Jesus. For the first time here the Son of man appears as the group spirit rather than the individual experience of evolution. Individuation has become Integration. "I" has changed into "We." The Son of man now is the oneness of men; he is love and collective creativity, raised into individual consciousness and realized as individual responsibility.

Whenever creation comes to a standstill between men—and human relationship is the main field of creation in our days—the reason for the breakdown is egocentricity. It is fear, greed, hatred, competition. But we have the ignition key to start the motor again. We ignite by forgiving.

Spiritual Laws, Inflexible

> Then Peter came up and said to him, "Lord, how often shall my brother sin against me, and I forgive him? As many as seven times?" Jesus said to him, "I do not say to you seven times, but seventy times seven.
>
> "Therefore the kingdom of heaven may be compared to a king who wished to settle accounts with his servants. When he began the reckoning, one was brought to him who owed him ten thousand talents; and as he could not pay, his lord ordered him to be sold, with his wife and children and all that he had, and payment to be made. So the servant fell on his knees, imploring him, 'Lord, have patience with me, and I will pay

you everything.' And out of pity for him the lord of that servant released him and forgave him the debt. But that same servant, as he went out, came upon one of his fellow servants who owed him a hundred denarii; and seizing him by the throat he said, 'Pay what you owe.' So his fellow servant fell down and besought him, 'Have patience with me, and I will pay you.' He refused and went and put him in prison till he should pay the debt. When his fellow servants saw what had taken place, they were greatly distressed, and they went and reported to their lord all that had taken place. Then his lord summoned him and said to him, 'You wicked servant! I forgave you all that debt because you besought me; and should not you have had mercy on your fellow servant, as I had mercy on you?' And in anger his lord delivered him to the jailers, till he should pay all his debt. So also my heavenly Father will do to every one of you, if you do not forgive your brother from your heart" (18:21–35).

Peter, our spokesman, has some experience of this sort. He ignited the engine many times, yet it stopped again. "How often, Lord . . . ?" Jesus looks at him with a strange fire in his eyes. The fathomless ambiguity of this moment still trembles in Matthew's words: "seventy times seven." Repeating the same performance *ad infinitum*? Has this ever helped any transgressor? Another joke! But a bitter one. Try it, Simon; forgive the same insult seventy times seven times. The dullness of your humiliation will paralyze you or ignite your own engine so that you explode in creative fury. Then you will learn the difference between the cringing appeaser and the creative peacemaker. Forgiveness must be creative, and if it is, there is no need for repetition: if it is not, it is not forgiveness at all; it is indulgence.

Did Jesus mean the opposite of what he said? He did not; he only meant by forgiveness something different from what his disciples meant. What, then, did he mean? Instead of an answer, Matthew tells the story of the king who delivered his debtor to the "tormentors." What a king! He looks as heartless as his heartless victim. We want to learn about forgiveness and we find ourselves face to face with the wrath of God.

The story is peculiar to Matthew; and often when Matthew resorts to his own material he stresses God's inexorable judgment. Matthew has lived through the Jewish war. It is possible that he was in Jerusalem when the Romans stormed and destroyed the city in a murderous battle. He knew something about the wrath of God and the inescapable judgment of history. He can help us to face the bloody throes of modern world wars and revolutions.

God, in the parable, knows what he is doing and why. He explains it to the debtor. God's victim has a chance to learn the lesson. The king's debtor did not learn anything when the debt was cancelled, and the king did not forgive him seven times, not even twice. The king's creative urge led him the other way. He knew that this man's hardboiled egocentricity could not be melted down by softness. Love, in the form of friendliness, is misinterpreted as weakness. Love, in the form of firm determination, is misinterpreted as cruelty. But the interpretation will change. What matters is the practical result.

God's firmness can force us to forgive our enemies.

Part Five

THE NEW WAY

Introduction

The fifth part of Matthew's Gospel corresponds to the third. Both describe a journey in the outer world and at the same time an inner development. Part Three could still be understood as the straight way up to success though it was filled with warnings and failures. The new voyage is definitely the paradoxical way leading down into physical destruction and up into spiritual evolution. It is the way to Jerusalem, the center and highest value of tribal life. But Jerusalem is bound to kill her prophets and to be destroyed herself in order to make room for the future.

The goal of our inner journey is the inner Jerusalem, the kingdom of heaven. In Chapter 18 we learned that forgiveness is an indispensable prerequisite for this journey; and forgiveness in a larger and deeper sense is the theme of the following chapters.

We know already that the right kind of forgiveness does something to the forgiver as well as to the one who is forgiven. This key of the kingdom opens two doors at once, changing bitterness and regret into cheerful cooperation in two opposite places: it releases creative power within the debtor and the creditor alike. We meet the king who forgives only when we are humble and loving enough to forgive others.

Matthew's next lesson is based on the broader meaning of the Greek word for forgiving. It includes the whole scope of the English words "sending away, letting go, giving up, renouncing, setting free." It refers to claims which we renounce, to hopes or fears we give up, to possessions we let go, and to forces or restrained reactions which we set free. If we learn to start and control the processes which are indicated by this concept, the coming of the kingdom and the inner birth of the Son of man will be assured.

Chapter 19

LOSS IS GAIN

Family Ties

> Now when Jesus had finished these sayings, he went away from Galilee and entered the region of Judea beyond the Jordan; and large crowds followed him, and he healed them there.
>
> And Pharisees came up to him and tested him by asking, "Is it lawful to divorce one's wife for any cause?" He answered, "Have you not read that he who made them from the beginning made them male and female, and said, 'For this reason a man shall leave his father and mother and be joined to his wife, and the two shall become one'? So they are no longer two but one. What therefore God has joined together, let no man put asunder." They said to him, "Why then did Moses command one to give a certificate of divorce, and to put her away?" He said to them, "For your hardness of heart Moses allowed you to divorce your wives, but from the beginning it was not so. And I say to you: whoever divorces his wife, except for unchastity, and marries another, commits adultery."
>
> The disciples said to him, "If such is the case of a man with his wife, it is not expedient to marry." But he said to them, "Not all men can receive this precept, but only those to whom it is given. For there are eunuchs who have been so from birth, and there are eunuchs who have been made eunuchs by men, and there are eunuchs who have made themselves eunuchs for the sake of the kingdom of heaven. He who is able to receive this, let him receive it" (19:1–12).

We are traveling with the Master to Jerusalem. Great decisions and great sacrifices lie ahead of us. We shall have to sell all in order to buy the treasure. There will be trouble between ourselves and our families. We are bringing the sword. We have to relinquish all tribal values, including our wives (Luke 14:26). Does this mean divorce? Is celibacy better than marriage? Our questions identify us once more with the Pharisees.

Jesus' answer describes the essence of man-woman relationship: they are "one flesh" (19:5, KJV). They can and should not separate.

The civil codes, not only of the ancient Jews but of all civilized peoples, have acknowledged divorce as a legal procedure. Does our civil law contradict the laws of nature and of God? Jesus answers: Divorce is allowed because of "the hardness of your hearts" (KJV)—in modern language, because of egocentricity. Rigidity, callousness, fear, greed, and selfishness are the outstanding symptoms of our egocentricity. And even where weakness and sentiment prevail, it is always our Ego which interferes with love and marriage and family life. Moreover, our egocentric blindness makes us choose the wrong partner. Many of us are legally wedded by the Justice of the Peace and by the Church without being "one flesh." And sooner or later we may find out that we never have been "joined together" by God. Legal divorce, then, is metaphysically an annulment. What seemed to be marriage actually was a mistake from the beginning.

Jesus insists that "unchastity" is the only excuse for divorce. There is unchastity wherever there is egocentricity. Sexual intercourse between husband and wife while they are not "one flesh" is unchaste. It leads to mere self-satisfaction, dead routine, and loveless duty. The end is impotence, frigidity, or adultery. Egocentricity is the suicidal poison of all sexual relationships, inside and outside of marriage.

Marriage in tribal life was a simple and happy affair. During feudalism it became difficult. Since the beginning of individualism, it is an endless struggle between selfishness and love. The original essence of man-woman relationship, to be "one flesh," has become a remote ideal. To reach it would mean to reach the kingdom of heaven.

Our question is: How can we become "one flesh" in spite of our egocentricity? Jesus answers, "Make yourself eunuchs for the kingdom of heaven's sake" (19:12). Complete sublimation of our sexuality, pulling out the eye, cutting off the hand? We know this leads to repression, neurosis, and crime. For centuries this mistake has been made in many religions. Sinister monks, sadistic rulers, and hysterical saints are the result. Is this what Jesus means? He is the calm and well-balanced representative of a higher life. Does he recommend the mortification of the flesh in order to make man and woman "one flesh" again? We puzzle and wonder. We need long hours of meditation to solve such a riddle.

Return to Innocence

> Then children were brought to him that he might lay his hands on them and pray. The disciples rebuked the people; but

Jesus said, "Let the children come to me, and do not hinder them; for to such belongs the kingdom of heaven." And he laid his hands on them and went away (19:13–15).

The heavy silence is interrupted by the merry laughter of little children. We are always disturbed when we come to the most decisive point of our considerations. These children are disgusting. But no, "Let the children come to me, . . . for to such belongs the kingdom of heaven." We are ashamed. We are praying for an answer to our insolvable sexual problem, and we are disturbed by—the answer. The answer rushed in, chattering and clamoring, then stopped, waiting to be accepted, smiling bashfully at our frown.

We learn our lesson. Face-to-face with little children, we shall discover what purity is and what it means to be "one flesh" on the natural as well as on the spiritual level. The spiritual "We-experience" presupposes the creative power of mature manhood and womanhood, together with the carefreeness and innocence of little children.

Silence

We meditate. To be one flesh was only the beginning. To be one spirit is more. It includes the beginning and adds the freedom of two independent personalities who complete and balance each other like double stars. But they cannot do this as long as they are enslaved to egocentric desires and selfish needs (which they describe as "natural drives"). Where sexuality, together with all other functions, becomes an expression of love, no mortification is needed, no sublimation, no repression; just love.

Let us make up our minds. Let us learn to love. Let us "take the kingdom by violence." Let us ask the Master, "What good deed must I do, to have eternal life?"

Detachment from Material Values

And behold, one came up to him, saying, "Teacher, what good deed must I do, to have eternal life?" And he said to him, "Why do you ask me about what is good? One there is who is good. If you would enter life, keep the commandments." He said to him, "Which?" And Jesus said, "You shall not kill, You shall not commit adultery, You shall not steal, You shall not bear false witness, Honor your father and mother, and, You shall love your neighbor as yourself." The young man said to him, "All these I have observed; what do I still lack?" Jesus said to him, "If you would be perfect, go, sell what you possess and give to the poor, and you will have treasure in heaven; and come, follow me." When the young man heard this he went away sorrowful; for he had great possessions.

> And Jesus said to his disciples, "Truly, I say to you, it will
> be hard for a rich man to enter the kingdom of heaven. Again
> I tell you, it is easier for a camel to go through the eye of a
> needle than for a rich man to enter the kingdom of God."
> When the disciples heard this, they were greatly astonished,
> saying, "Who then can be saved?" But Jesus looked at them
> and said to them, "With men this is impossible, but with God
> all things are possible." Then Peter said in reply, "Lo, we have
> left everything and followed you. What then shall we have?"
> Jesus said to them, "Truly, I say to you, in the new world,
> when the Son of man shall sit on his glorious throne, you who
> have followed me will also sit on twelve thrones, judging the
> twelve tribes of Israel. And every one who has left houses or
> brothers or sisters or father or mother or children or lands, for
> my name's sake, will receive a hundredfold, and inherit eternal
> life. But many that are first will be last, and the last first"
> (19:16–30).

Like the young enthusiast, once more we are ready to sacrifice
everything. But we are instantly checked: "keep the commandments." The proud human progress, our pioneering in spiritual
evolution, is discouraged. We have to become good tribesmen first.
Is there no other way, no shortcut? Yes, there is a shortcut: give
up all your possessions; renounce your position and reputation.
Here again loss will be gain. Give up, relinquish, let go. Rely on
your treasure in heaven.

Jesus looks at us: This is impossible for men, but anything is
possible for God. Are we discouraged or encouraged? All depends
on our faith.

Now, it dawns on Peter. Yes, it is impossible, for men. But
it has happened already. We did give up this, and this, and that.
In spite of all our relapses and doubts, sometimes, for a moment,
we seem to be already on the other side. Can this be? Is the reward already coming? Strange things have happened to us,
guidance, protection, new and dynamic relationships, the start of
the spiritual We-experience. A minute ago we thought we were
the last; now it looks as if we were the first. Some time ago the
joyous children rushed in and brought us the answer to our most
puzzling question. This time we find the answer within ourselves.
We have outgrown insolvable problems. Our own life history is
the best evidence of the power of creation.

Chapter 20

THE LAST WILL BE FIRST

Not for Reward but for the Kingdom

"For the kingdom of heaven is like a householder who went out early in the morning to hire laborers for his vineyard. After agreeing with the laborers for a denarius a day, he sent them into his vineyard. And going out about the third hour he saw others standing idle in the market place; and to them he said, 'You go into the vineyard too, and whatever is right I will give you.' So they went. Going out again about the sixth hour and the ninth hour, he did the same. And about the eleventh hour he went out and found others standing; and he said to them, 'Why do you stand here idle all day?' They said to him, 'Because no one has hired us.' He said to them, 'You go into the vineyard too.' And when evening came, the owner of the vineyard said to his steward, 'Call the laborers and pay them their wages, beginning with the last, up to the first.' And when those hired about the eleventh hour came, each of them received a denarius. Now when the first came, they thought they would receive more; but each of them also received a denarius. And on receiving it they grumbled at the householder, saying 'These last worked only one hour, and you have made them equal to us who have borne the burden of the day and the scorching heat.' But he replied to one of them, 'Friend, I am doing you no wrong; did you not agree with me for a denarius? Take what belongs to you, and go; I choose to give to this last as I give to you. Am I not allowed to do what I choose with what belongs to me? Or do you begrudge my generosity?' So the last will be first, and the first last" (20:1–16).

Again it looks as if the coming of the kingdom were dependent upon our cooperation. Does merit entail reward as the cause entails the effect? Somehow we understand that this is not so; God is free. We cannot force Him to reward us. On the other hand, we can buy the treasure if we "sell all." The relationship between freedom and causality is puzzling.

Matthew helps us by the great parable of the workers in the vineyard. We see clearly now that our endeavor is indispensable but its "success" is a free gift from Beyond. For a moment God seems to be unfair, unjust, arbitrary. But as soon as we leave behind our egocentric claims and make the growth of the kingdom our chief concern, the injustice disappears. God takes care of His kingdom; he does justice to His creation; and suddenly we recognize the infinite difference between Him and us. We think in terms of cause and effect; more work brings more reward. He lives in categories far beyond our grasp.

He is the father who rewards his children for their little achievements, not according to their contribution but according to their needs. Our work, therefore, should not be done for the sake of the reward, or for fear of punishment; that would keep us on the level of egocentric bargainers for higher wages. We should do what we do for the sake of the kingdom. Whether we are admitted or not, the purpose of creation must be achieved. The paradox that the first shall be last and the last shall be first loses its appearance of injustice.

On the basis of our new understanding, we are immediately forced to take the next step. Jesus' parables and his actions draw closer together.

Acceptance of Loneliness

And as Jesus was going up to Jerusalem, he took the twelve disciples aside, and on the way he said to them, "Behold, we are going up to Jerusalem; and the Son of man will be delivered to the chief priests and scribes, and they will condemn him to death, and deliver him to the Gentiles to be mocked and scourged and crucified, and he will be raised on the third day."

Then the mother of the sons of Zebedee came up to him, with her sons, and kneeling before him she asked him for something. And he said to her, "What do you want?" She said to him, "Command that these two sons of mine may sit, one at your right hand and one at your left, in your kingdom." But Jesus answered, "You do not know what you are asking. Are you able to drink the cup that I am to drink?" They said to him, "We are able." He said to them, "You will drink my cup, but to sit at my right hand and at my left is not mine to grant, but it is for those for whom it has been prepared by my Father." And when the ten heard it, they were indignant at the two brothers. But Jesus called them to him and said, "You know that the rulers of the Gentiles lord it over them, and their great men exercise authority over them. It shall not be so among you; but whoever would be great among you must be your servant, and whoever would be first among you must be your slave; even as the Son of man came not to be served but to serve, and to give his life as a ransom for many."

And as they went out of Jericho, a great crowd followed him. And behold, two blind men sitting by the roadside, when they heard that Jesus was passing by, cried out, "Have mercy on

> us, Son of David!" The crowd rebuked them, telling them to
> be silent; but they cried out the more, "Lord, have mercy on us,
> Son of David!" And Jesus stopped and called them, saying,
> "What do you want me to do for you?" They said to him,
> "Lord, let our eyes be opened." And Jesus in pity touched their
> eyes, and immediately they received their sight and followed
> him (20:17–34).

The great myth of the Son of God who dies, conquers death, and rises again—the Osiris myth—is about to become history. The myth is radiant with divine power; it is the way up. History is gloomy with human anguish; it is the way down. Jesus is willing and able to realize the way up while he is proceeding on the way down; the disciples are not. Mark describes their feelings during this journey. "They were amazed, and those who followed were afraid" (Mark 10:32). Jesus knows that "it would never do for a prophet to perish except in Jerusalem" (Luke 13:33, Moffatt). We have to make our sublime sacrifice in the right place, at the right time. *We* have to force the enemy to kill us when it serves the kingdom best and when it does the greatest harm to the enemy's cause. This is the difference between the conscious and successful strategy of Jesus and the blind and useless fanaticism of John the Baptist. The two of them represent the right and the wrong kind of "violence."

Jesus, or at least Matthew when he quotes him, says, "The Son of man will be delivered to the chief priests." Why does he not say "I"? The quotation does not only refer to the outer fate of the Master, but also to the inner history of his followers. Each one of us at the time of the final test will betray his inner Son of man, his divine spark, to his inner high priests. His inner desire is for security and peace. What little light we have will disappear in the dark night of our own Golgotha. We shall be lost in bewilderment and despair. Then, when we have given up all hope, the Son will rise (20:19).

When Jesus foretold his death earlier, the disciples did not hear the prediction of his resurrection. This time they do. Our understanding of the paradox has grown. Our eyes have improved; we can almost physically see the light in the darkness. We feel that the way down is the way up. But the result of our progress is disastrous. Our way up is our way down.

Our tribal inheritance, our family pride, represented by the sons of Zebedee and their mother, come forward with an amazingly childish request. Taking for granted now that we shall participate in immortality and eternal creation, we cannot help wondering what our share in this creative work will be. Did not the Master

promise something special to his special friends? Maybe we misunderstood him. Matthew himself may have misunderstood
(19:28), but wouldn't it be natural that our better training on
earth would entitle us to a higher commission in Heaven? Our
reasoning leads to the exact opposite of the vineyard parable.

Jesus' answer reminds us of the initiation fee which we have
not yet paid. It is the breaking away from our last earthly moorings, including our dependence on our "Lord Jesus." Spiritual
individuation presupposes the abolishment of spiritual feudalism.
Jesus must leave us alone; we must desert him, that the Son of
man within each one of us may break through into individual
maturity. The highest sacrifice of love is the acceptance of loneliness. It opens the door into the new brotherhood.

The closer we come to the understanding of the kingdom, the
more we are mortified by our mistake. We are so painfully aware
of our blindness because we have already seen the first glimpses
of the light. Matthew speaks about us though he pretends to speak
about other men, two unknown beggars. He changes Mark's and
Luke's text, replacing *one* blind man by two. He did the same thing
with the madman of Gadara (8:28) because of inner reasons;
this time his motive is an outer one: James and John, the erring
disciples who suffer from their spiritual blindness, are two.

The miraculous cure shows the eagerness and the desperate
zeal of the blind sufferers in cooperation with the compassion and
patience of the helper, while the bystanders are as unsympathetic
as the ten disciples in their competition with the two. We are
reminded of Jesus' advice: "Ask, seek, knock" (7:7); and the
miracle looks less miraculous if we think of the interplay between
the stirring life within the disciples, striving for its freedom like a
chick when it breaks through the shell of the egg, and the encouraging power of the helper who knocks hard at the egg shell
from outside.

However, we are disturbed by the feudalistic expression: "O
Lord, Son of David, have pity on us!" We have to regress into
feudalism as often as we sidestep the way of individuation.

THE MISSING CHAPTER

Silence

Jesus leaves Jericho and enters Jerusalem. But there is an inner gap. At Jericho we heard of the errors and quarrels of his main disciples; at Jerusalem we witness the victorious entrance of the king into his city. The situation has changed thoroughly.

There is a Sabbath in between. Jesus entered Jerusalem on Sunday morning. He could not travel all the way from Jericho on the Sabbath; he must have left Jericho Friday, spending the Sabbath near Jerusalem, probably at Bethphage, in rest and quietude. There it was that the disciples found a new adjustment to their task. It was the silence, instead of a discourse, that helped them.

We, his would-be disciples, are in a similar situation, moved by similar questions. He is the greatest peacemaker of all times. His religion is love. But he brings the sword. He knows that his enemies will kill him, and thousands of his followers after him. He sacrifices his men by the million. But he does not fight against anybody.

He is striving for the entrance into the kingdom of heaven. He throws everything into the boldest adventure of all times: the conquest of death.

The conquest of death must be general. It is not enough that one individual enters the new plane of evolution. Jesus is the pioneer. He makes the impossible possible, proving that it can be done. But his great experiment is useless unless we follow him. We have to go the same way. We have to drink his cup. It is easier for us since he has done it before us, but it is still difficult enough. The more we see what it means, the more we share the tragic mood and the dramatic tension of this journey to Jerusalem. It is expressed in Luke's quotation: "I have come to bring fire down to the earth, and how I wish it were kindled already! I have a baptism to undergo, and how distressed I am till it is over! Do you think I have come to bring peace to the earth? Not peace, I tell you, but discord!" (Luke 12:49–51, Goodspeed).

Chapter 21

ATTACKS

We are forced to neglect the traditional division between Chapters 21 and 22 because of Matthew's structure. Chapter 21 begins with three aggressive steps on the part of Jesus. He enters the city in triumph, cleanses the temple, and curses the fig tree. Then follows the argument concerning his authority which is the center of this section. The section ends with a trilogy of parables. Each parable corresponds to one of the aggressive steps at the beginning. The story of the two sons (21:28–32) balances the cursing of the fig tree. The story of the caretakers of the vineyard (21:33–46) is the counterpart to the cleansing of the temple; and the picture of the royal wedding (22:1–14) is painted in the same colors as Jesus' entrance into Jerusalem.

The Triumphant Entry

> And when they drew near to Jerusalem and came to Bethphage, to the Mount of Olives, then Jesus sent two disciples, saying to them, "Go into the village opposite you, and immediately you will find an ass tied, and a colt with her; untie them and bring them to me. If any one says anything to you, you shall say, 'The Lord has need of them,' and he will send them immediately." This took place to fulfil what was spoken by the prophet, saying,
>
> "Tell the daughter of Zion,
> Behold, your king is coming to you,
> humble, and mounted on an ass,
> and on a colt, the foal of an ass."
>
> The disciples went and did as Jesus had directed them: they brought the ass and the colt, and put their garments on them, and he sat thereon. Most of the crowd spread their garments on the road, and others cut branches from the trees and spread them on the road. And the crowds that went before him and that followed him shouted, "Hosanna to the Son of David! Blessed be he who comes in the name of the Lord! Hosanna in the highest!" And when he entered Jerusalem, all the city was stirred, saying, "Who is this?" And the crowds said, "This is the prophet Jesus from Nazareth of Galilee" (21:1–11).

The outer drama develops with breathtaking speed. Jesus' entrance into the city shows the ambiguity of all historical events. From the standpoint of political realism, it was a ridiculous demonstration, doomed to failure. The Romans, therefore, paid no attention. The Pharisees were aware of the paradoxical implications. They remembered Zechariah's vision: "Your king comes to you . . . riding on an ass . . ." (Zech. 9:9). They felt some misgivings. The Sadducees were seriously troubled. This "king"— or fool—did not think of riots and revolutions. But he aroused the hopes of the Jewish underground. Their shouts spread like a forest fire: "Long live the son of David!"—the battle cry against Rome.

Jesus' Declaration of Independence

> And Jesus entered the temple of God and drove out all who sold and bought in the temple, and he overturned the tables of the money-changers and the seats of those who sold pigeons. He said to them, "It is written, 'My house shall be called a house of prayer'; but you make it a den of robbers."
>
> And the blind and the lame came to him in the temple, and he healed them. But when the chief priests and the scribes saw the wonderful things that he did, and the children crying out in the temple, "Hosanna to the Son of David!" they were indignant; and they said to him, "Do you hear what these are saying?" And Jesus said to them, "Yes; have you never read,
> 'Out of the mouth of babes and sucklings
> thou hast brought perfect praise'?"
>
> And leaving them, he went out of the city to Bethany and lodged there (21:12–17).

Jesus' next step surpassed all ominous forebodings. Alone, without a weapon, but with authority as if he were the High Priest, he entered the temple and "drove out all who were buying and selling" (21:12, Moffatt). This shook the Jewish mind like an earthquake. The center of the old religion was attacked.

The selling of the animals in the temple court was big business, sponsored by the Sadducees, but with a definitely nationalistic implication. Foreigners could not bring their sheep and oxen from abroad; they had to purchase them in Judea, paying with Jewish coins, if they wanted them to be acceptable sacrifices. Thus, the superiority of the Jewish way of life was established once and forever. The temple commerce was an integral part of the national religion.

This was Jesus' "declaration of independence"—the independence of religion from political, national, legalistic, and economic ties. It was bound to provoke repercussions all over the world. He wanted the temple to be "a house of prayer for all the nations"[1] (Mark 11:17).

Grow or Perish!

> In the morning, as he was returning to the city, he was hungry. And seeing a fig tree by the wayside he went to it, and found nothing on it but leaves only. And he said to it, "May no fruit ever come from you again!" And the fig tree withered at once. When the disciples saw it they marveled, saying, "How did the fig tree wither at once?" And Jesus answered them, "Truly, I say to you, if you have faith and never doubt, you will not only do what has been done to the fig tree, but even if you say to this mountain, 'Be taken up and cast into the sea,' it will be done. And whatever you ask in prayer, you will receive, if you have faith" (21:18–22).

Jesus' third step was the worst of all. He cursed the fig tree which, according to Mark (11:13), could not yet be expected to bear fruit. As part of the outer drama, this is a petty misuse of miraculous power, but it helps us find the transition from the outer to the inner meaning of Matthew's report. Jesus found the expression, "the den of robbers" in Jeremiah's great "Temple Sermon" (Jer. 7:11). Jeremiah continues, speaking about those who do not find the Lord: "There shall be no grapes on the vine, nor figs on the fig tree, and the leaf shall fade" (Jer. 8:13, KJV). Jesus developed this figure of speech into a parable (Luke 13:6–9). The story of the cursed fig tree must have been another version of the same parable. We know already that we are the trees; we have to bear fruit or we shall be cut down (3:10); and by our fruits we shall be known (7:15–20). Here begins our understanding of the inner drama. Each one of us is the fig tree. We thought we had much time to develop our fruits, but that is not true. Suddenly we are asked to "bear fruit." But we are barren. It is a terrible moment of darkness. The presence of the Son of man makes our deficiencies evident.

The Son of man ignores our darkness. Then he speaks of our responsibility for others. In spite of our barrenness, we still carry the keys of the kingdom. "All that you ask in prayer you shall have," including leaves, blossoms, and fruits.

This climax of the inner drama follows after two acts of growing tension. The Son of man enters our inner city. We are the

---

1. This feature is blurred by Matthew's Judaic tendencies. He omits the words "for all nations," depriving his Gospel of one of the most important aspects of Christianity.

disciples who rejoice in his coming, but we are also the Pharisees and Sadducees who resent it. This is our old inner conflict: do we want him or are we afraid of him? Then something new happens: he arouses the multitudes; the national underground comes to the surface. Long repressed unconscious powers are stirred up. Primitive undifferentiated urges and drives rise into consciousness.

He enters the temple, the very center of our inner structure. Our "religious commerce," our habitual activities, are interrupted. The spiritual revolution begins. We can foresee that no stone of our inner structure will remain unturned. The new life emerges; utmost creativeness is required; we have to "bring forth fruit" immediately, or we shall perish. But we are not prepared. We are barren fig trees.

What Is Jesus' Authority?

> And when he entered the temple, the chief priests and the elders of the people came up to him as he was teaching, and said, "By what authority are you doing these things, and who gave you this authority?" Jesus answered them, "I also will ask you a question; and if you tell me the answer, then I also will tell you by what authority I do these things. The baptism of John, whence was it? From heaven or from men?" And they argued with one another, "If we say, 'From heaven,' he will say to us, 'Why then did you not believe him?' But if we say, 'From men,' we are afraid of the multitude; for all hold that John was a prophet." So they answered Jesus, "We do not know." And he said to them, "Neither will I tell you by what authority I do these things" (21:23–27).

The high priests had a right to ask for Jesus' credentials. They were responsible for what was taught in the temple. Jesus, like a good academician, names his teacher; but he adds his own question, "Where did John's baptism come from?" The high priests wanted to judge him, but they were forced to judge themselves. They wanted an answer, but they got a question, and this question they could not answer. Their counterattack was repelled.

The question of the high priests is our question. We feel doubtful when the Son of man appears within us. Who is he? Where does his power come from? What is his authority? Instead of an answer, we get a question. What was the power and authority of the spiritual leaders of the past? Did we believe in them or not? We cannot deny the values of tribal and feudal culture. We have outgrown them, but they still are valid. What is the basis of all these values, old and new, past and future? We have to find the answer within ourselves. We have to make the decision.

If we accept the Son of man, his credentials are clear. If we reject him, unanswered questions will torture us until we die.

The trilogy of Jesus' aggressive steps has awakened the dormant powers of our unlived life. We are confronted with the final question of humanity. Do we believe in the past or in the future or in neither one? The trilogy of parables following helps us to clarify our inner turmoil. The chaotic powers of our spiritual revolution will be channeled and clarified by a new system of values.

We think we are good, or at least we try to do what is right, but we do not do it. Paul was aware of this inner conflict between our conscious and our unconscious mind: "I do not do the good I want, but the evil I do not want is what I do" (Rom. 7:19). Our half-conscious tendencies which we disown may turn out to be more creative than our conscious decisions. We say "Yes" and do "No." They say "No" and do "Yes." We are barren fig trees, not because of a genuine lack of creative power, but because of our inner conflict. Two horses try to pull our wagon into opposite directions. They nullify each other. If we reconcile the opposite tendencies, their sum total will astonish us and the world.

Three Parables Mirror Our Inner Opposition

"What do you think? A man had two sons; and he went to the first and said, 'Son, go and work in the vineyard today.' And he answered, 'I will not'; but afterward he repented and went. And he went to the second and said the same; and he answered, 'I go, sir,' but did not go. Which of the two did the will of his father?" They said, "The first." Jesus said to them, "Truly, I say to you, the tax collectors and the harlots go into the kingdom of God before you. For John came to you in the way of righteousness, and you did not believe him, but the tax collectors and the harlots believed him; and even when you saw it, you did not afterward repent and believe him.

"Hear another parable. There was a householder who planted a vineyard, and set a hedge around it, and dug a wine press in it, and built a tower, and let it out to tenants, and went into another country. When the season of fruit drew near, he sent his servants to the tenants, to get his fruit; and the tenants took his servants and beat one, killed another, and stoned another. Again he sent other servants, more than the first; and they did the same to them. Afterward he sent his son to them, saying, 'They will respect my son.' But when the tenants saw the son, they said to themselves, 'This is the heir; come, let us kill him and have his inheritance.' And they took him and cast him out of the vineyard, and killed him. When therefore the owner of the vineyard comes, what will he do to those tenants?" They said to him, "He will put those wretches to a

miserable death, and let out the vineyard to other tenants who will give him the fruits in their seasons."
Jesus said to them, "Have you never read in the scriptures:
'The very stone which the builders rejected
has become the head of the corner;
this was the Lord's doing,
and it is marvelous in our eyes'?
Therefore I tell you, the kingdom of God will be taken away from you and given to a nation producing the fruits of it."
When the chief priests and the Pharisees heard his parables, they perceived that he was speaking about them. But when they tried to arrest him, they feared the multitudes, because they held him to be a prophet.
And again Jesus spoke to them in parables, saying, "The kingdom of heaven may be compared to a king who gave a marriage feast for his son, and sent his servants to call those who were invited to the marriage feast; but they would not come. Again he sent other servants, saying, 'Tell those who are invited, Behold, I have made ready my dinner, my oxen and my fat calves are killed, and everything is ready; come to the marriage feast.' But they made light of it and went off, one to his farm, another to his business, while the rest seized his servants, treated them shamefully, and killed them. The king was angry, and he sent his troops and destroyed those murderers and burned their city. Then he said to his servants, 'The wedding is ready, but those invited were not worthy. Go therefore to the thoroughfares, and invite to the marriage feast as many as you find.' And those servants went out into the streets and gathered all whom they found, both bad and good; so the wedding hall was filled with guests.
"But when the king came in to look at the guests, he saw there a man who had no wedding garment; and he said to him, 'Friend, how did you get in here without a wedding garment?' And he was speechless. Then the king said to the attendants, 'Bind him hand and foot, and cast him into the outer darkness; there men will weep and gnash their teeth.' For many are called, but few are chosen" (21:28–46; 22:1–14)

We need an eye-opener, a mirror, a tool which helps us or forces us to recognize and reconcile our inner opposites. The unconscious tendencies therefore must come to light. They must manifest themselves in all their destructiveness. Darkness must be challenged by the Light. Its resistance must be provoked. Error will beget error, light engender light. When the showdown comes, we may mistake the light for darkness and the approach of the Son of man for a curse. We will murder him in order to keep the vineyard which does not belong to us.

In spite of all our resistance, we are invited to the wedding feast. All our deviations will be forgotten and forgiven if we don the wedding garment. But we shun the invitation.

Our resistance becomes distrust. We are still in the attitude of the tenants who rented the vineyard and behaved as if they were the owners. In our egocentric enterprises we know what we have: farms, merchandise, and as Luke puts it, oxen and wives (Luke 14:19, 20). Regarding the invitation of the king, we are not so sure. He has the reputation of being very particular about his guests. Like all the ancient chieftains he will give us wedding garments and jewels when we come to his feast. The poorest of us can dress like a king. But we are afraid that by accepting his gifts, we may lose our independence. We prefer to remain as we are in spite of all our deficiencies and unsolved problems. We do not understand, in our egocentric blindness, that at the king's table the complete freedom of self-responsible individuals coincides with complete cooperation in creative teamwork. From the egocentric point of view, we cannot understand the meaning of individuation and integration.

However, the spiritual We-experience, the wedding banquet, is the very purpose of creation. We are not only the guests, we are the former stewards and future co-creators. We have been the adolescent boys who did not want to cooperate with their father (21:28). We shall be the adult sons who share the father's glory (22:3). But if we prefer egocentricity to individuation, refusing the royal wedding gowns, we shall be cast into "the outer darkness" where there is weeping and gnashing of teeth (22:13).

The Son of man comes to visit us: that is Jesus' entrance into Jerusalem. We are invited to his wedding feast: that is our entrance into the kingdom of heaven. The closer we come to the new phase of spiritual evolution, the more dangerous it is to reject the Son of man.

Chapter 22

COUNTERATTACK

What Is God's—What Caesar's?

> Then the Pharisees went and took counsel how to entangle him in his talk. And they sent their disciples to him, along with the Herodians, saying, "Teacher, we know that you are true, and teach the way of God truthfully, and care for no man; for you do not regard the position of men. Tell us, then, what you think. Is it lawful to pay taxes to Caesar, or not?" But Jesus, aware of their malice, said, "Why put me to the test, you hypocrites? Show me the money for the tax." And they brought him a coin. And Jesus said to them, "Whose likeness and inscription is this?" They said, "Caesar's." Then he said to them, "Render therefore to Caesar the things that are Caesar's, and to God the things that are God's." When they heard it, they marveled; and they left him and went away (22:15–22).

Jesus' aggressiveness provokes the total mobilization of his enemies. The Pharisees are determined to destroy him. They invent an excellent trap. If Jesus recommends paying tribute, he renounces his messiahship; if he decides against it, the Romans arrest him. But Jesus' answer traps the trappers. Since God and the emperor are not equals, we must give to the latter only what he deserves in the sight of the former.

The Pharisees' question, of course, is our question. We ask just as reverently and perfidiously as they. They wanted to annihilate Jesus' influence. We want to preserve the influence of old-fashioned patterns and habits. They and we are equally reactionary.

Jesus' answer turns out to be not an answer but a question. "What is God's?" Is not everything God's? We are forced to make decisions well beyond our capacities. Jesus helps us by not helping us. He forces us to take steps, to be independent, judging between the emperor and God.

Not only the answers of ancient oracles, but also the answers to modern prayers, the call of the "guiding voice" and the lack of answers and the silence of the "voice," with few exceptions, serve the goal of making us independent. We are only told in a general way and often in a puzzling form what we should or should not do. Then, we have to think and interpret and decide ourselves. If we receive detailed instructions, we are still in grammar school. There, the subject is "obedience." In God's High School obedience is replaced by cooperation, and in His College we are forced to create independently, and we create disaster because we have learned only obedience, and prefer disobedience, like rebellious little boys. The first counterattack has failed.

Is There Marriage in Heaven?

> The same day Sadducees came to him, who say that there is no resurrection; and they asked him a question, saying, "Teacher, Moses said, 'If a man dies, having no children, his brother must marry the widow, and raise up children for his brother.' Now there were seven brothers among us; the first married, and died, and having no children left his wife to his brother. So too the second and third, down to the seventh. After them all, the woman died. In the resurrection, therefore, to which of the seven will she be wife? For they all had her."
>
> But Jesus answered them, "You are wrong, because you know neither the scriptures nor the power of God. For in the resurrection they neither marry nor are given in marriage, but are like angels in heaven. And as for the resurrection of the dead, have you not read what was said to you by God, 'I am the God of Abraham, and the God of Isaac, and the God of Jacob'? He is not God of the dead, but of the living." And when the crowd heard it, they were astonished at his teaching (22:23–33).

Jesus' attacks were actually an invitation to come to God's wedding banquet, the We-experience beyond space and time. But we, together with the Sadducees, are reluctant. We want more information about that mysterious "Beyond." The strongest tie which connects us with eternity is the death of a truly beloved husband or wife. What about monogamy in heaven?

The Sadducees' case is stronger than they know. It raises not only the question of immortality, but also that of tribal life and individualism. Moses' law about the forcible marriage of brother and sister-in-law (Deut. 25:5), was a logical result of tribal consciousness. It is abolished by individualism. If there is immortality, shall we live beyond space and time in tribal or in individual consciousness?

Jesus' answer is amazingly simple. Beyond space and time there is no death and therefore no marriage, no procreation; they are "like angels." But Jesus does not say that the angels are neuters. Paul speaks of "sons and daughters" of God (2 Cor. 6:18). We begin to understand: the angels and the humans who have entered the kingdom seem to live like eunuchs without procreation; but not without the creative tension between masculinity and femininity: "God created them male and female."

The reinterpretation of "the God of Abraham" as God, not "of the dead, but of the living" sounds arbitrary at first. Soon, however, we discover its depth. If God were our God, we would be His; we would share His nature. Luke follows this idea through: "They are equal to angels and are sons of God, being sons of the resurrection" (Luke 20:36).

The Two Great Commandments

> But when the Pharisees heard that he had silenced the Sadducees, they came together. And one of them, a lawyer, asked him a question, to test him. "Teacher, which is the great commandment in the law?" And he said to him, "You shall love the Lord your God with all your heart, and with all your soul, and with all your mind. This is the great and first commandment. And the second is like it, You shall love your neighbor as yourself. On these two commandments depend all the law and the prophets" (22:34–40).

The second wave of our counterattack subsides. We are more interested now than hostile. In effect, Jesus told us that we can experiment with eternity, making the God of the patriarchs our own God. And we feel tempted to do so. The third wave of our counterattack looks like a peace-feeler: Which is the greatest commandment?

Regarding our present situation, it is the question how far "eternity" means "other worldliness." Are we bound to forget our neighbors, worshiping a transcendent God and laboring for the progress of our own private little soul? Or: how can we find eternity, immortality, the admission to the wedding banquet, while taking care of our earthly duties, farms, oxen, and wives? Was not just this the mistake of the wedding guests?

Again we tried to embarrass him with our question, and we are more embarrassed by his answer than we ever have been. In the awkward silence that follows we remember: he said "love" God and "love" your neighbor. Earlier he said, speaking of the Son of man: What you do to one of these little ones you do to me (18:5; 10:40). Loving the immanent Son of man within our neighbors (even if this Son of man is there only as a vague potentiality) seems to be identical with loving the transcendent God who created those neighbors. If the two commandments, being opposite in theory, turn out to be one in practical life, this would solve all our questions about the law and the prophets. Once more we are caught by the intriguing invitation: Try! The problem can be solved by experiment! Our counteroffensive is forgotten. We surrender, joining the army of creation.

"What Do You Think of the Christ?"

> Now while the Pharisees were gathered together, Jesus asked them a question, saying, "What do you think of the Christ? Whose son is he?" They said to him, "The son of David." He said to them, "How is it then that David, inspired by the Spirit, calls him Lord, saying,
> > 'The Lord said to my Lord,
> > Sit at my right hand,
> > till I put thy enemies under thy feet'?
> If David thus calls him Lord, how is he his son?" And no one was able to answer him a word, nor from that day did any one dare to ask him any more questions (22:41–46).

For the time being we are convinced. He has won the battle; we are his. But he asks us: "What do you think of the Christ?" (22:42).

A moment ago we felt like settling down with our feudalistic conviction that he is the Lord, and that he knows best. We must not argue with him. Now he forces us to do just this. We have to think independently, to study, and to decide. Feudalism is not permissible for more than a short minute of regression and rest. Then we are called upon to grow, take steps, and become of age.

Can Christ be understood in terms of tribal consciousness, as somebody's son? Is Christ a synonym for Jesus? Or is it a title which other people can acquire also? Or is it the same inner reality, a stage of spiritual evolution, which we tried to understand as "the Son of man"? Where can we find more information?

DEPTH CHARGES

Introduction

At first sight Chapter 23 appears as a part of a long discourse or collection of discourses (23–25) which corresponds to the Sermon on the Mount. Closer investigation, however, shows Matthew's characteristic closing phrase, "Jesus left," at the beginning of Chapter 24. The Sermon on the Mount of Olives, the sixth part of the Gospel, comprises only two chapters (24 and 25). Chapter 23 is the conclusion of the fifth part of the Gospel.

In one respect, however, this chapter corresponds to the beginning of the Sermon on the Mount. The seven Beatitudes find their counterpart in the seven Woes (23:13–19). An eighth Woe has been inserted later (23:14, RSV footnote).

If Chapter 23 belongs to the fifth part of the Gospel, it must be related to the problem of forgiveness. The seven Woes, then, cannot be accusations or curses; they must be meant as the necessary, though extremely painful, phases of a surgical operation. It takes all the knowledge of modern depth psychology to appreciate the masterly skill of the surgeon, and it takes the experience of a good counselor to understand that the seven Woes are seven phases of forgiveness. Criticism is helpful only if it originates in love. Its outer expression, then, can well be "Woe, thou hypocrite . . . ." As soon as we identify ourselves with the accused Pharisees, we shall feel that Jesus does not condemn us. He puts his finger on our sorest spots like a diagnosing physician: "Look here how bad this is, pus and decay; it will destroy you unless we remove it immediately."

Egocentricity

> Then said Jesus to the crowds and to his disciples, "The scribes and the Pharisees sit on Moses' seat; so practice and observe whatever they tell you, but not what they do; for they preach, but do not practice. They bind heavy burdens, hard to bear, and lay them on men's shoulders; but they themselves

will not move them with their finger. They do all their deeds
to be seen by men; for they make their phylacteries broad and
their fringes long, and they love the place of honor at feasts
and the best seats in the synagogues, and salutations in the
market places, and being called rabbi by men. But you are not
to be called rabbi, for you have one teacher, and you are all
brethren. And call no man your father on earth, for you have
one Father, who is in heaven. Neither be called masters, for
you have one master, the Christ. He who is greatest among
you shall be your servant; whoever exalts himself will be hum-
bled, and whoever humbles himself will be exalted" (23:1–12).

Jesus tells us how wrong the spiritual leaders are. The patriar-
chal era, with its healthy hierarchy, is over. All outer authority
nowadays separates us from our vital roots. What remains is
egocentricity.

We say "Yes" and do "No" like the "good" son in the parable.
We may be aware of our inner split but we cannot help it (Rom.
7:14–25). Therefore, we compensate our feeling of inferiority
and insecurity by outer successes. Social standing, good reputation, and flawless observance of all formalities give us at least an
outer appearance of dignity. We may finally even deceive ourselves, mistaking our social mask for our real being.

The era of individuation requires a new kind of leadership.
Democracy and hierarchy exclude each other. No earthly authority is recognized except the inner authority of "the Christ." The
father image, the symbol of power, must not be projected on any
human being. We are all brothers.

We understand this; we learned it already in the child sermon
(18:1–10). But why is it so difficult for us to achieve real
democracy? What can we do to replace our egocentric striving for
superiority by the creative authority of the Beyond Within? The
answer to this question and the fulfillment of this desire is a painful surgical operation, a very masterpiece of depth psychology.

The Seven Woes

"But woe to you, scribes and Pharisees, hypocrites! because
you shut the kingdom of heaven against men; for you neither
enter yourselves, nor allow those who would enter to go in.
Woe to you, scribes and Pharisees, hypocrites! for you traverse
sea and land to make a single proselyte, and when he becomes
a proselyte, you make him twice as much a child of hell as
yourselves.

"Woe to you, blind guides, who say, 'If any one swears by
the temple, it is nothing; but if any one swears by the gold
of the temple, he is bound by his oath.' You blind fools! For
which is greater, the gold or the temple that has made the gold
sacred? And you say, 'If any one swears by the altar, it is

nothing; but if any one swears by the gift that is on the altar, he is bound by his oath.' You blind men! For which is greater, the gift or the altar that makes the gift sacred? So he who swears by the altar, swears by it and by everything on it; and he who swears by the temple, swears by it and by him who dwells in it; and he who swears by heaven, swears by the throne of God and by him who sits upon it.

"Woe to you, scribes and Pharisees, hypocrites! for you tithe mint and dill and cummin, and have neglected the weightier matters of the law, justice and mercy and faith; these you ought to have done, without neglecting the others. You blind guides, straining out a gnat and swallowing a camel!

"Woe to you, scribes and Pharisees, hypocrites! for you cleanse the outside of the cup and of the plate, but inside they are full of extortion and rapacity. You blind Pharisee! first cleanse the inside of the cup and of the plate, that the outside also may be clean.

"Woe to you, scribes and Pharisees, hypocrites! for you are like whitewashed tombs, which outwardly appear beautiful, but within they are full of dead men's bones and all uncleanness. So you also outwardly appear righteous to men, but within you are full of hypocrisy and iniquity.

"Woe to you, scribes and Pharisees, hypocrites! for you build the tombs of the prophets and adorn the monuments of the righteous, saying, 'If we had lived in the days of our fathers, we would not have taken part with them in shedding the blood of the prophets.' Thus you witness against yourselves, that you are sons of those who murdered the prophets. Fill up, then, the measure of your fathers. You serpents, you brood of vipers, how are you to escape being sentenced to hell?" (23:13–33).

We are leaders. Whether we write books, teach Sunday school, or simply admonish our own children at home, we are responsible for the next generation. We should be able and willing to handle the keys of the kingdom. But being egocentric, we cannot help teaching egocentricity by action, though our words may be idealistic. That makes us hypocrites. Our words are pious but our influence on our fellowmen is injurious. Our good intentions do not excuse us; they make the result more disastrous.

This accusation is not limited to exceptional cases. It describes exactly the average person of our time. The more we understand the subtle poison of our unconscious Shadow, the more we discover that parental love and educational conscientiousness are thoroughly contaminated by egocentricity, fear, greed, and unbelief.

Nevertheless, our self-righteousness prompts us to give advice and teach and preach all day long. We send missionaries or go on missions, and present our contaminated message as the pure truth. People believe us, follow our leadership, and are excluded from the kingdom by our misuse of the keys.

The part and the whole. Verse 19 is the center of Chapter 23: "For which is greater, the gift or the altar that makes the gift sacred?" To modern ears it sounds like a meaningless rabbinic argument. To Matthew's students it may still have been an interesting issue. To the Pharisees it was a question of utmost importance. We have to grasp its principle before we can apply it to ourselves. But if we grasp it, it will prove as important to us as it was to the Pharisees.

What are we looking for? What is our highest value? The whole or the part? Mankind or a single nation? The nation or a single family? The family or a single person? The person or a single action? If we could see all things in their real perspective, we could immediately enter into the kingdom. In modern language: our whole thinking has become analytical instead of synthetic. Actually, the whole is prior to the part, the Creator is there before creation.

Our analytical thinking always leads from the spiritual aspect to the material aspect of reality (23:23). We lose sight of "judgment" (the inner crisis of our evolution), "mercy" (the We-experience on the spiritual as well as on the tribal level), and "faith" (the realization that the Creator is prior to all creatures).

Again the question arises, what can we do? The diagnosis of the disease does not yet help the sick. Matthew answers: "You try to clean only the outside of the cup; you whitewash the tomb. Your egocentric mask is beyond reproach. But inside yourself your unconscious tendencies, the unconscious part of your egocentricity, as well as the unconscious passions of your unlived life, are degenerating and decaying like corpses" (23:25–28).

We have to find and to redeem the Shadow side of our own case history. But how can we do it? For centuries religious people have searched their consciences, but they did not get rid of the "dead men's bones."

Again the diagnosis proceeds and indicates the spot where the exploration of the unconscious can evolve into constructive self-education. This point is our relationship to the past.

Our egocentricity separates us from the past and the future alike. We exploit our fellowmen or work for them in order to be praised, but we do not feel responsible for their actions. Yet we know our egocentricity is the result of the egocentricity of the previous generation. In order not to condemn ourselves, we have to condemn our ancestors. They were bad. They killed the prophets of the future. They cut themselves off from the past and invented the egocentric masks which they bequeathed to us. They are guilty of our guilt. The present is conditioned by the past.

This is not true, of course. It is a typical egocentric attempt to escape responsibility. Actually, we share their guilt as well as they share ours. We could have freed ourselves already of some parts of our bad inheritance. We have developed all kinds of wonderful theories of redemption, but we have not applied them to ourselves. We killed the prophets of the future as efficiently as our ancestors did. And we try our best to frustrate Matthew's surgery by identifying ourselves with the surgeon rather than with the patient (23:32).

Collective Guilt

"Therefore I send you prophets and wise men and scribes, some of whom you will kill and crucify, and some you will scourge in your synagogues and persecute from town to town, that upon you may come all the righteous blood shed on earth, from the blood of innocent Abel to the blood of Zechariah the son of Barachiah, whom you murdered between the sanctuary and the altar. Truly, I say to you, all this will come upon this generation.

"O Jerusalem, Jerusalem, killing the prophets and stoning those who are sent to you! How often would I have gathered your children together as a hen gathers her brood under her wings, and you would not! Behold, your house is forsaken and desolate. For I tell you, you will not see me again, until you say, 'Blessed be he who comes in the name of the Lord'" (23:34–39).

Our guilt is collective, but each individual has to accept it for himself. Each one has to pay his own debt, and, by doing so, he decreases the ancestral debt of mankind.

Each one of us is confronted with a final decision. The light is coming into the darkness; the prophet, the Son of man, the judge, is about to appear. If we accept him, our Ego must die. If our Ego wants to survive, we have to kill the prophet, the Son of man, and the judge.

Our exploration of the unconscious leads us back to the starting point. The debt is larger than we thought it was. The danger is more frightening; the decision, more urgent. But we have to decide consciously whether we want to enter the narrow gate or to drift through the wide gate into annihilation. So far our unconscious has swayed us clandestinely, and our egocentricity has controlled us openly. Now we are cornered. We have to reach a new decision against our Ego and against our unconscious. This decision, if we make it, is the first appearance of our true Self.

Each generation is the first one to be confronted with this final decision (23:36). Eternity knocks at the doors of time continually. If we open the door, the kingdom comes. If we keep it shut, the moment passes and another prophet is killed.

In this final decision, the difference between the individual and the collective disappears. Jerusalem (23:37) is the center of the nation as well as of the individual. Within each person the race comes to consciousness if the individual accepts the responsibility for the national debt. And within each individual the whole race can be redeemed if the individual pays his own debt.

The longer we postpone our individual crisis and escape the throes of our individual evolution, the more debts we accumulate for ourselves as well as for the race. Finally, the debts will be collected; and, since we are unable to pay, our house will be left "desolate"—but in the midst of the great tribulation the Son of man will appear.

Part Six
THE NEW CHART

The Mutation of Mankind Foretold

The "Sermon on the Mount of Olives" comprises Chapters 24 and 25. It is shorter, less elaborate in its structure, but not less important than its counterpart in the first half of the Gospel. The Sermon on the Mount prepares us for our spiritual growing pains and crises. It is the call to colors for volunteers who want to enlist for a daring expedition. The Sermon on the Mount of Olives is an emergency call. The last men are summoned, and the outline of our strategy, the "chart" of the great mutation of mankind, is foretold.

Some commentators have discarded these "eschatological horrors" as a merely Jewish experience or an outmoded superstition. Modern psychology, however, with its emphasis on personal crises as integral parts of human evolution, and modern history with air raids and poison gas and starvation, give them the lie. The "great tribulations" are the birth pangs of the new world. They began when Jesus was crucified and they have not reached their climax.

The first half of the discourse describes the tribulations (24: 1–41). The second half stresses our need for preparedness (24: 42–25:46). Here again the end of the chapter does not coincide with the division between the two halves.

Chapter 24

GREAT TRIBULATIONS

The False Christs

Jesus left the temple and was going away, when his disciples came to point out to him the buildings of the temple. But he answered them, "You see all these, do you not? Truly, I say to you, there will not be left here one stone upon another, that will not be thrown down."

As he sat on the Mount of Olives, the disciples came to him privately, saying, "Tell us, when will this be, and what will be the sign of your coming and of the close of the age?" And Jesus answered them, "Take heed that no one leads you astray. For many will come in my name, saying, 'I am the Christ,' and they will lead many astray. And you will hear of wars and rumors of wars; see that you are not alarmed; for this must take place, but the end is not yet. For nation will rise against nation, and kingdom against kingdom, and there will be famines and earthquakes in various places: all this is but the beginning of the sufferings.

"Then they will deliver you up to tribulation, and put you to death; and you will be hated by all nations for my name's sake. And then many will fall away, and betray one another, and hate one another. And many false prophets will arise and lead many astray. And because wickedness is multiplied, most men's love will grow cold. But he who endures to the end will be saved. And this gospel of the kingdom will be preached throughout the whole world, as a testimony to all nations; and then the end will come.

"So when you see the desolating sacrilege spoken of by the prophet Daniel, standing in the holy place (let the reader understand), then let those who are in Judea flee to the mountains; let him who is on the housetop not go down to take what is in his house; and let him who is in the field not turn back to take his mantle. And alas for those who are with child and for those who give suck in those days! Pray that your flight may not be in winter or on a sabbath. For then there will be great tribulation, such as has not been from the beginning of the world until now, no, and never will be. And if those days had not been shortened, no human would be saved; but for the sake of the elect those days will be shortened. Then if any one says to you, 'Lo, here is the Christ!' or 'There he is!' do not

believe it. For false Christs and false prophets will arise and
show great signs and wonders, so as to lead astray, if possible,
even the elect. Lo, I have told you beforehand. So, if they say
to you, 'Lo, he is in the wilderness,' do not go out; if they say,
'Lo, he is in the inner rooms,' do not believe it" (24:1–26).

Matthew's description of "the last things" is usually understood
as a forecast of the destruction of Jerusalem (A.D. 70). Luke's
parallel passage (Luke 21:20–24) has details which suggest that
eyewitnesses of the event have inserted them. Did Jesus prophesy
beforehand, or did the disciples write history afterwards?

It was not difficult to foresee the war between the Romans and
the Jews, nor was its outcome in doubt. Had Jesus' prophecy been
limited to the events of the years 70–71, it could hardly arouse
our interest. But what he described and what none of his disciples
could foresee then, or could have discerned later without his help,
was the inner crisis as it takes place within each one of us and
will take place as long as human beings are struggling for
maturity.

Jerusalem as the religious center will disappear, in the outer
world among the nations, and in our inner world among the
images—or idols—which we adore. The old visible center, the
temple, must be replaced by the new invisible center, the Christ.
But who is Christ? We do not yet know him.

Our uncertainty during the years of research and preparation,
after the loss of our former feudalistic security, makes us prone
to accept wrong Christs, wrong doctrines about Jesus, and wrong
hopes for a Messiah. The new prophet may pretend to be the son
of God or the leader of the master race, the bringer of culture, or
the bringer of the classless society. He may come in the name of
love or hatred. There will be many of them and they will destroy
each other. "By their fruits we shall know them."

In the service of the false Christs, nation will rise against
nation, race against race, and class against class; perhaps even
one sex against the other, "and there shall be famines, and
pestilences, and earthquakes" (24:7, KJV). Collective deviations
engender collective catastrophes. The goal of evolution, however,
is individuation. An outer crisis can bring the individuation of its
victims only if they are prepared for their private inner crises so
that the outer events are paralleled by inner developments of a
similar form.

Egocentricity, fear, greed, cruelty, and disintegration will grow
all over the world and within ourselves (24:12). But the gospel
will be spread (24:14), presumably by actions rather than by

words. It will grow in the outer world and within us. Light and darkness arrayed against each other will bring the last crises and the final decision.

The "end," however, is not the end of the world; on the contrary, it is the beginning of our real life. (The Greek word means "goal," "highest value," as well as "finish.") He who outlives the war will enjoy the peace.

Jesus' forecast holds good for all besieged cities, Jerusalem as well as Stalingrad. But the decisive point is that it holds good also for the besieged center within all the individuals, whether they live outwardly in war or peace. The sanctuary of our feudalistic past will be desecrated by "the appalling Horror" (24:15, Moffatt), the "abomination of desolation" (KJV). We should not try to save our old possessions (24:16–17).

Those, of course, who carry the future, the women with child, will be in an especially difficult situation. They need protection, but they are losing the protection of the past without yet finding it in the future. All the false little prophets therefore will have a field day. "Practice introversion," they will say, "he is in the inmost chamber!" "Back to nature!" others will cry, "he is in the wilderness" (24:26). But all of them will fail.

The Son of Man

> "For as the lightning comes from the east and shines as far as the west, so will be the coming of the Son of man. Wherever the body is, there the eagles will be gathered together" (24: 27–28).

The last word which any poet or prophet can say about the coming of Christ is formulated in Matthew's dual statement about the lightning and the carcass. The event is described twice, from inside and from outside.

The drama of mutation reaches its inner climax when the heavens are torn asunder and the power of the Spirit, like lightning, flashes from east to west. At Jesus' baptism and again at his transfiguration, the blinding light from Beyond had appeared. But the disciples had seen it as something that happened to their master rather than to themselves. Now their, and our own, experience is foretold. To us this will be like the end of the world. Struck by lightning, we shall see the light, but we shall not be able to stand it. (Thus it happened to Paul, Acts 9:34.)

Is this all we can know in advance about the most decisive moment of human life? Where, when, how will it happen? The disciples question Jesus. We question Matthew. What else can be

told? The answer is the gap of silence (between 24:27 and 28).
We shut our eyes, trying to be ready for the Light. The lightning
may strike any moment. What do we see, with closed eyes? The
vultures circling around a carcass. This is the outer aspect of the
climax: someone has died. Instead of the dove (3:16), we see
vultures.

Seen from inside: the Son of man. Seen from outside: a corpse.
Wherever it happens, at Jerusalem, or in the most luxurious
hospital of New York, the way down can be the way up; our death
can be the beginning of our life. However, the lightning of the
new life can also strike us while we are looking at the body of
someone else. If we can look at our brother's or sister's remains
as if it were our own body, we may undergo the transformation
from death to life "without tasting death." The crucifix, the
symbol of death, then changes into the symbol of new creation.
Physical destruction and spiritual growth merge into oneness, the
contrast of darkness and light disappears, and "old things are
passed away; behold, all things are become new" (2 Cor. 5:17,
KJV).

The Growing Pains of the Human Spirit

"Immediately after the tribulation of those days the sun
will be darkened, and the moon will not give its light, and the
stars will fall from heaven, and the powers of the heavens will
be shaken; then will appear the sign of the Son of man in
heaven, and then all the tribes of the earth will mourn, and
they will see the Son of man coming on the clouds of heaven
with power and great glory; and he will send out his angels
with a loud trumpet call, and they will gather his elect from
the four winds, from one end of heaven to the other.

"From the fig tree learn its lesson: as soon as its branch
becomes tender and puts forth its leaves, you know that summer is near. So also, when you see all these things, you know
that he is near, at the very gates. Truly, I say to you, this
generation will not pass away till all these things take place.
Heaven and earth will pass away, but my words will not pass
away.

"But of that day and hour no one knows, not even the
angels of heaven, nor the Son, but the Father only. As were
the days of Noah, so will be the coming of the Son of man.
For as in those days before the flood they were eating and
drinking, marrying and giving in marriage, until the day when
Noah entered the ark, and they did not know until the flood
came and swept them all away, so will be the coming of the
Son of man. Then two men will be in the field; one is taken
and one is left. Two women will be grinding at the mill; one
is taken and one is left. Watch therefore, for you do not know
on what day your Lord is coming. But know this, that if the

householder had known in what part of the night the thief was coming, he would have watched and would not have let his house be broken into. Therefore you also must be ready; for the Son of man is coming at an hour you do not expect" (24:29–44).

"Immediately after the tribulation" of our personal crisis, we shall have to face another one. But now we are on the side of the Light. To us the denseness of disaster has become transparent, and we realize "the sign of the Son of man" while the tribes on earth are wailing in despair. What is frightening to them, the loss of all their former values, now is encouraging to us, as the beginning of a new world. The "loud trumpet call" inaugurates the new phase of creation for those "who endure to the end," while it rings down the curtain for the rest of mankind.

The old values perish. Sun, moon, and stars disappear. Astrology and astronomy die together. New values arise: the Son and the angels, living beings instead of the dead planets with their unknown influences. It is not the universe, however, that changes; it is our understanding and our relation to it. We learn to look through matter and to see the living spirit everywhere. And therefore we recognize the agonies of tribes and nations as the growing pains of the human spirit when coming of age.

Do we look through matter, seeing the spirit, actually? Not yet. We cannot anticipate such an experience. Therefore there is no use in discussing it or debating theoretically about it, before we have been struck by the lightning ourselves. And when this has happened, no debate will be needed.

The crisis in question is the breakthrough of eternity into time and space. Where does it happen? Everywhere, but especially where human suffering accumulates, till "heaven and earth will pass away": in wars, revolutions, epidemics, earthquakes, and inundations. On the other hand, it happens nowhere, neither in the desert nor in the innermost room.

When does it happen? When history reaches the boundary of time; which is never, and always (24:36). To whom does it happen? To the now living generation (24:34); to those who know that they will be dead twenty or forty years from now. But it will not happen to all of us. One will be taken, and one will be left (24:41).

The coming of the Son, the beginning of the new aeon is real, indeed more real than anything else. But this reality is visible only to those who can see it. Light does not exist for the blind; space and time do not exist for a stone. The super-space and super-time of the coming world-age are not real for those who remain deaf and blind to eternity. For the others it is there already and has ever been.

However, our senses can be sharpened. Let us watch the fig tree (24:32). We shall learn to recognize the coming spring before the others are aware of it. We shall discover the presence of the Son as soon as we learn to see him. Where there is time there is eternity, waiting behind the door (24:33). The Son of man is entering unceasingly, if only we can see his sign.

The mutation of mankind is bound to come. Its smallest preparatory steps appear as destructive revolutions to those who eat and drink, who marry and give in marriage (24:38); that is, to the blind ones who cannot discern the "signs." Those, however, who "keep on the watch" (24:42, Moffatt) will learn to read the signs of the time. They will be prepared.

Chapter 25

PREPAREDNESS

Introduction

The center of the Sermon on the Mount of Olives is "Keep on the watch then, for you never know what day your Lord will come" (24:42, Moffatt). The urgency of this warning pushes away all theoretical questions. Do you want to know whether the Son of man is identical with the Son of God or how far the Spirit of Christ is different from the Holy Spirit? While lying on the operating table, you hardly ask which scalpel the surgeon will use. To be ready for the operation is the only thing that matters. The second half of the discourse, therefore, is dedicated to the problem of preparedness. Matthew gives another trilogy of parables parallel to the first trilogy (in 21:18 to 22:14).

The underlying question in both trilogies is: What are we doing with our freedom? Meticulous obedience, the Christian ideal of the Middle Ages, is not even mentioned. We are free, forced to rely on our own insight, and responsible for our own decisions, informed merely in general terms of the King's intentions. To be prepared for the coming of the Lord means to be neither a spineless slave nor a brainless rebel, but a wise and reliable steward who can become "the ruler over many things" (25:21, KJV).

A Faithful and Wise Servant

> "Who then is the faithful and wise servant, whom his master has set over his household, to give them their food at the proper time? Blessed is that servant whom his master when he comes will find so doing. Truly, I say to you, he will set him over all his possessions. But if that wicked servant says to himself, 'My master is delayed,' and begins to beat his fellow servants, and eats and drinks with the drunken, the master of that servant will come on a day when he does not expect him and at an hour he does not know, and will punish him, and put him with the hypocrites; there men will weep and gnash their teeth" (24:45–51).

The servants in this parable as well as the vinedressers in the first trilogy (21:33–41) behave as if they were, or could become, independent proprietors, though they know they are and always will be parts of a larger "household." However, they are actually free to do as they choose. Their lord wants them to act independently; and he will give them more power and more responsibility if they are faithful and wise. Individualism is their temptation. If they claim sovereignty, they are caught in egocentricity and will perish. If they find the way of individuation, they will grow into greater freedom.

From the egocentric point of view, the world of time and space is endless. Eternity will come after time has ended, and that means never. "My lord is long of coming" (24:48, Moffatt). From the point of view of individuation, eternity is the underlying reality which supports time and space as the table supports the tablecloth. We feel that we are living in eternity all the time. The Eternal is present; but we have to act, to form our life and to build our world as if we were little creators ourselves. God gives us a chance: "If you were in My place, what would you do?" We are trained as assistants in the laboratory of creation.

On the one hand we have to work, forming governments, making laws, improving or changing our economic system, as if time would last forever. On the other hand we should be aware of the breakthrough of eternity every moment. Creativeness is the capacity to draw space and time closer to eternity, until history in space and time expresses the Eternal as the human body expresses the human soul.

The Inner Light Cannot Be Given Away

"Then the kingdom of heaven shall be compared to ten maidens who took their lamps and went to meet the bridegroom. Five of them were foolish, and five were wise. For when the foolish took their lamps, they took no oil with them; but the wise took flasks of oil with their lamps. As the bridegroom was delayed, they all slumbered and slept. But at midnight there was a cry, 'Behold, the bridegroom! Come out to meet him.' Then all those maidens rose and trimmed their lamps. And the foolish said to the wise, 'Give us some of your oil, for our lamps are going out.' But the wise replied, 'Perhaps there will not be enough for us and for you; go rather to the dealers and buy for yourselves.' And while they went to buy, the bridegroom came, and those who were ready went in with him to the marriage feast; and the door was shut. Afterward the other maidens came also, saying, 'Lord, lord, open to us.' But he replied, 'Truly, I say to you, I do not know you.' Watch therefore, for you know neither the day nor the hour" (25:1–13).

In this parable the ten virgins are ready for the wedding feast. Their egocentricity is not so crude as to reject the invitation. But five of them have a problem similar to that of the wedding guest with the wrong robe. The waiting girls symbolize the introverted aspect of religious life. They should be prepared equally for the early arrival of the bridegroom and for his being late. The fearful servant thought his master would never come. The foolish virgins think they can meet him immediately, and he will take care of everything. "We should not rely on our own possessions or ideas or activities; we should not take thought for tomorrow. He is the eternal Light. Our little lamps are extinguished as a sign of humility."

They do not know that individualism and self-responsibility are required for the wedding banquet. Their cloak of meekness conceals the desire to shun creative and responsible activity. They do not dare to be "the light of the world and the salt of the earth." When the bridegroom comes, they will be recognized by their fruit: it is darkness.

The five wise girls refuse to share their oil with their unfortunate sisters. Alms, as we have seen, are good for the giver, but questionable for the receiver. Here sharing would mean dressing up the cowards as though they were courageous, leading them into greater disaster. The oil of the inner light cannot be shared. Our brothers and sisters can help us to light our lamps, but we have to provide the oil from within. The creative person, the individuated one, has access to the oil wells of eternity and therefore does not "take thought for the morrow" (6:34, KJV). The egocentric one cuts himself off from the well. The feudalist relies on the oil of his Lord, not noticing that he is in charge of a well of his own.

The Responsibility for Self-Development

"For it will be as when a man going on a journey called his servants and entrusted to them his property; to one he gave five talents, to another two, to another one, to each according to his ability. Then he went away. He who had received the five talents went at once and traded with them; and he made five talents more. So too, he who had the two talents made two talents more. But he who had received the one talent, went and dug in the ground and hid his master's money. Now after a long time the master of those servants came and settled accounts with them. And he who had received the five talents came forward, bringing five talents more, saying, 'Master, you delivered to me five talents; here I have made five talents more.' His master said to him, 'Well done, good and faithful servant; you have been faithful over a little, I will set you over much; enter into the joy of your master.' And he also who had the two talents came forward, saying, 'Master, you delivered to me two talents; here I have made two talents more.' His master said to him, 'Well done, good and faithful servant; you have been faithful over a little, I will set you over much; enter into the joy of your master.' He also who had received the one talent came forward, saying, 'Master, I knew you to be a hard man, reaping where you did not sow, and gathering where you did not winnow; so I was afraid, and I went and hid your talent in the ground. Here you have what is yours.' But his master answered him, 'You wicked and slothful servant! You knew that I reap where I have not sowed, and gather where I have not winnowed? Then you ought to have invested my money with the bankers, and at my coming I should have received what was my own with interest. So take the talent from him, and give it to him who has the ten talents. For to every one who has will more be given, and he will have abundance; but from him who has not, even what he has will be taken away. And cast the worthless servant into the outer darkness; there men will weep and gnash their teeth' " (25:14–30).

The girls know to a certain extent what they are expected to do. In the next story the servants are completely on their own. No instructions are given, and the suggestion which the master volunteers afterwards corroborates the impression that the whole experiment is a preparation for the emancipation of the servants. Each one gets a commission "according to his capacity" (25:15, Moffatt) and is promoted later according to his merits. There is no escape, we have our gifts and our freedom. We must use them or we shall suffer.

The defense of the timid servant is quite correct, from the standpoint of fear and immaturity. He projects his own rigidity on everybody, including God, and he cannot help it. He could have added that all the wealth and the talents, and all the creative forces which will change the world, are out of tune with the humbleness of the "poor in spirit." He would prefer, he could say, to be among the hungry ones, who mourn and shoulder the sufferings of mankind.

The logical dilemma is insoluble, from the standpoint of egocentricity. From the point of view of creation there is no dilemma at all. The failing servant does not co-create, he represses his talent into the unconscious where it degenerates into "dead men's bones," poisoning his whole life, chasing him into outer darkness and causing him to weep and to gnash his teeth.

The Last Judgment

> "When the Son of man comes in his glory, and all the angels with him, then he will sit on his glorious throne. Before him will be gathered all the nations, and he will separate them one from another as a shepherd separates the sheep from the goats, and he will place the sheep at his right hand, but the goats at the left. Then the King will say to those at his right hand, 'Come, O blessed of my Father, inherit the kingdom prepared for you from the foundation of the world; for I was hungry and you gave me food, I was thirsty and you gave me drink, I was a stranger and you welcomed me, I was naked and you clothed me, I was sick and you visited me, I was in prison and you came to me.' Then the righteous will answer him, 'Lord, when did we see thee hungry and feed thee, or thirsty and give thee drink? And when did we see thee a stranger and welcome thee, or naked and clothe thee? And when did we see thee sick or in prison and visit thee?' And the King will answer them, 'Truly, I say to you, as you did it to one of the least of these my brethren, you did it to me.' Then he will say to those at his left hand, 'Depart from me, you cursed, into the eternal fire prepared for the devil and his angels; for I was hungry and you gave me no food, I was thirsty and you gave me no drink, I was a stranger and you did not welcome me, naked and you did not clothe me, sick and in prison and you did not visit me.' Then they also will answer, 'Lord, when did we see thee hungry or thirsty or a stranger or naked or sick or in prison, and did not minister to thee?' Then he will answer them, 'Truly, I say to you, as you did it not to one of the least of these, you did it not to me.' And they will go away into eternal punishment, but the righteous into eternal life." (25:31–46).

This discourse closes with a vision of the last judgment which in its simplicity and grandeur outrivals the poetry of Dante and Milton. It is half prophecy and half parable, expressing metaphysical events.

The unique feature, which raises this description beyond all similar attempts, is the presence of the judge within the victims, and as we may add, within the defendants, too. The Son of man was there within the thirsty one, and came to life within the one who gave him drink.[1] He was challenging the selfish people by confronting them with those who needed help. "I was hungry but you never fed me" (25:42, Moffatt). He could not awake within the fortress of selfishness, but he would have been ready to do so if the selfish person had allowed it.

The sentence passed by the judge is the precise statement of

---

1. Here the Son of man appears as a superindividual entity, representing the principle of integration rather than of individuation, similar to Brahman: "I am the beggar, and the giver, and the gift."

what has happened already. "Come into your inheritance" is the formula of admittance for those who are prepared. "Depart from me, you cursed" is the statement of failure. The unlived life, the buried talent, is the cause of intense agony. Death is more painful for those who did not live a full life. Deviation and punishment stand in the simple relationship of cause and effect.

The "fire" which destroys the lost souls is "eternal" (25:41), not everlasting. The Greek describes it as "aeonian," related to the aeon, possibly dividing world-ages from each other: between the aeons, as it were, therefore without duration. There is good reason to assume that it is the same fire which Jesus came to kindle (Luke 12:49). This fire purifies and illumines those who can face it and destroys the others. It is a symbol as old as religion itself. Moses saw it in the burning bush (Exod. 3:2); it led the Israelites through the wilderness (Exod. 13:21); and it surrounds the Son of man in Matthew's story. This fire is eternity itself, showing its creative power where it is accepted, and its destructive effect when it meets with resistance.

Part Seven

THE NEW GATE

Meditation: The Two Gates

The discourse on the Mount of Olives gives a view of human history, thousands of years full of suffering and joy and growth condensed into a few prophetic visions. The standpoint of the discourse is neither earthly nor metaphysical; it is "religious." Our world of space and time is not the only thing that matters nor is it an illusion. Human life and history are "real," and extremely important, though they form only a small part of creation. Eternity surrounds and permeates us as a fruit surrounds and permeates each one of its seeds.

In all the parables, the entry to the wedding banquet and the coming of the Son of man seemed to coincide with the end of our earthly existence, or even with the end of the earth itself. The seed unfolds its creative nature only when it is disintegrating in the ground. This, however, would definitely separate our finite world from the eternal world beyond. We would have an "other-worldly" religion, but Jesus' religion is not "other-worldly." On the contrary, the new and powerful impact of his life is due to the fact that he lived here and beyond at the same time. He was at home in space and time as well as in eternity. He is the reliable steward who manages the king's business; he is the wise virgin and the well-dressed wedding guest.

He had reached the intersection of time and eternity long before he died. But he decided to do more. His followers could not distinguish between him and the power that was given to him. The oneness of Here and Beyond, so familiar to him, was incomprehensible to his disciples. His own evolution would have remained unique, a freak of history, had he not found a way which made it the beginning of a general human development. It would have remained an outstanding but single case of Individuation had he not completed it by Integration, drawing all darkness into the light and forcing all mankind into the new evolution. How he did this is told in the records of his death and resurrection.

Jesus' baptism was the gate through which he entered his earthly career; his death, the "baptism of fire," was the second gate through which he vanished from our sight. Between the two gates he worked hard to bring together heaven and earth, inaugurating a new phase of human life and a higher form of human consciousness.

His disciples remained "the little ones," disappearing in the blazing flames of the second gate. Then they woke up. His death became their birth. He baptized them with the fire of his passion and left them where the Baptist had left him: in the desert.

They had to find their own ways, each one by himself, through the dark night of Golgotha. And when they met again in the new brotherhood, they were grown up, independent pioneers, ready to face the second gate, as their master did. For the time being, however, we stand with them in the first gate, uncertain whether we can or should enter. We stare at Jesus; we see him disappear in the fire of the second gate. If the flames of his passion reach us, our future will be decided; if not, we shall have to wait until he calls again.

Jesus' way through this second gate, his death and resurrection, has proved to be the most decisive event in all human history. The records of this event show many discrepancies, especially with regard to the resurrection. But they all discern three stages:

1. Jesus' inner preparation, his way through the inner or psychological gate (Chapter 26).

2. His death on the cross, the way through the outer, physical gate (Chapter 27).

3. His appearance after his resurrection, "beyond the gate" (Chapter 28).

THE INNER GATE

Preparation

When Jesus had finished all these sayings, he said to his disciples, "You know that after two days the Passover is coming, and the Son of man will be delivered up to be crucified."

Then the chief priests and the elders of the people gathered in the palace of the high priest, who was called Caiaphas, and took counsel together in order to arrest Jesus by stealth and kill him. But they said, "Not during the feast, lest there be a tumult among the people."

Now when Jesus was at Bethany in the house of Simon the leper, a woman came up to him with an alabaster jar of very expensive ointment, and she poured it on his head, as he sat at table. But when the disciples saw it, they were indignant, saying, "Why this waste? For this ointment might have been sold for a large sum, and given to the poor." But Jesus, aware of this, said to them, "Why do you trouble the woman? For she has done a beautiful thing to me. For you always have the poor with you, but you will not always have me. In pouring this ointment on my body she has done it to prepare me for burial. Truly, I say to you, wherever this gospel is preached in the whole world, what she has done will be told in memory of her."

Then one of the twelve, who was called Judas Iscariot, went to the chief priests and said, "What will you give me if I deliver him to you?" And they paid him thirty pieces of silver. And from that moment he sought an opportunity to betray him.

Now on the first day of Unleavened Bread the disciples came to Jesus, saying, "Where will you have us prepare for you to eat the passover?" He said, "Go into the city to such a one, and say to him, 'The Teacher says, My time is at hand; I will keep the passover at your house with my disciples.'" And the disciples did as Jesus had directed them, and they prepared the passover (26:1–19).

The last part of Matthew's Gospel has three chapters. Chapter 28 is shorter than the others and has to be read very slowly. It contains several "gaps of silence." The division between Chapters 26 and 27 should be after 26:56: "Then all the disciples forsook him and fled." Chapter 26 then covers the events of Wednesday and Thursday; Chapter 27 begins with Jesus' trial before Caiaphas on Friday morning and ends with his burial Friday night.

The battle lines are arrayed. On both sides the general staff is in permanent session. On the side of the Light the commander arises: "Two days from now, at the Passover . . ." The time for the baptism of fire is set (26:2). The disciples know he will be crucified. They are speechless with awe and fear. On the other side, the high priests and the elders "take council." They want to kill Jesus, but it must be "not during the feast, lest there be a tumult . . . " It is a weird kind of scheming. Jesus and his enemies agree as far as the killing is concerned. He cooperates with them without their knowing it. But they disagree regarding the time. His strategy, however, is superior. He will have his way. In Jerusalem the politicians prepare his arrest. At Bethany his disciples arrange a secret supper for him. A few friends gather, depressed and fearful, and there is the woman who understands him better than anybody else.

Is she the clean, spiritual Mary, the sister of Lazarus (John 11:2 and 12:3), or the harlot (Luke 7:37), or Mary of Magdala (Mark 16:9)? It does not matter. Not any kind of Great Council of the Church, but a simple woman who loves, provides the last encouragement for his work. Mary does not speak, she acts. Her action expresses the spiritual meaning of the situation. Like a great artist she finds the unique form for an inner truth which could not manifest itself in any other way. That is why she never shall be forgotten.

The disciples again fail. Their sadness makes them pettier instead of greater. Jesus' answer should be remembered by all those who are afraid of beauty and refinement, because the costs might be given to the poor. If our situation expresses itself honestly, the material means, however expensive, will be there. If the expression is untrue, the material is wasted.

If we are identified with the disciples, let us discover Mary who is hiding in some corner of our soul. If we are identified with her, let us try to redeem the disciples whom we harbor in our unconscious. Or are we Judas?

Judas "sought an opportunity to betray him." Why did he suddenly turn against his master? And what secret, worth thirty pieces of silver, could he betray? Matthew does not answer this question. John's record (John 13:26–27) refers mysteriously to a silent understanding between Jesus and Judas. We have to find our own answer and we have to find it within ourselves.

The information which Judas sold to the authorities could not concern the place of Jesus' arrest. They certainly knew where he was. It must have been something about time, something that forced them to act immediately. Otherwise they would have waited until the festival was over. Only one thing would have been worse, prompting them to take the risk of riots: the proclamation of the Davidic kingdom by Jesus at the passover. Judas, as all the disciples, knew that Jesus had no intention of doing this. He told the high priests a lie. "The time for the baptism of fire is set," he reported, "two days from now, at the passover."

The Last Supper

> When it was evening, he sat at table with the twelve disciples; and as they were eating, he said, "Truly, I say to you, one of you will betray me." And they were very sorrowful, and began to say to him one after another, "Is it I, Lord?" He answered, "He who has dipped his hand in the dish with me, will betray me. The Son of man goes as it is written of him, but woe to that man by whom the Son of man is betrayed! It would have been better for that man if he had not been born." Judas, who betrayed him, said, "Is it I, Master?" He said to him, "You have said so."
>
> Now as they were eating, Jesus took bread, and blessed, and broke it, and gave it to the disciples and said, "Take, eat; this is my body." And he took a cup, and when he had given thanks he gave it to them, saying, "Drink of it, all of you; for this is my blood of the covenant, which is poured out for many for the forgiveness of sins. I tell you I shall not drink again of this fruit of the vine until that day when I drink it new with you in my Father's kingdom."
>
> And when they had sung a hymn, they went out to the Mount of Olives. Then Jesus said to them, "You will all fall away because of me this night; for it is written, 'I will strike the shepherd, and the sheep of the flock will be scattered.' But after I am raised up, I will go before you to Galilee." Peter declared to him, "Though they all fall away because of you, I will never fall away." Jesus said to him, "Truly, I say to you, this very night, before the cock crows, you will deny me three times." Peter said to him, "Even if I must die with you, I will not deny you." And so said all the disciples (26:20–35).

Light, harmony, and wholeness grow slowly, painfully, out of darkness, discord, and disintegration. We wish to follow Jesus and to run away at the same time. His wholeness reveals our disharmony. The outer conflict between his friends and enemies is superseded by the half-conscious conflict between light and darkness within his disciples and us.

During the last supper, the twilight dissolves into the full light, Jesus, over against the complete darkness, Judas. And there are his followers who feel the same process taking place within themselves: a center of light, the Christ, and a center of darkness, the Anti-Christ, both within us. Which center will prevail?

When Jesus says, "One of you is going to betray me" (26:21, Moffatt), we are paralyzed like thieves caught on the spot. Actually all of us will betray him a few hours later. "Woe to that man by whom the Son of man is betrayed." This describes not only the tragedy of Jesus and Judas, it sets the pattern for the inner tragedy between the center of light and the center of darkness, for many millions of people, through many centuries.

We are sitting at the supper table with the master who tomorrow will die for a great purpose which we cannot fully understand. We love him, admire him, but we know, and know that he knows, we shall betray him, all of us, without exception. If our inner Judas, the center of darkness, were to disappear, we should be in the light. This supper would be the wedding banquet. But we cannot rid ourselves of the inner Judas.

The Master gives us the bread: "Take, eat; this is my body." He knows our deficiencies and feeds us with his own life, sharing his strength. The captain looks at his men before the attack: "I shall go first, you follow. We shall all die. March." For a moment, all darkness disappears.

Jesus looks at us again and gives us the cup: "This is my blood." We are drinking his blood. We have betrayed him and shall betray him again. We are his murderers. We are killing the Son of man every day, within our own hearts. But he gives us his blood. He loves. He understands, He forgives. Why should we not forgive, understand, love? Let us drink our cup; let us become the bread, let us be eaten.

The hymn they sang was the "Great Hallel" (Pss. 115–118), describing the way of religious evolution: failure, suffering, and redemption. Creation must continue. It is the Creator's will: "Awake, O sword, against my shepherd and against the man that is my fellow, saith the Lord of hosts. Smite the shepherd, and the sheep shall be scattered: and I will turn mine hand upon the little ones" (Zech. 13:7, KJV). The mysterious words of the old prophet are suddenly as clear as day. The "scattering of the flock" is indispensable for the inauguration of the new phase of evolution. Individuation must begin with loneliness and despair.

Peter understands that he has to sacrifice his life, and he is ready to do so. The bread and the wine have given him courage. Yet it is still the courage of a feudal knight who wants to die for his king. The new way, however, is different. He must betray the feudal lord, thoroughly, three times, putting an end to spiritual feudalism, once and forever. Then, in bitterness, loneliness, and remorse, after days and nights of infinite darkness, he may find the new way: discovering the Son of man within himself and beyond space and time.

Gethsemane

> Then Jesus went with them to a place called Gethsemane, and he said to his disciples, "Sit here, while I go yonder and pray." And taking with him Peter and the two sons of Zebedee, he began to be sorrowful and troubled. Then he said to them, "My soul is very sorrowful, even to death; remain here, and watch with me." And going a little farther he fell on his face and prayed, "My Father, if it be possible, let this cup pass from me; nevertheless, not as I will, but as thou wilt." And he came to the disciples and found them sleeping; and he said to Peter, "So, could you not watch with me one hour? Watch and pray that you may not enter into temptation; the spirit indeed is willing, but the flesh is weak." Again, for the second time, he went away and prayed, "My Father, if this cannot pass unless I drink it, thy will be done." And again he came and found them sleeping, for their eyes were heavy. So, leaving them again, he went away and prayed for the third time, saying the same words. Then he came to the disciples and said to them, "Are you still sleeping and taking your rest? Behold, the hour is at hand, and the Son of man is betrayed into the hands of sinners. Rise, let us be going; see, my betrayer is at hand."
>
> While he was still speaking, Judas came, one of the twelve, and with him a great crowd with swords and clubs, from the chief priests and the elders of the people. Now the betrayer had given them a sign, saying, "The one I shall kiss is the man; seize him." And he came up to Jesus at once and said, "Hail, Master!" And he kissed him. Jesus said to him, "Friend, why are you here?" Then they came up and laid hands on Jesus and seized him. And behold, one of those who were with Jesus stretched out his hand and drew his sword, and struck the slave of the high priest, and cut off his ear. Then Jesus said to him, "Put your sword back into its place; for all who take the sword will perish by the sword. Do you think that I cannot appeal to my Father, and he will at once send me more than twelve legions of angels? But how then should the scriptures be fulfilled, that it must be so?" At that hour Jesus said to the crowds, "Have you come out as against a robber, with swords and clubs to capture me? Day after day I sat in the temple teaching, and you did not seize me. But all this has taken place, that the scriptures of the prophets might be fulfilled." Then all the disciples forsook him and fled (26:36–56).

The night was full of temptation. Jesus could go away before Judas arrived. Or he could fall asleep, as his disciples did, withdrawing into primitive dullness and inertia. Or he could accept his death in a rigid attitude of self-righteousness, blaming it on the "generation of vipers," as the Baptist had done. All this would have been equally wrong.

He had to find the new way, the way of loneliness. Despised by the Romans, cursed by the Jews, forsaken by his disciples, in complete isolation, he had to face the unknown.

Three times he came to the conclusion that this expedition into the unknown was the will of his Father. But God did not speak. Jesus had to find the way, to make his decision, to take the responsibility alone, independently, trusting God, but not directly and unmistakably guided by God's hand. To come of age means to be left alone by our whole tribe, including our father.

Jesus' statement, "The hour is at hand," in Matthew's Greek sounds infinitely stronger than any translation. It is as if he said, "I am ready; eternity can strike, the new world is approaching." The stroke of eternity was Judas's kiss.

Matthew gives us no respite. "While he was still speaking, up came Judas" (24:47, Moffatt). In an instant Jesus' attitude changes from passive sadness into active determination. The clouds of our fear and bewilderment are lit up by a flash of clarity; he, Jesus himself, acts while he is acted upon. The contrast of activity and passivity disappears. The higher consciousness coincides with higher action: we act, our enemies act, it is one action; history acts, the universe, the creator acts, blending all into infinite growth. *Amor dei, amor fati, amor creandi.* If we love God, we love our fate, and we love the creative event (which takes place within us).

Judas, in the grip of his own darkness, his egocentric ambition or nationalistic fanaticism (whichever it was), acted so promptly, was so reliable a cog-wheel in Jesus' strategy, that Jesus certainly has loved him profoundly. In John's veiled record (John 13:26–28) Jesus gives Judas a "sop," dipping it carefully into the dish; this is more intimate a "lord's supper" than sharing bread and wine. Jesus, more and more achieving the completeness of light, provokes more and more darkness in the man who carries his Shadow. Only by accepting and loving his own Shadow could Jesus redeem the Shadow of mankind.

The disciples (and we) are so poorly prepared that they have the choice only between two equally inadequate reactions. One is despair and flight; the other is relapse into feudalistic courage—

Peter's reaction. Jesus does not denounce such courage. He only states that "all who take the sword will perish by the sword" (26:52). For feudalists the death on the battlefield is the most desirable death. But Peter should outgrow feudalism.

This saying, together with the following about the twelve legions of angels, is from Matthew's particular source. The whole passage seems to be an answer to Judas and his messianic hopes. If Peter had to outgrow feudalism, Judas had to outgrow imperialism. Not only the means, the miracle, but also the goal, the replacement of the Roman by a Jewish empire, would have interfered with the evolution of mankind. All imperialism, all violence, greed, and fear had to be changed into something better whether it would take three hundred years or three thousand. The unadulterated power of spiritual evolution had to make its first appearance on earth. This was Jesus' mission.

Chapter 27

THE OUTER GATE

The Charge

> Then those who had seized Jesus led him to Caiaphas the high priest, where the scribes and the elders had gathered. But Peter followed him at a distance, as far as the courtyard of the high priest, and going inside he sat with the guards to see the end. Now the chief priests and the whole council sought false testimony against Jesus that they might put him to death, but they found none, though many false witnesses came forward. At last two came forward and said, "This fellow said, 'I am able to destroy the temple of God, and to build it in three days.'" And the high priest stood up and said, "Have you no answer to make? What is it that these men testify against you?" But Jesus was silent. And the high priest said to him, "I adjure you by the living God, tell us if you are the Christ, the Son of God." Jesus said to him, "You have said so. But I tell you, hereafter you will see the Son of man seated at the right hand of Power, and coming on the clouds of heaven." Then the high priest tore his robes, and said, "He has uttered blasphemy. Why do we still need witnesses? You have now heard his blasphemy. What is your judgment?" They answered, "He deserves death." Then they spat in his face, and struck him; and some slapped him saying, "Prophesy to us, you Christ! Who is it that struck you?" (26:57–68).

The Sanhedrin, the council of the high priests and elders, had decided that Jesus should die. According to Judas, the revolution was scheduled for the Sabbath. It was necessary, therefore, to have Jesus executed on Friday, publicly, with the full display of Roman military might. But the official reasons for the death sentence were still to be found. Neither his claim to Messiahship nor his plans for an upheaval against Rome were suitable accusations for public trial.

Jesus, however, wanted to be condemned on the charge of being "Christ." And he forced the elders to raise just the accusation which they wished to conceal. He waited in silence while the false witnesses brought forth their prearranged evidence. Hours passed. Finally, infuriated by the pressure of time, the High Priest rose and said with all the urgency and solemnity of his exalted office: "I adjure you by the living God, tell us if you are the Christ, the

Son of God" (26:63). The secret was out. The main witness for the prosecution, Judas, though now absent, had provided the only valid charge, exactly as Jesus had wished him to do. It was the word "Christ."

Jesus' answer, "You have said so," admitted that he was the "Son of God." Then he continued: "Hereafter you will see the Son of man seated at the right hand of Power, and coming on the clouds of heaven" (26:64). To the High Priest and the elders this was blasphemy, and it was more: it was their defeat. Their violent reaction made it clear that Jesus had won the battle.

His claim to messiahship was the only accusation which could compel the Roman governor, Pontius Pilate, to pass the death sentence instantly. To the Romans "Messiah" meant "the king of the Jews," the heir of David and the enemy of the emperor Augustus. Jesus forced the Sanhedrin to denounce messiahship, to desert the Jewish nationalist movement, and to acknowledge that a great Rabbi—loved by the crowds and recognized even by some Pharisees, such as Nicodemus—was to be considered a criminal. The Jewish authorities disowned the hope of the Jewish future. From now on messiahship was not a religious problem but a political crime.

The Betrayals

> Now Peter was sitting outside in the courtyard. And a maid came up to him, and said, "You also were with Jesus the Galilean." But he denied it before them all, saying, "I do not know what you mean." And when he went out to the porch, another maid saw him, and she said to the bystanders, "This man was with Jesus of Nazareth." And again he denied it with an oath, "I do not know the man." After a little while the bystanders came up and said to Peter, "Certainly you are also one of them, for your accent betrays you." Then he began to invoke a curse on himself and to swear, "I do not know the man." And immediately the cock crowed. And Peter remembered the saying of Jesus, "Before the cock crows, you will deny me three times." And he went out and wept bitterly. . . .
>
> When Judas, his betrayer, saw that he was condemned, he repented and brought back the thirty pieces of silver to the chief priests and the elders, saying, "I have sinned in betraying innocent blood." They said, "What is that to us? See to it yourself." And throwing down the pieces of silver in the temple, he departed; and he went and hanged himself. But the chief priests, taking the pieces of silver, said, "It is not lawful to put them into the treasury, since they are blood money." So they took counsel, and bought with them the potter's field, to bury strangers in. Therefore that field has been called the Field of Blood to this day. Then was fulfilled what had been

spoken by the prophet Jeremiah, saying, "And they took the thirty pieces of silver, the price of him on whom a price had been set by some of the sons of Israel, and they gave them for the potter's field, as the Lord directed me" (26:69–75; 27:3–10).

Peter, in his feudalistic faithfulness, followed the Master into the lion's den. He could have died in the glory of his loyalty before the High Priest. However he could not face the petty mockery of the servants. His individualism was budding already. Now it developed into egocentricity, and the way into individuation was blocked. Peter betrayed his feudalism, but he betrayed his egocentricity as well. When the cock crowed, he discovered that all egocentricity is bound to destroy itself.

Judas, as well as Peter, destroyed his own Ego. Had he been completely egocentric, he would have enjoyed his thirty pieces of silver. But we all harbor some old feudalistic loyalties, hidden under our egocentric shell. Judas may have hoped, without believing it, that Jesus would mobilize his twelve legions of angels to establish his kingdom. The betrayal, then, would have netted thirty pieces of silver for Judas's (conscious) Ego, and the honor of having started the national revolution for his (unconscious) feudalism.

Finally his feudalistic hope broke through into consciousness. Jesus refused to fight, and Judas, now the traitor of his feudal Lord, had to kill himself.

Judas regressed and perished. Peter wavered between regression and progress. His egocentricity broke down, but his guilt, the outer manifestation of his inner darkness, was balanced by the experience that Jesus had forgiven him his weakness many times. Once more Peter found himself on the side of darkness, weeping bitterly, and craving desperately for the light. He was not strong enough to reach the light, but his strength was just sufficient to endure the darkness.

The Condemnation

When morning came, all the chief priests and the elders of the people took counsel against Jesus to put him to death; and they bound him and led him away and delivered him to Pilate the governor. . . .

Now Jesus stood before the governor; and the governor asked him, "Are you the King of the Jews?" Jesus said to him, "You have said so." But when he was accused by the chief priests and elders, he made no answer. Then Pilate said to him, "Do you not hear how many things they testify against you?" But he gave him no answer, not even to a single charge; so that the governor wondered greatly.

Now at the feast the governor was accustomed to release for the crowd any one prisoner whom they wanted. And they had then a notorious prisoner, called Barabbas. So when they had gathered, Pilate said to them, "Whom do you want me to release for you, Barabbas or Jesus who is called Christ?" For he knew that it was out of envy that they had delivered him up. Besides, while he was sitting on the judgment seat, his wife sent word to him, "Have nothing to do with that righteous man, for I have suffered much over him today in a dream." Now the chief priests and elders persuaded the people to ask for Barabbas and destroy Jesus. The governor again said to them, "Which of the two do you want me to release for you?" And they said, "Barabbas." Pilate said to them, "Then what shall I do with Jesus who is called Christ?" They all said, "Let him be crucified." And he said, "Why, what evil has he done?" But they shouted all the more, "Let him be crucified."

So when Pilate saw that he was gaining nothing, but rather that a riot was beginning, he took water and washed his hands before the crowd, saying "I am innocent of this man's blood; see to it yourselves." And all the people answered, "His blood be on us and on our children!" Then he released for them Barabbas, and having scourged Jesus, delivered him to be crucified (27:1–2, 11–26).

In the meantime, Jesus stood before Pontius Pilate. "Are you the King of the Jews?" asked the Roman. Jesus said, "Yes," infuriating the Jews to the utmost. Pilate was not interested in religious quarrels about prophets and messiahs. His only question was whether the defendant represented a danger to the empire or not. According to Jesus' confession, he was dangerous and therefore had to be executed.

On the other hand, Pilate was astute enough to notice that the defendant was certainly no king like David nor rebel like Judas Maccabeus. Practically, he was not dangerous at all, especially as the Jewish authorities were against him. If Jesus had tried to explain the confusion between the religious Messiah, the son of God, and the political Messiah, the son of David, Pilate would have been glad to dismiss the case. Jesus did not speak. The confession stood, and the death sentence was unavoidable.

Pilate tried to release this unusual prisoner under the amnesty of the feast. The Jews, however, had to choose the one to be freed, and Pilate tried to force them to ask for Jesus. As the only alternative, he placed beside him a murderer, who certainly had no sympathizers among the Jewish authorities. Yet still the governor failed.

The populace, like the eleven disciples, were disconcerted by Jesus' arrest. A prophet who was not protected by the Lord against the Gentiles could not be a true prophet. It was easy for the elders, therefore, to make the mob shout for Barabbas. Pilate, now losing all interest in a cause which was to him unimportant and merely embarrassing, did something unusual for a Roman official: he surrendered to the crowds. "Then what am I to do with Jesus the so-called 'Christ'?" (27:22, Moffatt). The final death sentence was formulated by the populace: "Have him crucified!"

Pilate made a weak attempt to argue with them, as though he were Jesus' lawyer. The governor was under the spell of a power he could not understand. He washed his hands of it to satisfy his forebodings, and the mob, bold in their ignorance, assumed the full responsibility. They spoke the truth when they screamed, "His blood shall be on us and on our children!" They surrendered themselves to their fate. Jerusalem went down in blood and fire, forty years later.[1]

The Crucifixion

Then the soldiers of the governor took Jesus into the praetorium, and they gathered the whole battalion before him. And they stripped him and put a scarlet robe upon him, and plaiting a crown of thorns they put it on his head, and put a reed in his right hand. And kneeling before him they mocked him, saying, "Hail, King of the Jews!" And they spat upon him, and took the reed and struck him on the head. And when they had mocked him, they stripped him of the robe, and put his own clothes on him, and led him away to crucify him.

As they were marching out, they came upon a man of Cyrene, Simon by name; this man they compelled to carry his cross. And when they came to a place called Golgotha (which means the place of a skull), they offered him wine to drink, mingled with gall; but when he tasted it, he would not drink it. And when they had crucified him, they divided his garments among them by casting lots; then they sat down and kept watch over him there. And over his head they put the charge against him, which read, "This is Jesus the King of the Jews." Then two robbers were crucified with him, one on the right and one on the left. And those who passed by derided him, wagging their heads and saying, "You who would destroy the temple and build it in three days, save yourself! If you are the Son of God, come down from the cross." So also the chief priests, with the scribes and elders, mocked him, saying, "He saved others; he cannot save himself. He is the King of Israel; let him come down now from the cross, and we will believe in him. He trusts in God; let God deliver him now, if he desires him; for he said, 'I am the Son of God.'" And the robbers who

---

1. Matthew, in spite of his Jewish sympathies, does everything in his power to excuse Pilate and heap the responsibility on the Jews. The dream of Pilate's wife (27:19) is another item serving this tendency.

were crucified with him also reviled him in the same way
(27:27–44).

The execution took its course, cruel and impersonal. First there
was a serious scourging, and then a long time to wait. Someone
had the cynical idea of a crown of thorns; the soldiers crowned
Jesus and bowed to him as "the king of the Jews," then spat at
him and struck him on the head.

The political betrayal of the Sanhedrin bore fruit; the dignity
of the Jewish nation was abased and ridiculed. But from the
peculiar point of view which the prophets of the Old Testament
had discovered, and which later has become the outstanding
characteristic of Christianity, the mockery became a great symbol. The "King" was worshiped by Roman soldiers who did not
know what they did. His powerlessness was the true form of his
success, and his lack of resistance was his means to conquer the
world. He actually was "the King of the Jews" in the sense of
transcending and fulfilling the Jewish mission, enlarging it from
nationalism into universalism.

The Roman cohort started the march to Golgotha. Jesus was
too weak to carry his cross. The soldiers, in their careless way,
seized on one Simon of Cyrene to do this for him. It was not compassion on the part of the Romans, just a routine job, to save time.
But it gives us some information about Jesus. He was not a robust
man, but sensitive, and of delicate health. The scourging seems to
have broken his strength.

In spite of his weakness, Jesus refused the drink the soldiers
offered. Was it the ordinary beverage for marching troops, given
to the criminals in order to invigorate them and so lengthen their
agony? Or was it, as most interpreters think, a narcotic drink, to
dull their consciousness for the ordeal? Whichever it may have
been, Jesus wanted to avoid both. He wished to face death as
speedily as possible and in complete consciousness.

He wanted to remain awake, to experience the transition from
life to death, or from one life to another, in full awareness and
presence of mind. He did not drink any wine during the last supper (Luke 22:17) because he wanted to be as alert and watchful
as possible. Later, however, when he was exhausted to the point
of fainting, he took the drink which kept him conscious for a few
more minutes. He braved anguish and pain in order to retain
through all changes the continuity of his existence.

Thus he was crucified. Matthew mentions the appalling procedure only in an indirect way: "And when they had crucified

him" (27:35). There is silence between 27:34 and 27:35. Nothing is said. But there are the hammer blows which pierce the silence, and the nails which pierce hands and feet. The unbelievable now is reality: This sensitive, alert, active man has given himself voluntarily, to be killed, slowly, in the most painful of all possible ways. And he tries to remain conscious, drinking the cup of human suffering to the very last dregs.

Matthew expresses the horror and solemnity of this hour by the quotation of the most awe-inspiring psalm (Ps. 22:19) whose words Jesus later used at the climax of his agony. The veil between time and eternity now is worn so thin that even the average human eye is able to glimpse the light behind the darkness. History took its decisive step exactly as the prophets had foretold. What happened, however, was not less terrible because it was foreseen. On the contrary, when the vision became reality, it turned out to be darker and more painful than even the greatest poet could have visualized.

The common people laughed. The Jewish authorities joked in a more subtle way. The thieves who were crucified with him "denounced him in the same way" (27:44, Moffatt). The record of the crucifixion is flanked by two passages describing the scorn of Jesus' enemies, just as his cross is flanked by the two crosses of the thieves (27:27–31 and 39–44).

Death

> Now from the sixth hour there was darkness over all the land until the ninth hour. And about the ninth hour Jesus cried with a loud voice, "Eli, Eli, lama sabachthani?" that is, "My God, my God, why hast thou forsaken me?" And some of the bystanders hearing it said, "This man is calling Elijah." And one of them at once ran and took a sponge, filled it with vinegar, and put it on a reed, and gave it to him to drink. But the others said, "Wait, let us see whether Elijah will come to save him." And Jesus cried again with a loud voice and yielded up his spirit.
>
> And behold, the curtain of the temple was torn in two, from top to bottom; and the earth shook, and the rocks were split; the tombs also were opened, and many bodies of the saints who had fallen asleep were raised, and coming out of the tombs after his resurrection they went into the holy city and appeared to many. When the centurion and those who were with him, keeping watch over Jesus, saw the earthquake and what took place, they were filled with awe, and said, "Truly this was a son of God!"
>
> There were also many women there, looking on from afar, who had followed Jesus from Galilee, ministering to him; among whom were Mary Magdalene, and Mary the mother of

James and Joseph, and the mother of the sons of Zebedee (27:45–56).

From the sixth to the ninth hour, that is, from noon to 3:00 P.M., Jesus was hanging on the cross in agony. The chief source of pain in this type of execution is the difficulty in breathing, the result being an extremely slow process of suffocation. The suffering is increased if the delinquent is nailed to the cross, instead of being tied to it by ropes. Loss of blood deepens the agony. The southern sun, burning the naked body, does the rest.

According to early Christian tradition, however, there was darkness all over the earth during these three hours. It corresponded with the inner darkness of the disciples. The shepherd had forsaken his sheep, and the sheep had forsaken their shepherd. Now they had to live, to make decisions, to find their way without his guidance.

Then Jesus cried: "My God, my God, why hast thou forsaken me?" He went through the same inner eclipse as his disciples, only on a higher plane. He quoted the twenty-second psalm, but not in Hebrew (as the psalm was read in the synagogues). The words are Aramaic. He said in his mother tongue what he suffered. His contact with his heavenly Father had been so intense, his access to the Beyond so easy for many years, yet now in the moment of unbearable anguish, this contact failed. The Father forsook the adolescent son, forcing him through utmost darkness into the new light, the light of adult sonship.

Burial

When it was evening, there came a rich man from Arimathea, named Joseph, who also was a disciple of Jesus. He went to Pilate and asked for the body of Jesus. Then Pilate ordered it to be given to him. And Joseph took the body, and wrapped it in a clean linen shroud, and laid it in his own new tomb, which he had hewn in the rock; and he rolled a great stone to the door of the sepulchre, and departed. Mary Magdalene and the other Mary were there, sitting opposite the sepulchre.

Next day, that is, after the day of Preparation, the chief priests and the Pharisees gathered before Pilate and said, "Sir, we remember how that impostor said, while he was still alive, 'After three days I will rise again.' Therefore order the sepulchre to be made secure until the third day, lest his disciples go and steal him away, and tell the people, 'He has risen from the dead,' and the last fraud will be worse than the first." Pilate said to them, "You have a guard of soldiers; go make it as secure as you can." So they went and made the sepulchre secure by sealing the stone and setting a guard (27:57–66).

When the Christians of the first generation collected and organized their memories about Jesus, they may not have been aware of the peculiar fact that at his grave, as well as at his cradle, there was a Joseph and a Mary to care for the beloved charge. At the grave, however, there were two Marys and the Joseph was a stranger whose name occurs here for the first time. It is as if the gospel proves Jesus' statement that whoever gives up father and mother for the sake of the kingdom will find himself surrounded by a hundred fathers and mothers (19:29).

Joseph of Arimathaea saw to it that Jesus' body was buried before the Sabbath began; and the Marys watched him doing it. Their love transcended death, but it was still the old dependent and dependable love of the tribal community. They had not yet learned to be without him, yet they learned "to die with Christ" while they buried him. The male disciples had to learn the same lesson while hiding in fear and depression, but for all of them "the veil was rent" (27:51, KJV). They slowly began to see the light.

The High Priest and the elders wanted to safeguard the grave against theft. Pilate agreed, scarcely giving a thought to the consequences. To the Romans it did not make any difference how this "King of the Jews" was buried, and whether his body was stolen or not. That he could not rise from the dead was, of course, beyond doubt for the Roman mind.

For millions of people, however, and for many centuries to come, it was to be a question of utmost importance: Was the grave empty on Sunday morning because the body was stolen, or because the Lord had risen from the dead, physically? Was his resurrection physical or spiritual, or was there a third way of understanding it?

Matthew is the only one of the three synoptics who tells about the rumor that the corpse might have been stolen and about the eagerness of the high priests to prevent this theft. In this way Matthew seeks to prove that the theft was impossible. The Lord must have risen physically. Strangely enough, however, Matthew's account leaves a gap and does not prove anything. Jesus was buried Friday evening, and the high priests did not file their petition for the guards before Saturday morning (27:62). The night between gave ample opportunity to remove the body and replace the stone.

Could Matthew not have said that the guards were posted at the grave immediately after the burial? Here, as in several other places, the records of Jesus' death and resurrection are in a strange way inconsistent and blurred. We may regret it, but it forces us to make our own decision, to find out the truth, or to wait until it is taught to us from Beyond. If we had complete and officially ascertained documents about all the details of Jesus' death, burial and resurrection, we should be forced to accept the content of Christianity exactly as the Jews were forced to accept their Law. Then there would be no real Christianity, no religion for free and maturing individuals and nations coming of age.

Meditation: Golgotha Within

We are identified with Peter, aware of the Light, watching it, protecting it, accompanying it on its way into sacrifice and death. We recognize and admire this Light, this divine spark in Jesus and in other men who, like him, are able to give up their lives in the service of a new creation. And we find the same spark within ourselves. It is our treasure, the Beyond Within, the Son of man who begins to speak and wants to guide us, leading us to our own crucifixion. The goal is Golgotha. We look around, and we discover: there is darkness all over the place, our inner darkness, and darkness closing in from outside. The darkness threatens to crush the Light. Shall we fight and die in the battle against our darkness?

We thought the Light was leading us straight into the kingdom. When "the Christ" comes to life within us, we should expect to be saved and safe forever. We hoped to enjoy the Light and to help our brothers and sisters who are still struggling in darkness. But Jesus went to Jerusalem to be crucified. *The only way to overcome darkness is to walk right into it.* Challenged by the Light, it will arise in self-defense, unfolding all its cruelty and recklessness. If we can face the darkness, the Light will be victorious. But can we face it?

The struggle takes place within us. We are Peter, following our inner Light into the deadly battle against our inner darkness. "Love your enemies," says the Light; "do not fight back; be killed if necessary, but love the killer. If you lose your life, you will save it." "This is nonsense," shouts Darkness. "Protect yourself and your children; fight for justice and right; do away with illusions and dreams; be realistic!" Our inner Judas has tangible and limited goals: Thirty pieces of silver, or national independence, or perhaps a farm and a wife and a healthy family. Our inner Christ wants us to challenge the authorities and to change our inherited religion. Our conscious mind, Peter, is torn between the opposites: the dazzling Light of Christ and the solid darkness of Judas.

Peter draws his sword, fighting for the Light with the weapon of darkness. We argue for the irrational power of the future with the rational means of the past. We pretend to serve the future; actually—though unconsciously—we take sides with the past. We explore, describe, criticize, and judge the Light from the point of view of its opponents, using their terms and symbols and categories. We drag the Light, now fettered for scientific investigation, before the Sanhedrin of our contemporary philosophy. We cannot help doing so. Indeed, Jesus himself warned us to discriminate between "the false Christs" and the real Son of man (24:24). We must judge, and we shall fail.

We give up our identification with Peter. There is no use in defending the Light unless we are certain the Light is divine. It hurts; it is betrayal; we weep when the cock crows; but there is no other way. We are the High Priest. In desperation, we ask our inner Light, "Tell us if you are the Christ, the Son of God" (26: 63). If the inner voice says "no," darkness has won the battle. If it says "yes," we shall accuse it of blaspheming. How can anything within our miserable human nature be divine or creative or good?

We have the right to be on the side of darkness, and to silence our inner voice, calling it blasphemous. And we prove our right by appealing to Pilate, our sense of orderliness and practical decency. Pilate tries to exonerate the Light. He is not afraid of it because he does not believe in its existence. But we are afraid. We shout, "Let him be crucified!" We must destroy our inner Light completely, or we shall repent and accept it; and that would mean to accept our own crucifixion.

It is the final contest between us and our inner Light. We are identified with darkness, with Caiaphas, the elders, and the crowds: "His blood be on us and on our children." In order to avoid our own crucifixion, we crucify our inner Light, every day, every moment. We destroy the new creation which wants to begin within ourselves.—

The Light is dead. The madness of our Ego-defense subsides. We are exhausted, empty, in utter darkness. If the Light was not divine, life was futile from the beginning and creation was a mistake. If the Light was divine, we have quenched it, we are the murderers of God. In either case, it was suicide, the end of our former existence. — Can this be the beginning of something new? Is it true that the divine is immortal? Can we survive after having extinguished the divine spark within ourselves? Can the Light itself survive in spite of all our darkness?

Chapter 28

BEYOND THE GATE

The Resurrection

Now after the sabbath, toward the dawn of the first day of the week, Mary Magdalene and the other Mary went to see the sepulchre. And behold, there was a great earthquake; for an angel of the Lord descended from heaven and came and rolled back the stone, and sat upon it. His appearance was like lightning, and his raiment white as snow. And for fear of him the guards trembled and became like dead men. But the angel said to the women, "Do not be afraid; for I know that you seek Jesus who was crucified. He is not here; for he has risen, as he said. Come, see the place where he lay. Then go quickly and tell his disciples that he has risen from the dead, and behold, he is going before you to Galilee; there you will see him. Lo, I have told you." So they departed quickly from the tomb with fear and great joy, and ran to tell his disciples. And behold, Jesus met them and said, "Hail!" And they came up and took hold of his feet and worshiped him. Then Jesus said to them, "Do not be afraid; go and tell my brethren to go to Galilee, and there they will see me."

While they were going, behold, some of the guard went into the city and told the chief priests all that had taken place. And when they had assembled with the elders and taken counsel, they gave a sum of money to the soldiers and said, "Tell people, 'His disciples came by night and stole him away while we were asleep.' And if this comes to the governor's ears, we will satisfy him and keep you out of trouble." So they took the money and did as they were directed; and this story has been spread among the Jews to this day.

Now the eleven disciples went to Galilee, to the mountain to which Jesus had directed them. And when they saw him they worshiped him; but some doubted. And Jesus came and said to them, "All authority in heaven and on earth has been given to me. Go therefore and make disciples of all nations, baptizing them in the name of the Father and of the Son and of the Holy Spirit, teaching them to observe all that I have commanded you; and lo, I am with you alway, to the close of the age" (28:1–20).

When we first started our religious expedition, Matthew was a perfect guide. He conveyed to us so completely what he had learned from his teacher and what his teacher had learned from

Jesus that we received an unfailing chart for the perilous night-sea-journey.

Jesus had to "forsake" his disciples to teach them self-reliance and independence. Matthew did not know that he would forsake his later readers at the very point where he tells them how the disciples were left alone. It is a superhuman and therefore unconscious accomplishment.

Jesus was raised from the dead, they say, physically, lived in the flesh, eating and drinking, forty days, until he was lifted up into the Heavens, physically. This Lord Jesus has never ceased to exist. He is reality, as long as there is spiritual feudalism on earth; but he exists, he is reality, only in the feudalistic mind of men. If we outgrow feudalism, this Lord Jesus dies; indeed, he dies for us. He disappears from our mind, leaving us alone in darkness and despair. The flock is scattered, the shepherd is slain. But he said, anticipating our crisis: "My going is for your good. If I do not depart, the Helper will not come to you: whereas, if I go, I will send him to you," (John 16:7, Moffatt).

Who is the Helper? As we study the records, we find him at work in them.

The discrepancies between the five accounts are so striking that we are forced once more to set out on our own journey, to make our own discoveries, and to draw our own conclusions. The records here vary more than in any other part of the Gospel. The five accounts which we have allow us to distinguish four different levels regarding the existence of the resurrected Christ.

(1) Paul's account (1 Cor: 15) must be valued as the oldest, best-founded evidence we possess. He was not influenced by amplifications of the oral tradition, but he might have omitted some parts which he considered unimportant. He does not mention the empty grave. To him the resurrected Christ was a spiritual entity, having no body in the material sense. And he assumes that Christ appeared to the first disciples on Easter morning in the same way that he appeared to him at Damascus.

(2) Mark and Matthew tell us that the resurrected Christ not only spoke (as Paul too maintains) but also could be seen. However, Matthew's remark that "some doubted," indicates that neither the appearance nor the speaking voice were completely convincing. That the women touched his feet is inconsistent with the rest of the description. But the remark that some were in doubt must be authentic. That is one of the things which no writer could have invented.

(3) & (4) Luke and John describe a kind of materialization:

the resurrected Christ can be touched, can eat and expound the scriptures (Luke 24:42; John 20:27).

An additional factor contributes to the insecurity of the records. That is the fact that the end of Mark's Gospel was lost before the book could be copied. The verses nine to twenty of his sixteenth chapter are a later addition. His original text ends before the resurrected Christ appears to anybody. History itself sees to it that Christianity be based on faith and not on historical evidence.

The Light from Beyond

The two Marys stare into the infinite darkness of death. The grave, the womb of the earth, is empty. Then they are seized with fear and joy. They see the light. "Like lightning!" And instantly to them it becomes an angel.

We too gaze. Yes, there is light. The dark cave, the nothingness of the hollowed rock, opens, like a tunnel, into blinding light. The grave is a gate. We cannot yet walk through it; but like Moses we can see through it into the promised land beyond.

The women, carrying the mystery of unending life within themselves, are more ready than men to respond to the mystery of metaphysical rebirth. The grave, the womb of mother earth, as the cradle of spiritual life, to them, is but another higher form of their own experience of motherhood. Therefore they are sent to tell the disciples: "He has risen from the dead."

The message first of all is an experience, a fact that the two women realize with absolute certainty. When this experience enters their consciousness, it is transformed into words, "He has risen." Who said that? Neither one of them did. The words were formed, without their conscious help, as the expression of their inner certainty. What is this new power which they realize as a source of joy and fear? The power itself seems to say: "Not fear, joy!" Perhaps it is the angel, or Jesus himself? They know: Christ is alive.

Without the audacity of the two Marys, our concept of immortality would still be vague and impersonal. If, on the other hand, we had nothing but the report of the women, Christianity would be based on the "concretistic" belief that they not only saw and heard the Lord, but also touched his feet.

However, what the two Marys have contributed to Christianity is more than it seems to be at first sight. The experience of the light can be found in many religions. It is either objective and external: the light is seen as the sign of God's presence in the outer world (e.g., Exod. 3:2); or it is internal and subjective: it fills the soul of the mystic with eternal bliss (2 Cor. 12:2–4).

The two women at Jesus' grave realized the outer and the inner light at the same time. The Beyond broke like lightning through the outer continuity of space and time, exactly as Jesus had said the Son of man would appear. And the inner structure of their minds gave way: they felt the earthquake, the change of the internal world, and then were able to hear the voice, announcing the change in the outer world: This man "has risen from the dead . . . you will see him." Mankind outgrows materialism, and that means the limitations of space and time, only if those who have not yet died are aware of their immortality and live accordingly.

The sudden experience of the light—the lightning—then becomes the basis of a lasting change, an organic growth of human nature. The individual, from now on, can reach a degree of maturity which enables him to join, through death, the immortal Spirit beyond space and time. And this process can be seen by those who, still in space and time, grow mature enough to realize the Beyond Within. This is what happened to the two Marys.

Meditation: Easter Within

Easter, rebirth, the new phase of creation, is either a convincing inner experience which changes our character and our life, or it is nothing at all. We do not need the empty grave. To us every grave is empty, every corpse is darkness. But darker than all this is our own failure. We know what love is, but we do not love: we only want to be loved. We know responsibility and self-sacrifice and creativeness, but we choose to be arrogant or evasive, indignant or apologetic, greedy or frightened. We do not help to create the new world. We only complain that the old world disintegrates. Thus, we destroy ourselves.

This darkness of ours, however, is changing. The more we recognize its nature, the more it turns into regret and remorse. We were close to the Light, but we preferred darkness. We stood at the entrance to the kingdom, but we were afraid to give up our former security, our private claims, resentments, and goals. In order not to be crucified with Christ, we committed moral suicide. Now we are dying every hour and every moment from the horror of our darkness and from the longing for the Light which we quenched. Hopeless and dejected, with the two Marys, we come to the grave. At least we are honest enough, now, to look at the great friend we have killed. What we see is so terrible that it destroys our mental structure. We die with him. The earth is shaking. The lightning strikes. Are we dead or alive? We know and see, feel and think. Creative power fills our soul. The debt is canceled. "I live; yet not I, but Christ liveth in me" (Gal. 2:20, KJV). Life, and Light and Love begin anew.

The Voice from the "Beyond Within"

Matthew's Gospel closes with the solemn last commandment of the glorified Christ. This meeting with the dead who is alive has changed the fearful, blundering disciples into independent and fearless apostles. According to Matthew, they met in Galilee. Luke tells us it was in Jerusalem (Luke 24:36–53). The event was similar to the experience of the two Marys. The outer light appeared and was seen through the inner eye. Then there was a voice, heard through the inner ear. And what the voice said was understood and shaped in human language by the minds of eleven men. The wording would have differed had they compared their experiences instantly. But the deeper meaning was the same. They could honestly say that they all heard him say this. It does not matter whether they were in Jerusalem or in Galilee, eleven of them or a hundred. The same voice which initiated them into apostleship, that inner voice, as objective, indeed more objective than any outer voice can be, has spoken to innumerable initiates since, and will speak to many more. What the voice says is always the same, though the words we hear change with the historical situation. Since Jesus' death, this voice, the voice of Christ, is calling unceasingly. When we are prepared, we shall hear it: "I am with you alway, even unto the end of the world" (28:20, KJV).

Bibliography

I. THE TEXT

Goodspeed, E. J. *The New Testament, An American Translation*. Chicago: Univ. of Chicago Press, 1923.

Lamsa, George M. *The New Testament According to the Eastern Text*. Philadelphia: A. J. Holman Co., 1940.

Moffatt, James. *The Bible: A New Translation*. New York: Harper & Bros., 1935.

Nestle, Eberhard. *Novum Testamentum Graece*. New York: American Bible Society, 1927.

Scofield, C. I. *The Holy Bible, Authorized Version*. New York: Oxford Univ. Press, 1917.

Westcott, B. F. & Hort, F. J. A. *The New Testament in the Original Greek*. New York: The Macmillan Co., 1940.

Weymouth, R. F. *The New Testament in Modern Speech*. Boston: Pilgrim Press, 1939.

II. COMMENTATORS

Eiselen-Lewis-Downey. *The Abingdon Bible Commentary*. New York: Abingdon-Cokesbury Press, 1929.

Heard, Gerald. *The Code of Christ*. New York: Harper & Bros., 1941.

Heard, Gerald. *The Creed of Christ*. New York: Harper & Bros., 1940.

Jones, Stanley. *Christ of the Mount*. London: Hodder & Stoughton, 1931.

Morgan, G. C. *The Gospel According to Matthew*. New York: Blakiston Co., 1929.

Robinson, T. H. *The Gospel of Matthew*. New York: Harper & Bros., 1927.

Sharman, H. B. *Records of the Life of Jesus*. New York: Harper & Bros., 1917.

Sharman, H. B. *Son of Man and Kingdom of God*. New York: Harper & Bros., 1943.

Sharman, H. B. *The Teaching of Jesus About the Future*. Chicago: Univ. of Chicago Press, 1909.

Streeter, B. H. *The Four Gospels, A Study of Origins*. London: Macmillan, 1936.

Tittle, Ernest. *The Lord's Prayer*. New York: Abingdon-Cokesbury Press, 1942.

Wilkens, Dr. T. *Der König Israels*. Berlin: Furche-Verlag, 1937.

III. PSYCHOLOGY

Adler, Alfred. *Understanding Human Nature.* New York: Green-berg, Publisher, Inc., 1927.

Freud, Sigmund. *Introductory Lectures on Psychoanalysis.* New York: W. W. Norton & Co., Inc., 1933.

Jacobi, Jolan. *The Psychology of Jung.* New Haven: Yale Univ. Press, 1943.

James, William. *Varieties of Religious Experience.* New York: Modern Library, 1902.

Jung, C. G. *The Integration of the Personality.* New York: Farrar & Rinehart, 1939.

Jung, C. G. *Modern Man in Search of a Soul.* New York: Harcourt, Brace & Co., 1939.

Jung, C. G. *Psychological Types.* New York: Harcourt, Brace & Co., 1938.

Jung, C. G. *Psychology and Religion.* New Haven: Yale Univ. Press, 1943.

Jung, C. G. *Psychology of the Unconscious.* New York: Dodd, Mead & Co., 1937.

Kunkel, Fritz & Dickerson, Roy. *How Character Develops.* New York: Charles Scribner's Sons, 1940.

Kunkel, Fritz. *In Search of Maturity.* New York: Charles Scribner's Sons, 1943.

Ligon, E. M. *Psychology of the Christian Personality.* New York: Macmillan, 1940.

Wickes, Frances. *Inner World of Man.* New York: Farrar & Rinehart, 1938.

IV. HISTORY, LITERATURE

Bewer, J. A. *The Literature of the Old Testament.* New York: Columbia Univ. Press, 1922.

Durant, Will. *Caesar and Christ.* New York: Simon & Schuster, 1944.

Goodspeed, E. J. *Problems of New Testament Translation.* Chicago: Univ. of Chicago Press, 1945.

Klausner, J. *Jesus of Nazareth.* New York: Macmillan, 1927.

McCown, Chester C. *The Search for the Real Jesus.* New York: Charles Scribner's Sons, 1940.

Olmstead, A. T. *Jesus in the Light of History.* New York: Charles Scribner's Sons, 1942.

Schweitzer, Albert. *Quest of the Historical Jesus.* London: A & C Black, 1931.

Scott, E. F. *The Literature of the New Testament.* New York: Columbia Univ. Press, 1936.

V. MISCELLANEOUS

Asch, Sholem. *The Nazarene.* New York: G. P. Putnam's Sons, 1939.

Austin, Mary. *The Man Jesus.* New York: Harper & Bros., 1915.

Barton, Bruce. *The Man Nobody Knows.* Indianapolis: Bobbs-Merrill, 1925.

Kelly, Thomas. *A Testament of Devotion.* New York: Harper & Bros., 1941.

Meister Eckhart, A Modern Translation (ed. R. B. Blakney). New York: Harper & Bros., 1941.

Waley, Arthur. *The Way and Its Power.* London: George Allen & Unwin Ltd., 1934.

White, Bouck. *Call of the Carpenter.* New York: Doubleday Page & Co., 1912.

About the Author

Fritz Kunkel studied medicine in Munich and received his license as a physician and surgeon in 1914—just in time to serve in the German army as a surgeon during World War I. In those years he experienced the brotherhood of man among his comrades and his enemies. A shell explosion cost him his left arm, but gave his life a new direction.

As Joseph Havens says in *Inward Light* (Spring 1966), "the death of the physician was the birth of the psychotherapist; resurrection was a theme of his life from that moment." Dr. Kunkel studied psychology first with Alfred Adler in Vienna, later he added C. G. Jung's depth psychology and his own growing insights. In the next ten years he wrote eleven books, among them a six-volume work on Personality Development. The center of his productive practice was in Berlin, but the demand for his lectures spread to Holland, Sweden, England, and the United States.

Fritz Kunkel called his approach "We-psychology." He developed a technique of creative introspection in which the daily difficulties as well as the major crises of life are seen as man's greatest opportunities for the development of emotional maturity. He was concerned with life itself rather than with psychopathology.

His psychology was deeply religious and philosophical. In his use of "thesis-antithesis-synthesis" he anticipated Assagioli. He was an existentialist and a transpersonal psychologist but used the language of his time which he called "religious psychology." He wrote nineteen books of which only two are presently available in English.

His wide interest in art, literature, philosophy, his study of Latin and Greek source material, plus his lifelong work in psychiatry, made him a great humanitarian and psychiatrist. In his modesty, however, he called himself simply "a psychologist."

One of his outstanding traits was his great sense of humor. With his fine wit and hidden smile he saved many a difficult situation, made people laugh, and gave to a serious talk a light flavor. Solitude was his creative time, helping people was his great call.

Fritz Kunkel came to the United States in 1939 to lecture at Pendle Hill, a Quaker adult study center near Philadelphia, and at the Pacific School of Religion in Berkeley, California. World War II separated him from his family. He decided to remain in the United States and became an American citizen in 1947. The family was reunited after the war. Thereafter he and his wife, a certified psychologist, practiced psychotherapy in the Los Angeles area. Together they developed techniques of joint and group therapy until his death in 1956.

Joseph Havens says of Dr. Kunkel: "I suspect that his lasting contribution lies . . . in four . . . areas, namely, his delightful and edifying use of symbols and images, his redemptive use of personal crisis in his own and patients' lives (the 'trauma treasure' theory), his contagious faith that men can nurture their own growth, and his creative synthesis of the religious and the psychological." In relation to the last point, Haven says that Kunkel insisted on an integration rather than a coalition of the two perspectives; on a *religious psychology*, as he called his own approach. In . . . *Creation Continues*, he spells out his conviction that the New Testament is 'the great text-book of depth-psychology.' "